EXTRA INNINGS

Also by David Whitford

*A Payroll to Meet: A Story of Greed,
Corruption and Football at SMU*

EXTRA INNINGS

A SEASON IN THE SENIOR LEAGUE

David Whitford

 Edward Burlingame Books
An Imprint of HarperCollins*Publishers*

FOR MY BROTHERS,
ROB AND BRAD

"But it's a fantasy," Keyes said.

Tommy Tigertail smiled handsomely, his caramel face brightening. "Of course it's a fantasy. Of course it is!" He laughed softly, a laugh full of irony. "Ask anybody," Tommy said. "Florida is the place where fantasies come true."

From *Tourist Season* by Carl Hiaasen

Acknowledgments

Secretly, I've always wanted to be a baseball beat writer. I had fun pretending during the three months I was in Florida, and I'm grateful for the help and friendship given me by the real baseball beat writers I met while I was there, among them Roy Cummings, Paul Dzimitrowicz, Ed Giuliotti, and Mike Pryson. Special thanks to Tom Jones of the *St. Petersburg Times,* who definitely deserves a staff job. And my buddies in Fort Myers, Glenn Miller of the Fort Myers *News-Press,* Randy White, and the Card Wizard (I know who you are).

The idea for this book came from my agent, Ned Leavitt. Were it not for Ned, it never would have been written, and that would have been my loss. Ed Burlingame at HarperCollins never panicked (or if he did, never let me know about it), and let me write the book I wanted to write. Sam Perrigo was always helpful. Christa Weil was a pleasure to work with. Mike Anderson was an able research assistant, unearthing clips I would not otherwise have found. John Rolfe answered countless queries and never once complained.

While I was in Florida, far from home, the Muellers—Hans, Terri, Sarah, and Anna, and baby Paula, too, who arrived after I left—saved me from a steady diet of ballpark hot dogs and even remembered my birthday. Thanks for keeping me company and letting me talk about something besides baseball for a change.

For whatever interest this book may hold, I owe deep thanks

to the players. All but one (and that's all right) tolerated my presence with professionalism and good grace and shared generously of themselves with a stranger. I'm not supposed to have favorites, but I do: Bill Lee, Fergie Jenkins, Scipio Spinks, and all the members—front office included—of the late, lamented Winter Haven Super Sox. It was good while it lasted.

Sara, thank you for urging me to go. Emma, thank you for waiting until I came home.

PREFACE

I WASN'T LOOKING TO ESCAPE, NOT AT ALL. AFTER MOVING FOUR
times in less than three years, my wife, Sara, and I were settled
at last in a sunny apartment outside Boston with family and
friends all around. My first book had just been published. I was
busy—writing magazine stories, helping my brother-in-law tear
down half his house and then rebuild it, fixing up my own apartment. I painted the kitchen. I refinished the oak floor in the
hallway, a messy job but well worth the labor. Life was good. I
had no plans to go anywhere.

Then one raw, hard-wind afternoon in late October my agent
called. Big news: a publisher had offered me an advance to write
a book about the first season of the senior league. Of course I'd
have to go to Florida for three months, November through January. And I'd have to make up my mind fast. It was the night
before Halloween. The games would start November 1.

Sara and I went for a long walk. What I haven't said yet is
that Sara was pregnant with our first child. The baby was due
in February, about a week after the season would end. Now, I
could imagine fates worse than spending the winter in a sub-
tropical climate with no obligations other than to show up at the
ballpark every day and talk to many of the same players I had
worshipped as a kid. I just wasn't sure how to justify something
like that in terms of my responsibilities as a husband and father-
to-be. In the end, Sara said go. She could take care of herself.
The baby would probably wait until I got home. As long as I

remembered that the main reason I was doing this was to support my family, I was free to have fun. Two days later I was on a plane to West Palm Beach.

I rented a car, a lap-top computer, and a pink, one-room cottage on the bay side of Pass-A-Grille Beach, near St. Petersburg. Apart from one three-day break for Christmas, I spent the next three months, it seemed, traveling to the ballpark, at the ballpark, or on my way home from the ballpark. I drove ten thousand miles and saw a hundred games; at least one a day, sometimes two, and once, insanely, three. I collected ninety hours of taped interviews and filled a dozen notebooks. I was seldom sure what day of the week it was.

As soon as the season ended, I flew home, landing at Logan Airport on a bright, cold morning in February. It was the day after a storm. Snow was piled up between the runways. Three weeks later Emma was born. Where I had been, what I had done all winter, began to seem unreal. Whenever I thought about it, I found myself returning to one particular day. It was a Tuesday afternoon, late in the season. I was in Bradenton at McKechnie Field, watching the middle game of a three-game series between the Bradenton Explorers and the Orlando Juice. I don't remember much about the game. Both teams were fighting for the last available play-off spot in the southern division. Bradenton won, I think.

What I do recall clearly is what it felt like to be there on that day in that ballpark. By then I knew all the ballparks, and McKechnie was my favorite. One of its charming features was that it had three separate grandstands. I preferred the one on the third-base side, with its back to 9th Street. The box seats at McKechnie were lousy—unforgiving metal chairs that must have been salvaged from a church basement. Higher up, though, in the reserved-seat section, were rows of wooden benches softened and made smooth by thick succeeding layers of brown paint. The bench in the very last row—where I sat whenever I could— had a backrest attached to it, inclined at just the right angle.

Whatever McKechnie was, it wasn't cozy or intimate or any of the other adjectives so often used to describe grand old baseball theaters such as Wrigley Field or Fenway Park. McKechnie was too insubstantial for that, too much a part of a setting that had nothing to do with baseball. That day, as I sat alone in the upper right-hand corner of the third-base grandstand, I had a feeling of being suspended between two worlds. Behind me and directly below me was 9th Street, a dusty, gritty strip on the dowdy side of town, clogged with midday traffic. There was Popi's Place, a workingman's café that advertised "homemade breads and pies"; Community Tire Service, a red-and-white-striped concrete box with a sheet-metal awning that made a shady place for changing flats; Superior Automotive Detailing, which specialized in "upholstering, landau tops and seat covers"; and a used-car lot, where the sales pitches were written in script on the windshields: "1978, 40,000 Miles," "1988 Make Offer," "Classy Ride."

When I turned to face the field I saw a pale blue sky streaked with clouds and felt the breeze blowing in from right field. The wind brought with it a sick-sweet aroma from the Tropicana plant, whose belching smokestacks could be seen on the horizon; it fluttered the crowns of the few lonely palm trees that stood outside the low, green outfield fence. The fence was made of tin, a thin dividing line. Inside was the wide swath of outfield grass, the grass a darker, more textured green than the fence, and inside that the dirt collar of the infield, a vivid orange tinged with pink.

The baseball players in their clean white uniforms made their familiar pattern on the wide-open field. The sounds they made were small, precise, distinct; leather against leather, leather against wood. They seemed like children, utterly absorbed, playing, but with a seriousness that in that moment I felt as plainly as I felt the hard bench and the soft wind, oblivious to the combustive roar and rattle, the workaday confusion of 9th Street in Bradenton on a Tuesday afternoon.

I was strongly affected, for reasons I'm not sure I understand. But I believe it had to do with my sudden grasp of how profoundly separate the two worlds were, though physically very little stood between them. I know I felt privileged, even if I was only an observer. Maybe, too, I felt a little wistful. My place was on the outside, and soon I'd be going home.

EXTRA INNINGS

ST. PETERSBURG, FLORIDA • November 3, 1989

OPENING NIGHT AT AL LANG STADIUM, INSIDE A HARSHLY LIT CINDER-block cubicle beneath the home-plate grandstand. Cardboard boxes stacked halfway to the ceiling, filled with hats, T-shirts, sweatshirts, scorecards, and yearbooks. Three or four busy people gathered around a table in the center of the room, coming and going all the time. A small metal box on the table, lid open. Bank notes piled all around—fives, tens, and twenties.

"I need ones!" came a voice through the open door to the ticket office. Oh, boy. Ones, ones, who's got some ones? (Palms patting pockets, shoulders shrugging.) No ones. Baseball was a cash business. When you ran a cash business, you learned to carry ones. Oh, well, they'd know tomorrow.

"What's nineteen and twenty-six?" A pause, a grimace, "Forty-four. Put down Linda for forty-four hats." Someone scribbled on a yellow legal pad. The vendor grabbed her hats—maroon with gold insignia, one size fits all—and ran.

The man who couldn't add straight was Jim Morley, owner of the St. Petersburg Pelicans and founder of the Senior Professional Baseball Association. Morley was thirty-two years old, but he looked younger; anyone meeting him for the first time was likely to be taken aback and Morley, a salesman by profession and temperament, capitalized on the effect. "Jim Morley," he'd say, shaking hands. "Surprised, weren't you?" For one brief, significant summer after college, Morley was an outfielder in the

San Francisco Giants farm system. After ten years of selling real estate, his sandy brown hair was not as thick as it once was, but otherwise he looked as if he could still play. He was dressed for opening night in running shoes, blue shorts, and a white T-shirt that said "Way Bad" across the chest.

"All right," said Morley to his troops, "I'm gonna go take a shower and get ready and then I gotta go out on the field and do all the bullshit. You wanna lock this up? I'll be in the locker room."

Morley opened the door to the public corridor and found himself face to face with a woman who was very happy to see him—not because she found him attractive (she may well have, most women did) but because she had a bone to pick and Morley was the man in charge.

"Where are my tickets?" she wanted to know. She had sent in her money ages ago, but she was still waiting for her season tickets.

Morley was polite, charming, apologetic—"we didn't get the tickets until *Saturday*"—and managed to satisfy the customer without stopping, without even slowing down. And so across the corridor, through the unmarked door, down the steps, right turn (running now) and into the locker room.

While Morley showered, I looked around. The room was empty, the players were all outside. They'd left behind their street clothes and their colorful big-league duffel bags—Phillies, Expos, Dodgers, Orioles, Padres—baggage from a former life. Morley's locker was in the center of the room, along the far wall; "J. Morley," it said on the piece of masking tape above. M. Morley, Jim's thirty-year-old brother, Mark, was the team's vice president and general manager.

Scrubbed and shampooed, J. Morley emerged from the shower, toweled off, and quickly donned his owner's uniform: khaki pants (pleated), a pink button-down shirt (the collar lined in contrasting blue), and a pair of brown leather pumps by Bally of Switzerland (no socks). A glance at his watch (twenty minutes before game time), a lingering look in the mirror, then it was back down the hall, up the stairs, through the door, across the corridor, around the turnstile, and out into the night air, where Morley paused for a moment and took stock. He beheld a perfect St. Petersburg evening, the sort to make a chamber-of-commerce man teary with gratitude.

Sleepy old St. Petersburg (named by the Russian immigrant who brought in the railroad in 1885) was once known mainly as a place where old people from colder climates came to die. In those days, the city's most recognizable urban features were the hundreds of green wooden benches that lined the sidewalks on Central Avenue. Almost all the benches were gone now, but signs of St. Petersburg's geriatric roots remained: in the stark black-and-white billboard out on Interstate 275, for example, with its itemized list of services available at a local discount mortuary.

Lately, though, St. Pete was trying hard to appear youthful. Farther south on I-275, a spanking-new all-sports arena—the Suncoast Dome, paid for with civic funds on the daring assumption that it made sense to build now and find a tenant later— was nearing completion. Because Tampa, just across the bay, already had a football team, St. Pete pined for a baseball team. Two years ago it almost got the White Sox; only a special midnight session of the Illinois state legislature halted the move. These days, the big push was toward winning an expansion franchise. The National League had promised to add two new teams by 1993, although it hadn't said where. St. Pete was hopeful, but then so were at least a dozen other cities, including Miami and Orlando. Meanwhile, the empty dome waited.

Sports were a big part of St. Pete's new self-image. Like some middle-aged divorcée who one day traded in his family sedan for a sports car, every October the city hosted a grand-prix automobile race. The event took place downtown on city streets, shattering the tropical peace and rattling the benches where elderly couples once gathered at dusk and listened to the wind in the palms. Tonight the streets were quiet again, but refuse from the race remained; Morley had spent much of the afternoon clearing tires out of the parking lot.

St. Petersburg had become "a city on the fast track," to quote the chamber of commerce, "setting the new pace of progress." A few years back, Al Lang Field—overlooking the water at the edge of the downtown district—was given a concrete make-over and renamed Al Lang Stadium; the Mets were gone now, but the Cardinals still played there in the spring. From where Morley stood tonight just outside the main gates, his gaze took in the forest of masts bobbing peacefully in the yacht basin and the sparkling lights of the new pier: shops, bars, restaurants—a yuppie playground—extending half a mile into Tampa Bay. To his left was the high-rise Hilton Hotel and behind him the big new Bayfront Center auditorium.

And so many people! Morley was quoted in the newspaper today with a prediction of twenty-five hundred for opening night. Here it was, twenty minutes before the start of the game, and already there were at least that many fans right here in front of him, streaming through the turnstiles and lining up for tickets. The ticket line was so long, in fact, that Morley made a snap decision. He dashed inside and came back out with a fistful of grandstand tickets.

"VOUCHERS!" Morley cried, weaving his way through the crowd. A voucher was good for two free tickets. "VOUCHERS! Vouchers to redeem? How many, sir? One, two, three. One, two, three. All right, there you go, sir. VOUCHERS OR BONUS BOOKS TO REDEEM!"

Then a little girl with curly brown hair walked up to Morley and asked him, "How much are tickets?" Clenched in her tiny fist were dollar bills.

"Boy, I could do this, but I don't know if I want to," Morley said to himself. Then, "I'm gonna do it! ANYBODY BUYING GRAND-STAND TICKETS WITH EXACT CHANGE, RIGHT HERE!" Hesitatingly at first, then in a rush, fans came to him with their money.

"How much?"

"Four dollars. One, two, three, four, five, six, seven. Twenty-eight dollars. Thank you very much, sir!"

"Are you an employee?"

"I own the goddamn team!"

Morley worked the crowd right up until 7:00. At the last possible minute he sprinted back inside to the cinder-block office, pounded on the door, dumped the bills on the table by the metal box, ran across the hall, rattled the locker-room door (it was locked), turned, bounded up the ramp, wiggled past the fans clogging the portal, and entered the arena.

It was dark. Something was wrong with the lights. Morley would have worried, but there was no time for that. Impatiently, he made his way down to the field. Next to the home dugout, Curt Flood, commissioner of the senior league, was waiting with his hands behind his back, rocking back and forth on his heels. The players were all lined up along the foul lines in their strange new uniforms. The stadium was full. The crowd, over four thousand, was on its feet and making noise. As they stood there together—Morley and Flood, the founder and the commissioner—

taking it all in, Flood tapped Morley on the shoulder, lightly, as if to be sure that neither of them were dreaming.

MORLEY WAS LOOKING TO MAKE A BUCK. THAT'S REALLY HOW THIS whole thing got started. Sure, he'd played baseball. And he loved the game. He was moved by the poetry of the diamond, he was a sucker for nostalgia, he felt the pull. All of that. But Morley was a businessman—real estate was his game now—and at the time the idea first came to him, business was not so good.

"I got big overhead, big interest payments, big real estate payments," Morley said, remembering. "So I'm thinking of another way to generate some dough."

This was early 1989. The go-go decade that had been so kind to Morley and all the others like him was just winding down. Morley had landed in Colorado Springs in 1980, one year removed from the University of Arizona. He was twenty-three years old, competitive, opportunistic, eager to the point of impatient, confident on the verge of cocky—your basic yuppie, I suppose—and he arrived just in time to catch a killer wave in commercial real estate.

At Schuck/Grubb & Ellis, Morley dealt land, leased big chunks of office space, sold buildings. "He got there right at the right time," said Gary Feffer, a childhood buddy who followed Morley to Colorado. "He struggled for a couple of years, but when things started to really roll in '83, '84, '85, he did real well and made a lot of money and really established himself as one of the best brokers in town.

Life in those days was all deals and dough—you did a deal, you made some dough. "I was making a ton of dough" is the way Morley put it, "and a lot of my buddies were making a ton of dough."

In 1984, the year Morley turned twenty-seven, he was Schuck's top producer. His personal share of the commissions he generated for the firm came to seven hundred thousand dollars. Then the wave crashed, and Morley's earnings plummeted.

"In '84, the market was real hot," Morley said. "Then in '85 the market was pretty good and I made about four hundred. Then in '86, the market—I mean, we're talking like right off the table. The year before we had nine or ten guys make over a hundred grand; in '86 we had two. I was still number one and I only did about a hundred and seventy-five. In '87 I was up around a couple hundred thousand, but I had a ton of bad deals as well."

By this point Morley was well into the second stage of capital accumulation. No longer just a broker, he was buying and selling on his own, real estate, mostly, but also anything else that looked good at the moment. When frequent-flyer miles were hot, he sold miles. When silver was up, he sold silver. He took a few hits—"I lost a hundred fifty thousand in a building deal, lost about two hundred thousand in a piece of land, seventy thousand in an oil deal, fifty thousand in a commodities deal"—but nothing overly worrisome, not by his standards. Win or lose, you kept on going. There was always another deal.

In 1987, Morley left Schuck/Grubb & Ellis to form his own company. His friends thought he was crazy. It was definitely a gamble. Before, he'd been working on a sixty-forty split, a generous arrangement that nevertheless meant he turned over 40 percent of every commission he earned. Now the commissions were all his. On the other hand, he had his own office now, and employees, so his fixed costs were way up.

"It probably wasn't a very good time [to start a business] because the market was going to shit," Feffer said. "While he was still making money, he had a lot more going out than he had coming in." For the first time in his career, Morley was feeling squeezed.

In January 1989, Morley and his girlfriend, Annie Schmidt, flew to Australia for a two-week vacation. They planned to do some gambling and some diving along the Great Barrier Reef, but mostly this was supposed to be a beach break, a chance to lie around in the sun and drink beer. Morley, though, was preoccupied with business. The cash-flow problem had reached the point where he felt he had to come up with a way to "generate some dough," enough to carry him through the slump until the market turned up again. Annie suggested branching out. Maybe open a restaurant, or a bead store, or a balloon-delivery service. Morley thought those were "goofy ideas." His mind was still on real estate. He knew that when the market went sour, a lot of people in his business got into property management on behalf of banks and lending institutions. It was a way to generate some fees, that's all. Boring but maybe necessary.

Then one day on a beach near Sydney, as Morley sat reading the sports page, he happened upon a story about a seniors' golf tournament in Brisbane. The seniors tour, Morley knew, was for professionals age fifty and older. Arnold Palmer had played for years; now with stars like Lee Trevino and Jack Nicklaus about to come of age, the tour was beginning to attract more attention than ever before from fans, corporate sponsors, and television executives. In golf, clearly there was a market for nostalgia.

If golf, then why not baseball?

Morley looked up from his newspaper. "There should be a senior league for baseball," he said to Annie.

"I WASN'T NERVOUS," MORLEY SAID TO FLOOD TEN MONTHS LATER, while they waited to take part in the pregame festivities. "But why does everybody have to show up at seven for a seven-o-five start?"

There were three speeches (all short), three first pitches (Morley, Flood, the vice mayor of St. Petersburg), a moment of silence for the late commissioner of baseball, Bart Giamatti, and finally the singing of the national anthem.

Together with the opening strains of the familiar old song, the powerful stadium lights began to flicker. By "the dawn's early light," a light like dawn filled the air. It was the dawn of a new season and a new league.

ST. PETERSBURG • November 4

I FOUND BAKE (DON'T CALL HIM ARNOLD) MCBRIDE IN A CORNER OF the Pelicans' locker room. He was reaching up to adjust the volume (also up) on the stereo, a move beyond the reach of most of his teammates. McBride looked a little thicker in the trunk—they all did—but he still had the same high waist and narrow hips I remembered from his days as an outfielder with the Cardinals and the Phillies. He was a fixture in right field for the Phillies during their championship years in the late seventies and early eighties. McBride and center fielder Garry Maddox (taller and skinnier even than McBride, and just as fast) let few balls fall between them and together helped make up for the fact that Greg Luzinski over in left played like a dog chained to a stake.

McBride was driven out of the game before his time by a chronic case of bad knees. They were so tender at the end that it hurt the rest of us to watch him walk. It didn't help that the stadiums he played in for the first nine years of his career all had artificial turf, which was little more than a thin plastic carpet laid down on a concrete floor. McBride finished up in Cleveland, which had grass, but by then this knees were too far gone. He batted .291 in seventy games in 1983 and then he retired. He was thirty-four years old.

McBride's short-clipped hair still grew low on his forehead and had not yet begun to turn gray. The day I talked to him, he looked studious in gold-rimmed glasses and was smoking a cigarette.

"It's tough to leave the game," he said when I asked him why he was here. "The idea of being able to *play* again is the main thing. I just wanted to try it one more time. I wanted to see what it would be like. It's strange, all of a sudden I'm starting to think about that slider and that curveball again." He laughed. "That's one reason I got out of the game, so I wouldn't have to think about that slider and that curveball. Strange."

"How are your legs?"

"Oh, they're sore. My knees are very sore. That's why I only been able to DH. Throughout my whole career I had problems with my knees so I guess it's no different now. I hadn't run on 'em since I got out of ball. The doctor checked 'em out last night. He said, 'I'd like to drain 'em for you,' and I said, 'I gotta think about it first.' But I'll probably do it. I already have arthritis so it's really not gonna make a whole lot of difference."

"What's holding you back?"

"The needle, man, that's the thing. The needle. Now if they could do it some other way, no problem. But it's tough to sit in there on a table while he's sticking a needle in you and he's telling you not to move."

"Is it a big needle?"

"Yeah, it's a big needle! Hah! It's not the kind you sew with. Hah-hah!"

HERE, AS ELSEWHERE AROUND THE LEAGUE, ATTENDANCE FELL OFF sharply after opening day. Despite glorious weather and a Saturday 1:00 start, only about one thousand fans showed up for the game between the Pelicans and the Orlando Juice, the second of a three-game series. If Morley was disappointed he didn't show it. He worked the spread-out crowd like a preacher working a revival, patting strangers on the back, leaning over for little kids, smiling at women who smiled at him. Periodically, he sat down and watched a half inning or so with a group of rowdy friends from Colorado, here for the weekend to join in the celebration.

Morley's buddies—all men in their thirties who looked like actors in a commercial for imported beer—were working hard at having fun. They staked out a section in the grandstand behind home plate, took off their shirts in the first inning, kept the beer man working all afternoon, and cheered loudly, sometimes for the Pelicans and sometimes for the University of Colorado, to whose showdown with Nebraska for the right to go to the Orange Bowl they kept their portable radios tuned.

"We're talking goddamn eleven months ago," said Gary Feffer. "Shit, less than that. Sitting on the *beach*. That's the amazing thing. And here he is, got a goddamn baseball team!"

Feffer roomed with Morley at the University of Arizona. That was long before Morley ever thought of owning a baseball team. Morley was still a player then, dreaming of a pro career. At Central Arizona Junior College in 1976 he led his team to the junior college national championship. The following year he transferred to Arizona. Morley made the team as a walk-on and played two seasons. In 1978, his senior year, he batted .351 and was the starting center fielder. That winter he signed a free-agent contract with the San Francisco Giants.

Morley had a decent spring training and was assigned to the Fresno Giants of the Class A California League. But "he was just a very average minor-league player," according to Bob Brenly, a former teammate and ex–major leaguer. "He was a good contact hitter with little power. If I remember right he was pretty slow afoot. He always had a good time, that's one thing I remember about him."

Morley's own analysis was even more blunt. "I wasn't good enough, period." He played sparingly and was released in midseason, which was far from being a tragedy because immediately afterward he moved to Colorado Springs and started making money hand over fist. For ten years, he claimed, he never gave baseball another thought. Until that day on the beach. It was as if he awoke from a decade-long dream. Suddenly baseball mattered again.

Morley decided the first thing he had to do as soon as he got back from Australia was round up some players. "There was no use in spending any money if the players weren't interested in playing," Morley explained while we sat watching the middle innings of the game together. "If the players don't want to play, okay, deal's done, let's go down the road to the next one."

Morley called a man named Jack Smalling who lived in Ames, Iowa. Smalling published a book that listed the names and last-known addresses of everyone who ever played major-league baseball, living or dead. Morley sent Smalling a check for fifteen dollars. When the book arrived (together with a refund check of $2.05), he went through it name by name. "I wish it had their ages," Morley said, "but all it had was when they entered the league."

Morley figured anyone who started his career between 1969 and 1978 ought to be about the right age by now. He marked those names with a yellow highlighter. Any other name he recognized but that fell outside the limits of his search he marked in pink. Then he gave the book to his secretary and asked her to enter all the names and addresses in the office computer.

"So I send all these guys a letter, twelve hundred fifty of them. I'd composed this letter that said basically, 'Dear David, my name's Jim Morley. I'm a former minor-league player with the San Francisco Giants. I'm starting a league, senior league, players over thirty-five, catchers over thirty-two, are you interested in playing? Here's the deal: it's five-to-fifteen thousand per month.' The way I figured that, I just took the amount of fans you could expect and what it would cost and then I misinterpreted a lot of things but I was reasonably close. I put the league together in my mind where we didn't need TV money to make it work. I didn't want to be like the USFL where when the TV check was supposed to arrive they're waiting at the mailbox for it.

"Then in the very last paragraph of the letter I put, 'Enclosed is an already addressed stamped postcard. Just fill it out, find any post box in America, put it in it, and it will find its way back to me."

"How long did it take for replies to start coming in?"

"About a week. I got like a hundred. I'm looking through 'em and I'm seeing a few big names. I got like Vida Blue early and I was excited."

Before he had the names, the senior league was more like another of Annie's goofy ideas than a legitimate deal. But now it was starting to take shape. "I think it's got a chance," said Morley, "so I start down the road."

After players, what next? Well, places to play. Morley knew there were lots of places to play in Florida, all those ballparks where the major-league teams trained in the spring. He figured they were probably empty all winter. He assumed, as one who owned property might, that whoever owned those ballparks would at least *listen* to a deal that held out the possibility of some out-of-season rental income. But Morley had never been to Florida, and he didn't really know. So in early February Jim and his brother, Mark, flew to Miami. They rented a Lincoln Town Car and drove the state from Miami to Dunedin, from Daytona to Fort Myers, looking at ballparks and talking to the people—mostly city officials—who owned them.

While the Morleys toured Florida, more cards from interested players arrived every day back at the office in Colorado Springs. Morley's letter had tapped a vein . . . of what? Nostalgia? Playfulness? Desperation? Who knew? The fact was that within the first few weeks, over three hundred fifty ex-players wrote back to say sure, they'd leave their families, their jobs, their lives, whatever they had going, and come play baseball again. One even scribbled in the margin of his reply card, "My dream's come true."

Morley decided it was time to go public. He sent out a press release on a business wire service—"Colorado Springs real estate broker James F. Morley announces the formation of the Senior Professional Baseball Association"—and a couple of newspapers picked it up, one in Evansville, Indiana, another in Allentown, Pennsylvania. "I'm really excited," said Morley, " 'cause now I got the press calling me."

By the time big-league camps opened that spring, Morley's new league was on everybody's lips. A lot of the players he'd contacted were working in baseball anyway—as scouts, coaches, minor-league managers—and they helped spread the word. Everybody wanted to know what was going on. Eventually the national media picked up the story. There were articles in the Chicago *Tribune, Sports Inc.,* and *The Sporting News.*

"Now we're getting about two hundred calls a day," said Morley, "from press, players, people who said, 'Oh, I thought of this already, maybe we should get together.' Amazing how many guys called me and said they thought of this already."

In April, Morley hired his first two employees, Peter Lasser and Charles Yancy. Like Morley, Lasser and Yancy were in their early thirties. Lasser had won a shelf full of Emmys directing sports programs at ABC; he would work on a TV deal. Yancy's task was to sound out potential corporate sponsors. And in May Morley hired Curt Flood to be the league's first commissioner. By now more than six hundred players had sent back their reply cards.

Lasser and Yancy wanted to have a press conference. "Well, hey," Morley asked them when the subject first came up, "how much is this deal gonna cost us?"

"Oh, about thirty grand."

"Guys, I don't know."

Morley, remember, had a cash-flow problem. That was the whole reason he got started on this deal in the first place. Instead, all he was doing so far was spending—on postage, phone calls, trips to Florida, trips to New York. He had a commissioner on the payroll at five thousand dollars a month. Lasser and Yancy had agreed to work for nothing—for the first month only, after which (and the day was fast approaching) Morley would have to pay each of them *eight* thousand dollars a month. But Morley had a strategy for dealing with all that.

"The way I financed the deal," Morley explained, "was by not paying mortgage payments some months. Typically a lender, especially when the market's bad, they'll let you slide a month or two. So I'd collect all my rents—about thirty-five, forty grand—and then I have three American Express cards. I mean, without American Express, this league wouldn't be here.

"I gotta gold, a platinum, and a green. One month I'd use only the green for the whole month, all the flying around and the hotels, everything, put it all on the green. The next month I'd use only the gold and the next month I'd use only the platinum and I'd run those babies way up. Well, by the time I'm using the platinum, they're calling me on the green. I have good credit, I pay my bills. Over a short period of time they just send you a little letter—'Mr. Morley, have you forgotten?'—that kind of thing.

"This is February, March, April, May, June, July. Until I got the first payment from the owners, which was like the first week of August, this is what's supporting me—taking the money from not making my mortgage payments and shuffling the cards."

The press conference was held at Gallagher's restaurant in New York on May 31. That same day, Deion Sanders was re-called by the Yankees and Mickey Mantle threw a video party. Still, the senior-league affair attracted more than one hundred reporters and television people. Morley's major expense was airfare and accommodations for twelve former major leaguers—including Bill Lee, Graig Nettles, Luis Tiant, and Bert Campaneris. It turned out to be money well spent. "The media picked up on the players," Lasser said later. "That's what excited them."

Several hours later, while Morley was sitting down to a star-struck lunch with Howard Cosell (Lasser had worked with Cosell at ABC), he took the first of several phone calls that day from people who had heard about the new league and were interested in buying a franchise. First the players, then the ballparks, now the owners. "Everything that Mark and I thought back in February—that if we did it this way the owners would come to us—was starting to come true."

The cost for the first five months had been high. Would there ever be enough dough in this deal to make it all worthwhile? Morley was about to find out.

"You KNOW, FOR A LOT OF THESE GUYS IT'S JUST A BALLMARK." This was one of Morley's buddies speaking. I had no idea what he was talking about. Down on the field, Joe Sambito was on his way in from the bull pen. There were two outs in the ninth inning. Bill Madlock, who represented the tying run for the Juice, was on first. Ken Landreaux was waiting at the plate.

"You know, a pimple on an elephant's ass."

I understood now. He meant that most of the other owners in the league had so much money that for them to buy a baseball team was nothing. Unlike Morley, who was definitely reaching. All the buddies were impressed by that—by the fact that he reached and especially by what he grabbed hold of.

Sambito retired Landreaux on an infield grounder for the last out of the game. The Pelicans had won their fourth straight. The buddies all cheered.

"What a way to make a living!"

ST. PETERSBURG · November 6

Two days later I saw Bake McBride again, this time out on the field. It was changing-of-the-guard time at the batting cage. A Winter Haven player on his way to the locker room passed McBride on his way to the cage, bat in hand. The Winter Haven player looked up.

"I heard you got your knees drained," he said.

"Yeah," McBride said. "Same old shit."

Indeed. The season was less than one week old and already the sentimental veneer was beginning to wear thin. Injuries were piling up, mainly pulled hamstrings, "the official injury of the senior league." In the locker room before and after games, the constant traffic in and out of the whirlpool was a daily reminder of age and limits. "Your mind says yes," said Bill Madlock, "but your body snaps you by the ass, says stop!"

Everywhere around the league, players were taking the measure of what they imagined it would be like to play again and what it was really like. Pelicans outfielder Alan Bannister, a twelve-year major-league veteran, was the manager of the Expos AA affiliate in Jacksonville. He looked like a skipper, something to do with cool eyes and a level gaze, someone you'd rather not disappoint if you could help it. On the day we spoke, Bannister was disappointed mainly in himself. He was struggling with two hits in his first eleven at-bats and was temporarily out of the lineup.

"Nobody likes to be put in a position where you're not going to succeed," Bannister said. "It's aggravating. Baseball's always like that, at any level. It's a game of failure. That hasn't changed. Now, here there's not the press, there's not the fifty thousand people, there's not the contracts you're trying to shoot for, there's not a lot of variables that you have in the big leagues. But there's still your own pressure.

"I think the biggest worry for me and a lot of the other guys is staying healthy. I don't have the faith in my legs and my arms that I once had. When you're on first base and somebody hits the ball in the gap and you're used to running at a certain speed, only now you're not getting there so you try to push it a little more—that's where I have my biggest fear that something's gonna snap or break or pull. You can't expect to be as aggressive as you once were."

"Is it fun?"

"I've been putting on the uniform for a long time. Only time will tell how long it will be before this gets a little old. We don't have a lot of the things that get old in the big leagues. We don't have long road trips. We don't have night after night in a hotel room. We don't have coast-to-coast flights and all-night travel. And we have a lot of days off, seven or eight days a month, so that will break it up. Just when it might start to get a little bit tiresome, I think it will be over."

With Bannister watching from the bench, St. Pete got by Winter Haven that night, 10–9, running their division-leading record to 5–1. For Ron LeFlore, who was originally signed out of prison by the Detroit Tigers, it was a night to relive the glory of the past, not with words but with deeds. Since he retired in 1982, LeFlore had stumbled trying to find his way. For a while he worked as a baggage handler for Eastern Airlines and even earned a promotion to ticket-counter duty, but the job didn't last. "I couldn't go and get a nine-to-five job," he explained ingenuously. "It doesn't seem to be in my make-up." But tonight, appearing in his first game for the Pelicans, LeFlore went three-for-five and drove home the winning run with a bases-loaded single in the bottom of the ninth.

"This was exciting," he later told reporters who gathered at his locker. "It feels like the big leagues. It felt great to contribute."

It was, however, another disappointing crowd, only six hundred twenty-eight on a warm Monday night. Jim Morley watched the game from high up in the grandstand behind home plate. He was joined in the late innings by Rick Langford—the former A's pitcher, now general manager of the Bradenton Explorers— who had driven across the Skyway Bridge on an off day to look over the competition and maybe make a deal. Langford was curious about Pelicans relief pitcher Sammy Stewart.

"Does he still set like this?" Langford asked Morley, bringing his fists together at chin level.

"He still sets like that."

Stewart, a former relief pitcher with the Orioles, Red Sox, and Indians, was off to a rough start with the Pelicans. He had given up six hits and four walks in only four innings of work. Moreover, he was getting on people's nerves. It seemed like he was always hitting somebody up for a loan—teammates, the owner, everybody. Very casually, Morley asked Langford, "How much would you give me for him? C'mon, right now."

"I'll give you two thousand," Langford said.

"Make it twenty-three."

"Make it two, that's fair."

Morley hesitated, but only for a second. "Okay, two. I'll check it with Bobby [Tolan, the manager] after the game."

"Bullshit," Langford said. "You're the owner, you make the deal."

"Okay," Morley said. "Two."

Sold, for two thousand dollars to the Bradenton Explorers, Sammy Stewart. The deal took all of thirty seconds to arrange. They didn't even shake hands.

"I'm taking your word for it he can still throw," Langford said.

"He can still throw. If he can't throw, you don't have to pay me."

After LeFlore's game-winning hit, I followed Morley down to the Pelicans' locker room. Everyone was in a good mood, including Stewart, who hadn't played. He stripped down to a pair of knee-length stretch shorts, white sanitaries, maroon stirrups, and a gray Red Sox T-shirt that said on the back, "53 will always be #1 in Boston." He took two beers from the cooler and filled a paper plate with salad and lasagna from the postgame spread. When he sat down to eat it was not in front of his locker, like most players, but at the picnic table, where there was company. "All right, fellas!" he said. "Way to play!"

Morley was already down the hall, talking to Bobby Tolan.

After he finished eating, Stewart took off the rest of his clothes, stepped into a pair of flip-flops, and trudged off toward the communal shower. A minute later, Tolan emerged from his office. He motioned to pitching coach Dock Ellis and whispered something in his ear. Ellis heard without expression, then went to the shower, pointed at Stewart, and wiggled his index finger, like a teacher calling a delinquent student to the front of the class. Stewart came out—naked and dripping and carrying a towel that was too small anyway to circle his waist—and followed Ellis down the hall and into Tolan's office. The door closed behind them.

Five minutes later, the door opened. Stewart, still naked, walked straight to his locker and began to dress.

"I heard you're going to Bradenton," I asked him. "Is it true?"

Stewart looked at me with an unnatural face. It wasn't anger, and it wasn't pain. It was more like the face of a little kid who was being picked on by older kids at the playground and was pretending, pathetically, that he didn't care. He actually made a smile. "Yeah," he said. "I don't want to talk about it right now."

That's okay, I understood. Same old shit.

ST. PETERSBURG • November 7

TONIGHT WAS WADE BOGGS NIGHT AT AL LANG STADIUM. THE Pelicans had invited the Red Sox star, who lived across the bay in Tampa, to throw out the first pitch and lend a little of his big-league panache to the senior league. Before the game, he stood around the batting cage like everybody else and watched the players hit.

"Bernie!" he called out in greeting.

"Boggsie!" said Bernie Carbo, stepping in. "I been watching you on TV. Let me show you how to go to left."

Boggs smiled in acknowledgment. He was dressed for leisure, Florida style, in a pink-and-orange polo shirt, pants that didn't need a belt, and a pair of palomino, soft-leather pumps. His whole being was enveloped in an invisible mist of sweet-smelling cologne, strong enough to induce nausea. Which reminded me— Gary Carter had smelled nearly as fruity when he walked into the press box at West Palm Beach last week. Was that what made you a big leaguer these days, you wore perfume?

The atmosphere around the batting cage was loose and easy, as always. If there was anything I envied the ballplayers, it was their swings. Hitting is more than just a lot of fun; it's the basic skill you need to play the game. Practice is the only way to improve, and that's the problem. Think of it—all a basketball player needs to practice *his* game's most fundamental skill is a ball, a hoop, and a patch of asphalt. Is it any wonder they score so many points? But a baseball player, just to hit, needs *many* balls, a bat, a backstop, a pitcher (willing *and* capable), a catcher (optional but recommended), several fielders, and about two level acres of grass. These things in combination are hard to come by. To have played baseball at all is to regret never having had nearly enough opportunities to swing the bat.

Suddenly Bill Lee sprang from the direction of the on-deck circle, cut a sharp corner into the mouth of the cage, dug in on the left side of the plate, waved his bat aggressively, and when the pitch came straight and hard slapped a line drive out over second base. Ordinarily managers don't take batting practice. Neither do pitchers in leagues that play with the designated-hitter rule. Lee was both the manager of the Winter Haven Super Sox and one of their starting pitchers, but he also loved to hit. He had been among the first of the potential players contacted by Jim Morley to mail in his reply card and on it he scribbled this message: "What do you mean DH? I hit .350 my last year with the Expos. I could be the best hitter in this league."

The DH was a big issue with Lee. He'd fought it from the start, and he wasn't about to let up now. Lee hated the DH mainly because he loved baseball, loved all the varied skills it required. "You should play the game *totally*," he insisted. "You should hit, run, throw, bunt, and field your position." But with the DH, as with everything else on which Lee had an opinion, there was a larger issue. "The DH rule," he said, "is probably the most scrupulous"—I think he must have meant *unscrupulous* but with Lee you could never be sure—"rule created by the owners to decrease rosters and instigate specialization, and according to Buckminster Fuller all forms of specialization lead to extinction. He was a great thinker."

There were many reasons Lee was chosen to manage the Super Sox: he'd had seven memorable years in Boston in the 1970s, which fit with the Red Sox theme the team was promoting; he had a cult following among fans in the age group the senior league was trying to reach; he was accommodating to reporters, as well as entertaining; and most of all he was a baseball misfit, a philosopher in double knits, a humanist and an existentialist, a socialist and a libertarian, a contrarian, a reader, a *thinker*—qualities which invariably led to friction between Lee and baseball managers, front-office types, and, surprisingly, many players,

but which Mitchell Maxwell, the Super Sox owner and a producer of movies and off-Broadway plays, found immensely ap-
pealing.

"I think Bill Lee is a fantastic person," Maxwell gushed. "He's
a genius, he's a great spirit, and he's what this league is all about."

True geniuses are tolerated their excesses. In Winter Haven
five days ago, after the last out of a disastrous two-game series
in which the Super Sox were outscored by the Pelicans, 21–4, a
reporter had asked Lee for his assessment of the Pelicans. "I
think they're assholes," he said. "They're good ballplayers, but
that doesn't make them nice men. It's a damn militaristic regime
over there. [Pelicans manager Bobby Tolan] makes them shave
their mustaches. He's a Hermann Goering. He's an anal-retentive
black man. He should take a shit somewhere and relax."

Lee had said so many outrageous things over the years that
his currency was devalued; he probably couldn't offend anyone
if he tried. Steve Henderson, the Pelicans' right fielder, got such
a kick out of Lee's tirade that he asked the reporter from the St.
Petersburg *Times* to read him the quote twice. "He's always been
like that," Henderson said, laughing. Tolan, on the other hand,
didn't know what to think, a reaction which probably pleased
Lee more than any other. "I'm not going to respond to him,"
Tolan said stiffly. "Bill Lee says what he wants to say. I don't
know what he's trying to do." (Jim Morley was miffed, but he
quickly recovered and organized Boo Bill Lee Night—free Boo!
placards for every fan.)

Lee began tonight's game like every other manager, watching.
Then in the top of the third inning, with one out, a man on
second, his team down by a run, and cleanup hitter Leon Roberts unable to bat because of an upset stomach, Lee went to his
bench for a pinch hitter and sent out . . . himself. The fans
hooted and howled. Some who had been here last night waved
their Boo! cards.

Lee's unorthodox move was an affront to everything that is
written in The Book of Baseball and the ghost of Abner Dou-
bleday made him pay. First Lee struck out looking. Then in the
bottom half of the inning, playing left field, Lee stumbled twice
on a line drive by Jerry Martin and got crossed up on a fly ball
by hot-hitting Ron LeFlore. Aided by Lee's misplays, the Pelicans scored seven runs that inning and won going away, 16–3.

After the game, I went looking for Lee in the visitors' clubhouse. I found him at the first locker on the left, just inside the door, expounding to a writer from *Sports Illustrated.* Lee had his hat off and showed a full head of gray hair, cut boyishly in a style that made me think both of Andy Warhol and Peter Lynch. His lower half looked solid enough to fill a pair of football pants, with muscle, not fat. Later I learned that he did more running (including sprints) than the rest of his teammates combined. When I walked in, Lee was busy briefing the national press on the state of the Super Sox.

"It's been a weird start," Lee was saying. "If something could go wrong, it would go wrong. I'm just trying to help keep the guys together for seven more days. I told 'em when the moon loses its horns, you got six days to get in shape. Chief Joseph of the Nez Percé Indians said that, before he beat General Sheridan in the battle of Big Hole, Montana, the last Indian chief to defeat an American."

Lee paused while he reached into his pants pocket and pulled out a silver money clip, thick with bills. "You shouldn't play the game with your money clip in your back pocket," he said, and dropped the clip on the floor. He grinned in a way Cheech and Chong would have recognized.

"They may be doing good, but they're gonna get worse and we're gonna get better. LeFlore's hot, [Lenny] Randle's hot, Henderson's hot. What's the other guy, Martin, he hit the dog shit out of the ball. This game has a way of equalizing its way out. Make good pitches, they don't hit 'em. Make bad pitches, they rope 'em. Team ERA's gotta be way up there. One thing we don't have is we don't have one sore arm. Pitchers' arms are very sound." Lee was silent for a beat, then "Their ERAs are very high. Hah!"

I was working on a theory I wanted to test with Lee. I thought that when a player looked back on his career, he would tend to recollect mostly the days when he went three-for-three or struck out the cleanup hitter with the tying run on second. That is, until he joined the senior league and had his first night like Lee had tonight. Then he'd remember that baseball was a hard game and that it was not fun to mess up in front of other people. "Do you ever wonder why you got yourself into this?" I asked him.

"No!" Lee said. He looked at me like I was nuts. "Shit, no. It's a way of getting in shape and reducing my insurance premiums. I had a long talk with Equitable. They owe us. Heck, there's guys around here that coulda been dead in ten years and now they're gonna live for another fifteen or twenty."

"Has anybody been paid yet?"

"I don't care if they never pay us. Pay is irrelevant. Just cover my expenses and let me stay down here and have a good time. Money is totally irrelevant in this situation."

"But you have to be paid," I said. "Otherwise the owners make all the money."

"I'm a socialist," Lee said seriously. "I believe a worker should be paid his fair share. I'm a worker-oriented guy. But I don't think of money in my life. I'm an Indian. I just read a lot of philosophy books, kiss flowers and babies." Lee grinned like Cheech and Chong again. "You all right?" he asked us. We nodded and put away our pens.

Lee took a deep pull on his can of beer and turned to face his teammates. They were crowded together in the cramped space in various stages of undress, some standing, some sitting, and they all looked tired. "Get in the pool, guys!" Lee hollered.

Across the room I noticed Bernie Carbo. He'd had his turn in the whirlpool tonight and was already showered and dressed and well beyond his first beer. Carbo had started the game at DH but lost his spot in the fifth inning when Lee brought himself in from left field to pitch. An inning later, Carbo was up in the press box with wild eyes, saying "Where's Jim Morley?" and "We gotta talk!" The two went off to an empty section of the stands, and while Morley sat calmly with his legs draped over the seat in front of him, Carbo leaned into Morley's ear. Whatever it was they were talking about, Carbo was definitely hot.

"I'll tell you exactly what's going on," Carbo said when I asked him about it. "I was talking to him about how we wish it had been a better game. Yesterday we played a good game and we lost. Today we played a horseshit game and that's not professional. We want to stay in the ball game. We did things wrong today."

Not all of Carbo's words were fully formed by the time they came tumbling out of his mouth. His eyes were wet. Without being prompted he launched into a recitation of his recent life story, the same one I'd overheard him deliver to several other reporters in the last few days. "My last year was 1980. I gave my glove and spikes away and I started cutting hair and going to school and bartending and running dry wall. I was trying to work for a living and I found out how the real people live."

The last year had been the worst. His mother had committed suicide. Three months later his dad died. Carbo was fat and depressed, and his blood pressure was way up. Then he heard about the senior league. He lost weight, his blood pressure went down. Recently he'd sold his house and salon in Detroit and moved with his wife and three daughters to Winter Haven. The senior league was his salvation.

"We have to realize how fortunate we are to be playing the game that we love best," Carbo said. I wished he wasn't standing quite so close. "I don't care if this league ends right now. If it ends today, I've enjoyed myself."

On the way home, I stopped in at the Pelicans' downtown office on Central Avenue. It was late and Morley was alone at his big wooden desk, which was positioned like a throne in the middle of the room. He was writing checks. I asked him what was up with Carbo.

"He's just mad 'cause we whipped their butts," Morley said, and smiled like a winner.

As it turned out, Carbo was mad at his own team more than anything else. He had complained to Morley that the players never knew what time they were supposed to hit (how could they; Bill Lee didn't even own a watch), or when they were supposed to stretch, or whether or not they had to take infield practice before a game; in short, the kind of information that was posted every day for all to see in Bobby Tolan's clubhouse.

Morley thought the whole thing was pretty funny, as well as a sign of where the league was headed. Less than one week after Bill Lee blasted the Pelicans for being a "damn militaristic regime," here was Carbo confiding to Morley that at least some of the Super Sox players were hungry for a little military discipline themselves. They may have come down here to have fun or make money, but as long as they were here they wanted to win.

The Super Sox were off for the next two days—plenty of time to contemplate their record of one and seven and consider what they might do about it.

BRADENTON, PORT ST. LUCIE • *November 8*

THE SIGN AT MCKECHNIE FIELD SAID, "VISITORS WELCOME AT YOUR own risk." Like all the really old parks, McKechnie was tucked into the corner of a city block, in this case, the northeast corner of 9th Street and 17th Avenue in Bradenton. The ball yard was just shabby enough to fit logically into its setting: a dowdy, edge-of-downtown neighborhood long since given over to used-car lots and public housing. McKechnie was bordered on the south by an eight-foot-high concrete wall, which gave way to a corrugated tin fence when it reached the right-field foul pole, the tin running all the way around the outfield to the third-base side, where it hooked up with a chain-link fence. The press entrance was through a gate in the concrete wall. As I showed my pass and was waved through, I had the uncomfortable feeling that I was entering a prison.

But once inside I was charmed. I couldn't imagine a friendlier setting for baseball. The green tin fences ran straight out from either foul line, following the line of the base paths and the city streets rather than the rounded perimeter of the infield. Three miniature grandstands with sharp tin roofs were pulled up close to home plate like chairs around a fire. And there were no lights. McKechnie, the spring-training home of the Pittsburgh Pirates, was probably the last place left in America where professional baseball was played exclusively during the day. Since the kids were all in school and everybody else had to work, it was mostly retirees who showed up at McKechnie these winter afternoons. Between innings, they tapped their feet in time to the big-band sounds of Glenn Miller and Artie Shaw.

The Orlando Juice were in town today for the first of a two-game series. The only other game on the schedule was a night game in St. Lucie between the Legends and the West Palm Beach Tropics. The season was young and I was feeling ambitious. Foolishly, I thought I'd try to see them both.

I ran into Sammy Stewart in the Explorers locker room before the game. He apologized for brushing me off the other night in St. Petersburg. He wanted me to know that he was happy now in a Bradenton uniform. Manager Clete Boyer had told Stewart as soon as he arrived that he was looking for one more starter and Stewart thought he had a shot at eventually winning the job. Meanwhile, he was content to be the setup man and work on strengthening his arm.

"I wanna play professional baseball next year," he said in a thick Appalachian accent. Stewart was from Swannanoa, North Carolina, east of Asheville in the Smoky Mountains. He was tall like a mountain man and wore a big, bushy mustache. "I wanna go to spring training with somebody, hopefully the Atlanta Braves, Cincinnati Reds, St. Louis"—he said it "St. Looey"— "Cardinals, somebody. You just don't want to fool yourself. I don't want to start off like a ball of fire. I wanna be able to compete the whole year long."

Stewart last pitched in the big leagues in 1987 with Cleveland. He worked just twenty-seven innings that year, all in relief, and wound up with a record of four wins, two losses, and three saves. At thirty-five, Stewart was young for the senior league, but he was awfully old to be talking about winning an invitation to spring training, especially after having sat out a full year. He wanted to hope, and I wanted to be hopeful with him, but I knew the chances were next to nothing that any big-league team would be interested in a senior-league setup man who'd already been sold down the river for two thousand dollars. The fact that the three teams he'd mentioned were the ones closest to his home—as if he could choose—made me wonder about his grip on reality.

Stewart also made a point of mentioning that what with payday not until the sixteenth, he was kind of hard up. "It's hurt me," he said. "I don't know about a lot of other people, but it's hurt me. I had a lot of bills before I left the house anyway." He also left a lot of loans unpaid in St. Petersburg, which Jim Morley had made good as a favor to his players.

It was more than a week into the season and all I'd seen so far were two home runs. Today in Bradenton I saw six—two by Bill Madlock of the Juice, one each by teammates Dave Cash and Larvell Blanks, and one each by Explorers Gene Clines and Jim Morrison. Part of the reason for the sudden explosion was McKechnie Field's odd dimensions: three hundred forty feet down the lines and four hundred ten to center but only three hundred fifty-nine feet to the power alley in left-center—a chip shot by big-league standards. On the other side of the left-field fence there was a boy's club, one large plate-glass window of which was shattered by Clines's homer in the fourth. I assumed the boys would make him pay.

You never realized how much you remembered about a ball-player until you saw him in uniform again, and then it all came back—the habits, the mannerisms, the thousand details every fan kept stored away on a back shelf of the mind. I felt that way about Dave Cash. It had been ten years since I last saw him play and yet I knew the moment he appeared on the field that every-thing about him was exactly right—the bowed legs, the fussy way he wore his hat high on his head, the finger's width of stirrup that showed between his sanitary socks and his pants, the flip-up sunglasses that always seemed to be flipped up, details that in their sum connected what was taking place here and now with what had happened years ago in big-league stadiums, and so guaranteed the senior league some measure of legitimacy.

By the eighth inning, the Juice were comfortably ahead, 11–5. If I was going to make it to St. Lucie—about one hundred sixty miles east of here, mostly on back roads—I had to leave now. (I saw in the box score the next day where Hal McRae of the Explorers hit a solo homer in the ninth, the seventh of the day for both teams. Unfortunately for the Explos, as they were dubbed by the local headline writers, McRae's homer was too little, too late. Final score: Orlando, 11, Bradenton, 8.)

Spring training was big business in Florida. The state esti-mated that baseball was directly responsible for three hundred million dollars in annual spending, a figure which didn't begin to measure the overall economic impact. As that impact grew, developers and local governments fought hard to attract teams to their area. The most obvious winners were the teams them-selves. Recently the Rangers left Pompano for a new playground in Port Charlotte, the Reds quit Tampa for Plant City, and the Royals abandoned their home in Fort Myers for Boardwalk and Baseball, an amusement park (recently closed) on the interstate between Tampa and Orlando. Spurned by the Royals, Fort Myers was readying a new complex for the Twins, who planned to depart Orlando. Rather than lose the White Sox to God knows where, Sarasota had graciously provided them with fancy new

digs, built with taxpayers' money. And in Bradenton, city officials were bracing for the inevitable announcement that the Pirates had decided definitely to take their business elsewhere.

The St. Lucie County Sports Complex was eight miles from
the town of Port St. Lucie in a doomed stand of piney woods
between Interstate 95 and Florida's turnpike. The Mets moved
here from St. Petersburg just last year, seduced by the promise
of a custom-built $11.2 million stadium and training facility, plus
a piece of the action in adjacent St. Lucie West, "A New Town
Where You Can Live, Work and Play." If you believed the pro-
moters, St. Lucie West was "taking shape quickly," although
most of what was promised—schools, churches, office parks, golf
courses, "secure, private neighborhoods," a mall, and *two* college
campuses—remained in the planning stages. For now, the dom-
inant feature on the landscape was the ballpark. Floodlit, surrounded on three sides by a vast moat of asphalt, it shone coldly
in the darkness like a highway rest stop.

The Legends were owned by Burt Abrams and Joe Sprung,
two accountants from New York City whose vision of what a
senior-league team should be was probably the same as that of
most fans. Some of the Legends really were legends, or almost—
names like Felix Millan, Jerry Grote, George Foster, Bobby
Bonds, Fred Stanley, Oscar Gamble, Vida Blue, Rollie Fingers,
and player-manager Graig Nettles. The Legends had marquee
value, no question about that, but whether they had the talent
to match was not yet known. Early indications were not good.
With a record of one and five, the Legends were tied right now
with Earl Weaver's Gold Coast Suns for last place in the league's
southern division.

The Tropics, on the other hand, were alone in first place, with
a perfect record. They had their share of big names, too—Dave
Kingman, Mickey Rivers, Toby Harrah—but it was obvious that
in putting together his team, manager Dick Williams meant to
win some ball games. He had a lot of guys like Ron Washington,
Rodney Scott, Tito Landrum, and Jerry White, marginal big
leaguers but all-stars in the senior league. The Tropics were by
far the fastest team in the senior league, *and* they had the best-
looking uniforms. Tonight they wore the road version—orange
stirrups, gray pants, a gray buttoned shirt with Tropics written
across the chest in blue-green script trimmed in orange, and
an orange hat embroidered with a blue-green palm tree in the

shape of a T. The colors went together beautifully, like grass and clay.

Not much of a crowd. Only eight hundred thirty fans showed up at the park tonight, which meant there were about six thousand five hundred empty blue-plastic seats. With so few voices, those that were raised were easily heard.

"WE GOT A WHOLE FIELD OF DINOSAURS OUT HERE!" yelled a man sitting behind me along the first-base line. "I THINK WE OUGHT TO MAKE GASOLINE OUT OF THEM!"

He was right. The Legends, especially, looked their age. First baseman Steve Ontiveros left the game early with a pulled muscle in his rib cage. Third baseman Nettles went down with a pulled groin. And Grote, who came in to play first base, looked fat and slow and every one of his forty-eight years; with his full gray beard he resembled an old sea captain.

Legends, yes. But living? Barely. When thirty-seven-year-old John D'Acquisto surrendered three runs on five hits in an inning and a third—and looked miserable doing it—Leather Lungs lit into him: "C'MON, BONEHEAD, DON'T YOU REMEMBER WHY YOU RETIRED?"

In the top of the second, with two outs, runners on first and third, and Kingman at the plate, Legends starting pitcher Don Cooper tried an old high school trick, one that never worked even then: you step off the rubber, you fake the throw to first, then you turn and throw to third and hope to catch the runner leaning toward home. Well, tonight it worked. What's more, the embarrassed victim was Jerry White, who made his living teaching Expos minor leaguers how to run the bases. "Oh, man," he said after the game. "I made a boo-boo. I'm glad none of them was here tonight to see that."

But the evening was far from a wash. I got a good look at Walt Williams, the original Kirby Puckett, retired since 1975. "Now batting," the PA announcer said, "Walt 'No-Neck' Williams." Williams was only five-six, most of it muscle. When he stood at the plate waiting for the pitch, his chin fell below his shoulders. Not only did he have no neck, he had no knees, no calves, and no ankles. His legs were like a pair of square posts. But he still swung hard and smiled doing it.

Also, I saw George Foster hit a home run. Toward the end of his career when he was with the Mets and the White Sox, Foster's swings all looked late to me. But when he turned on reliever Doug Capilla in the seventh inning, he looked like the same

George Foster who in 1977 hit fifty-two homers and drove in one hundred forty-nine runs for the Reds. It was an illusion, no doubt, but the effect was pleasing.

By the bottom of the ninth, the Tropics were coasting with an 8–3 lead. Fingers—who had acquired a biker's beer gut to go with his handlebar mustache—was on the mound, looking to wrap things up for starter Tim Stoddard. After Foster reached base on an error, Clint Hurdle grounded into a double play. One out to go. But then Williams doubled, and that brought Bonds to the plate, pinch-hitting for Gamble.

Bonds hit a home run that was the last and longest of a day filled with home runs. It was one of those magical blasts, the ball seeming to climb for as long as it could be seen until it pierced the bubble of light and disappeared above the pines. "Anything that flies that far," a player remarked after the game, "ought to have a flight attendant on it."

After Bonds's homer, Stanley flied out to left. The ball game was over. Another win for the Tropics, another loss for the Legends. It was after 10:00 and I was three hours from home.

On lonely roads in the pale light of a quarter moon I drove fast and without stopping, through Basinger, Lorida, Crewsville, and Zolfo Springs, across the Kissimmee River, the Peace and the Horse, past farmhouses with palm trees growing in their yards, through swirls of mist that rose to meet the car like a swamp tide, home to bed in my pink shack on the beach.

BRADENTON · November 10

A BRIGHT WINTER DAY IN BRADENTON, HOT IN THE SUN AND COLD in the shade. I arrived at the visiting clubhouse not long after the team bus. The players were taking their time getting ready. A card game was in progress. Newspapers, coffee, and doughnuts were spread out on top of a picnic table.

I found Bill Lee in the manager's dressing room, off the main clubhouse. He was eating a bran muffin and drinking coffee. Between bites, he let his mouth hang open, showing a gleaming row of perfect (false) incisors. Like his teammates, Lee was still in street clothes, in his case, jeans, a T-shirt, and a Ducks Unlimited cap. The cap's what got me. Was that possible? Was Bill Lee—environmentalist, political liberal, well-known Bohemian—also a hunter?

"Yeah, we're all hunters," he said, looking up at me tiredly from under his cap. His eyes were like a blue sky on a muggy day. "Of our thirty-two teeth, four of them are eyeteeth. Those eyeteeth are in our body for one reason—ripping of flesh. Anybody that says he's not a hunter is a liar."

Lee's nickname was The Spaceman. He got it when a reporter said something in the Red Sox clubhouse one day about the latest lunar launch, or so the story goes. John Kennedy, a utility infielder, pointed at Lee and said, "We don't need to watch that. We have our own spaceman right over there." Lee didn't mind the nickname. "I just thought it was off the mark," he wrote in his autobiography, *The Wrong Stuff.* "I would have preferred to be known as Earth Man."

When Lee first heard about the senior league, he was living with his second wife in Craftsbury, Vermont, a town with less than one thousand population, twenty-five miles south of the Quebec border.

"What have you been doing?" I asked him.

"Running for President and making maple syrup. One of the two is an honest job. Also been running around south Florida warning people to move away from the coastline. Like Chicken Little, 'The sky is falling, the sky is falling.' The tide is rising, the tide is rising!" Lee demonstrated by raising his voice and waving his arms. "This is the first year I didn't play organized ball, but now that I'm organized I've gone since 1955 when I was ten. I play hardball for the town of Newport and I been playing senior ball in Canada since 1982. I can play twenty-four hours a day, twelve months out of the year."

"Are you working?" That was really what I had meant by my last question.

"Building a house for my wife."

"What do you do for *pay?*"

"Oh, I go to the University of Saskatchewan and speak and they give me five hundred dollars. I go to the University of Alberta and speak. I sign autographs. Subsistence, more or less."

Lee was from southern California. He went to college at USC. Knowing this, I wondered how he ended up living in a place that was geographically, politically, and culturally the opposite of where he came from. Northern Vermont, as Lee described it, was a place with "no billboards, no road signs. If you wanna get somewhere, you gotta ask somebody. You ask somebody, you have to have patience 'cause Vermonters go, 'yeah, nope.' They don't offer anything else."

"Unlike you."

"Nope. Well, you're right. I been portrayed as someone that gets involved in everything. If that's the case, to maintain sanity I have to live in a place that gives me total freedom and peace. That's why I picked Vermont."

That made a certain amount of sense, but then Lee was just getting started.

"It also happens to be geographically located between Boston and Montreal, where I played my whole major-league career. It also happens to be in New England. It happens to be in the mountains of New England, where all revolutionary ideas came from. Revolution did not spring up in Philadelphia, it did not spring up in Virginia, it did not spring up in New York. Revolution sprung up in the hills of Vermont and the hills of Massachusetts. Revolution did not come out of the valleys or the cities of China, it came out of the mountains of China with Mao Tse-tung. Revolution always springs up in the mountains, never on the cities or the plains. They're always too involved in commerce, trying to make money. Ideas always come out of the mountains."

Lee was off and running. He had "developed a way of answering questions," as he admitted in his book, "that often had little to do with the question being asked." In 1979, Bowie Kuhn sent three goons to the Expos clubhouse to question Lee about his admission that he "used" marijuana. One of them wanted to know exactly how he "used" it, that is, if he didn't actually smoke it.

Lee replied that he sprinkled marijuana on his pancakes, strictly for medicinal purposes. "That THC makes me impervious to all the toxic bus fumes and other forms of air pollution I may encounter while running," he told them. The amazing part was, the goons wrote it all down.

All his life, Lee had resisted, even mocked authority. How then could he turn around suddenly and be the man in charge?

"Do you *like* being manager?" I asked him.

"I don't," he said. "Don't like it. I don't believe in managers.

But the other twenty-four on the ball club do so we're bringing in Ed Nottle now, i.e., to be the manager that they want."

Without meaning to at all, I had stumbled onto a piece of real news. Lee was not the manager anymore. After only seven games, he had become the first senior-league manager to be fired. Later I found out what happened. On Wednesday, the day after the fiasco in St. Petersburg, general manager Rick Maxwell had called his brother, Mitch, the owner, in New York to tell him that the situation on the team had reached the crisis stage. It wasn't just Bernie Carbo anymore; now everybody craved more discipline. If they didn't do something right away, Rick feared, the team was going to fall apart. Mitch flew in from New York the next day. Together the Maxwells talked to Lee. The meetings lasted late into the night. Eventually, Lee agreed to step aside, on the understanding that he be given the nebulous title of co-manager.

The Maxwells wanted an older, wiser, more experienced manager to replace Lee. Ed Nottle, manager of the Red Sox AAA farm team at Pawtucket, fit the bill. He had left Winter Haven only four days earlier at the conclusion of the Red Sox winter instructional league and was back home in Evansville, Indiana. But as soon as he got the call, he was on the next plane. The team Nottle inherited was in last place with a record of one and six. Today would be his first game.

"My theory," said Lee, "is just come to the ballpark, get ready and play, and I expected everybody else to work as hard as I did. But baseball players need regimentation. Most ballplayers do. I was an antiregimentation guy, but that theory does not work in this situation and everybody brought it to my attention. They couldn't handle that concept. They had to have a manager who's always sitting down, rocking back and forth like Danny Murtaugh"—Lee demonstrated again, rocking back and forth on a stool with his arms tightly folded—"so we're giving them Danny Murtaugh. We brought in a person of regimented nature to sit on the bench and everybody can go, 'Yeah, we got organization.'"

Lee would never admit it, but discipline was not the only issue. Some of Lee's teammates, even if they did not actively dislike him, were at times resentful of him. He was always stirring things up. The business with Bobby Tolan was a big kick for Lee; it was *fun* to make people angry. He even got to show off the fact that he knew who Hermann Goering was and what it meant to be anal-retentive. But Bernie Carbo was bitter. He let it be known that he couldn't concentrate on baseball when everybody in the ballpark was booing Bill Lee. Lee's second mistake was putting himself in the lineup. In baseball, even in the senior league, pitchers pitch and position players play their positions. When Lee inserted himself in left field, twice, his teammates fretted about becoming supporting actors in the Bill Lee Show. Lee insisted he was only doing what was best for the team, but the others weren't so sure.

Then there was the compatibility factor. When it came right down to it, a lot of Lee's teammates just thought he was too damn weird. Darrell Brandon, who was born in 1940, had a word that, for him, perfectly expressed Lee's otherness. "He's a Communist," Brandon said.

Lee had originally been hired, he reminded me, as much for "my political stance and my beliefs on humanity" as for any reason having to do with baseball. "We were trying to make a ball club that was different than any other ball club," he said, "different from the thing we all got released from." Lee's definition of the word "released" was more like a convict's than a ballplayer's.

A noble experiment, perhaps, but it had failed. In the end, Lee was fired for the same reason managers have always been fired: he lost too many ball games. That was no different at all.

ORLANDO · November 12

ON MY WAY TO ORLANDO FOR A LOOK AT THE JUICE IN THEIR OWN ballpark. East of Tampa on Interstate 4, beyond the urban sprawl, the speed limit kicked up to sixty-five. This was big-blue-sky country. Grapefruit and orange trees—planted in perfect rows in white, phosphate-rich soil—fanned out from both sides of the highway. The trees were green and thick with winter fruit.

There was a time when this part of Florida was all agriculture and mining. Apart from the ubiquitous alligator farms, tourism was a coastal phenomenon. The snowbirds who flocked south in winter followed predictable flight patterns. Easterners gathered on the Atlantic coast, around Miami and Fort Lauderdale. Midwesterners gravitated toward St. Petersburg on the Gulf of Mexico. The draw, in either case, was the beach. Sand, surf, and swaying palms, a tropical paradise that didn't ask for your passport.

By 1990, close to forty million tourists were visiting Florida every year. Other than through the window of an airplane, millions never even saw the ocean. Why bother, when for $23.95 per person you could visit Sea World and stroll through a clear plastic tube at the bottom of a six-hundred-thousand-gallon saltwater tank stocked with three dozen man-eating sharks?

Sea World was only one among hundreds of packaged attractions that drew tourists by the car, bus, and plane load from all over the world to vacation in central Florida. For a complete listing, all you had to do was check the billboards that sprouted above the orange trees along I-4: Busch Gardens, Cypress Gardens, Arabian Nights, Medieval Times, Boardwalk and Baseball, Alligatorland Safari Zoo, Super Seminole Greyhound Park, Mystery Fun House, Wet 'n Wild, Water Mania, the new Universal Studios theme park, and my favorite, the Tupperware Museum, with its fascinating collection of "containers from many cultures." Altogether too much fun.

The sales pitch built to a thundering climax on the final approach to Orlando, where time began in 1965, the year Walt Disney announced plans to build a "Vacation Kingdom" on twenty-seven thousand acres of proverbial swampland. No more open skies from here on in, no more sweet smell of citrus. Time now to roll up the windows. The traffic thickened as the highway entered a glass canyon of high-rise luxury hotels. A computerized signboard blinked an urgent message to all motorists: "TWO MILES TO MICKEY!"

But where was Tinker Field? No less than four different toll collectors on two sides of town had never heard of Tinker Field, nor the Orlando Juice, nor senior baseball. I scanned the horizon for telltale light standards. Eventually, by dumb luck, I landed before the looming, concrete bulk of the Citrus Bowl. There in its shadow, hunched over and forlorn, sat tiny Tinker Field.

The Twins played their spring games there, or would for one more season. In 1991 they were moving to a multipurpose, all-in-one, state-of-the-art (yeah-yeah) training complex in Fort Myers, built, as they all were now, with public money. Tinker

Field—with its pretty blue grandstand and scary, unprotected front-row seats—was safe for the time being; the Twins' Southern League affiliate, the SunRays, were staying on as summer tenants. But this town had its sights set on a big-league expansion franchise, and already there was talk of a new stadium.

Poor Tinker Field. It looked like it was about to be steamrolled anyway by a football stadium. The Citrus Bowl's massive west wall backed up to within a few feet of the right-field fence and jutted over the outfield grass. It blocked out the sky. If you sat through a game, at some point, out of the corner of your eye, you'd see it move. Left-handed hitters were the most affected. It taunted them, and they ended up overswinging, striving always to knock it down.

There was plenty of that going on as the visiting Pelicans took batting practice. Dwight Lowry, a left-handed-hitting catcher who spent parts of three seasons with the Tigers in the mid-eighties, had just finished taking potshots at the construction workers readying the Citrus Bowl for New Year's Day. Lowry was taking his turn around the bases when a booming voice called to him from the first-base dugout: "Hey! You didn't hit like that for Sparky!"

Lowry looked over. He didn't have to squint. "Yes, I did!" he said.

"Oh, okay, all right," said Gates Brown, the Juice's manager. He smiled concedingly and waved Lowry on.

The Juice players were in their locker room; they were free until infield practice. Brown was out here all by himself—meaty hands tucked under enormous thighs, rocking back and forth on the bench, eyes scanning the field. Most managers try not to let on how much fun they're having. If they act bored or exasperated half the time, it's because they want you to think that their job is demanding and unpleasant and a horrible routine, just like yours. But not Gates Brown. A man his size would be intimidating if it weren't for that trigger-happy big-league grin.

"I look forward to each and every day," he said, his voice so deep it resonated in the wooden bench and could be felt. "When I went home, people asked me, 'Do you like it down here?' What the fuck kind of question is *that?* You *gotta* like it, if for no other reason than for the weather, especially this time of year up north. Jesus, I even got a fucking *tan,* man. Can't beat the weather.

Can't beat the *hours*. Shit, come out to the ballpark at five, you're done at ten. I *like* it."

Gates Brown made his debut with the Tigers in 1963 when he was twenty-four years old. The first time he came to the plate, as a pinch hitter, he hit a home run. That's not as rare as you might think; through 1989, sixty-one others had done the same thing, and usually it was just a tease. In Brown's case, he came back in 1964 and won a job in the outfield, batting .272 for the season with fifteen home runs and eleven stolen bases. But his defense was lacking, and one year later he lost his starting job.

"You know," said Brown, "you work hard in the minors, then you get up to the big leagues and you say, 'Damn, am I here?' See, that's only half the battle. The battle is trying to stay for a certain length of time."

Though never again an everyday player, Brown lasted thirteen seasons with the Tigers. He won the battle by adapting to the difficult role of pinch hitter and accepting it as his fate. His best season was 1968—the year Denny McLain won thirty-one games and the Tigers beat St. Louis in the World Series—when he pinch-hit for a .450 average. Overall, he collected one hundred seven career pinch hits and sixteen career pinch homers, both American League records. He retired in 1975.

"I coulda played longer than what I did," he said. "It wasn't about the money. It's just, I wasn't having any *fun*, man. It ain't no fun when you lose, especially when you get thirty-five years old, man. It ain't about just drawing a paycheck with *me*. I like to think I earned it, and being that I wasn't booming the ball like I thought I should, I got out."

Later, Brown returned to the Tigers as hitting coach. He was still with them in 1984 when they won the World Series. The Tigers led the majors in runs scored that year, and naturally Brown expected a reward. This time, it *was* about a paycheck. When management balked, he quit. "You can't win a pennant and draw three million people and offer me a three-thousand-dollar raise," he says. "I ain't gonna take that from nobody. If that's what they thought of me, then to hell with it."

After twenty-five years in the game, Brown found a job as a salesman for a metal-stamping company in Detroit. "It's nice," he said. "Keeps me busy, always moving around. I'm not stuck behind no desk. Being in one spot fucks with me."

Brown was reasonably happy "in the real world," making good

money, spending time with his wife of twenty-seven years, enjoying the grandchildren. A return to baseball, if not the farthest
thing from his mind, was not something he dwelled on. Then
along came the senior league. Phil Breen, who bought the Orlando franchise, turned out to be a Tigers fan. Breen asked
Brown to be his manager, Brown's boss agreed to a three-month
leave of absence, and that's how Brown came to be in the dugout this afternoon, watching batting practice and rhapsodizing
about baseball.

"I believe baseball is like a ballet," Brown said. He spoke like
a preacher, always with the right emphasis, pausing frequently
to lend weight to his words. "You take a lot of basketball and
football players and try to get *them* to play *this* fucking game.
Put a bat in *their* hands and let 'em swing. Some of 'em six-foot-
six, two hundred fifty pounds, look like *sissies* up there. You
don't have to be big and strong to win. I mean, it's—it's an *art*.
It's not about brute strength."

The silences between sentences were filled with the metro-
nomic crack of the bat, like a clock ticking. "When I was in the
big leagues, it was hard for me to sit and watch a game. I'd be
in the clubhouse, I'd be anywhere but on the bench. The way I
played—you know, pinch-hit seventh, eighth, or ninth inning
and that was it—I never really got into the flow of the game.
Sixty-four was the most I got up, four-hundred-and-some times.
Then, well, three years in a row I didn't get up a hundred
times. That's not a hell of a lot of playing. You got to be out
there every fucking day to really get in the flow. That's the fun
part. Ain't no fun sitting here, not for me it wasn't.

"But managing, I'm *in* it, you know? The blood is pumping,
the adrenaline is flowing. Oh, boy, you have a lot of sleepless
nights. I mean, I'll be *keyed up*, man. Be so goddamn tired just
thinking all the time. What they gonna do? Should I bring the
pitcher in? Should I bunt? But that's the good part about it—
you can *control* it. I *enjoy* being in it for nine innings. I like it. I
like it, man. I'm telling you, I *like* it."

Wynne Dillard, investment banker turned Juice general manager, had come up quietly on Brown's blind side and listened to
the last part of his monologue. "Show me how much you like it,
Gates," he said now, "and don't cash your check."

Brown turned halfway and glanced over his shoulder at Dillard. "You know what I do with mine, I send it to Mama. I'm

like the cactus—I can live on nothing." Then he said to Dillard, "Sometimes I think you want out there in a uniform with the boys."

"No," said Dillard, "I want *your* job."

ONLY FIVE HUNDRED SEVENTEEN SHOWED UP FOR TONIGHT'S GAME, sparing Orlando the double indignity of being slaughtered in front of a big home crowd. Gary Rajsich, the Pelicans' left-handed-hitting first baseman who was a flop with the Mets, Cardinals, and Giants but found fame and fortune in Japan, homered twice off the upper deck of the Citrus Bowl (which remained standing). Both times, the ball caromed off the concrete facing and fell back to the outfield grass, where it was retrieved by right fielder Ike Blessitt—who knew a soft ball when he felt one—and casually returned to the pitcher.

By the ninth inning, the Pelicans were way out in front, 11–4. Jamie Easterly, the Juice's fifth pitcher, was trying to wrap things up so we could all go home. He had one out, with runners on first and third, when Alan Bannister hit a pop-up in foul territory—a routine play for the first baseman. Routine, except that Bill Madlock shuffled after the ball with about as much enthusiasm as a punk on a street corner who'd been told by the cops to move along. The ball dropped in front of the dug-out. The fans, what few were left, groaned loud enough to be heard.

Madlock, a lifetime .305 hitter who won three National League batting titles, would ordinarily have been the kind of player that people paid to watch. During his fifteen-year career in the majors, he had a reputation among fans and peers alike for always playing hard. His teammates called him Mad Dog. But so far in the senior league, Madlock had looked tired, like he was just going through the motions. Until tonight, he had been used strictly as a designated hitter, and he was under orders from Gates Brown to lose weight. Orlando made no secret of wanting to get rid of Madlock and his five-figure monthly salary; the team just couldn't find any takers. "He's more than ten thousand dollars' worth of pain in the ass, I guarantee you that," said a member of the Juice front office.

Saved by Madlock's lack of effort, Bannister drew a walk. That was all for Easterly, and, on his way to the showers, he passed within a few feet of first base. Madlock just stood there planted in the dirt, arms folded across his chest, eyes unfocused, looking straight ahead. He blew a big pink bubble and managed to look bored.

WINTER HAVEN • *November 13*

"WHATTAYA GONNA GIMME?" VIDA BLUE WANTED TO KNOW. I found him sitting alone in front of his locker, already dressed, not visiting with anybody or playing cards or reading the paper— approachable. So I approached, stated my business, said I'd like to talk. No hand, no smile. Just that answer. I had to assume he was serious.

"How about my undying love and affection?" I improvised. That's what my dad always said he was giving us for Christmas.

"I just got married. That won't do."

"Okay, how about everlasting respect and admiration?"

Blue didn't even look up. "You're gonna give me that anyway, I'll beat your ass if you don't. You and every motherfucker that gets in my way—*without* going to get my gun."

Still no smile, not even a hint. I was stumped.

"How about you just owe me?" he said finally.

Deal. We shook hands. Blue grabbed his blue Legends warm-up jacket, and I followed him outside. The air was raw and humid; it was always cooler in the interior. We sat down on a low wall behind the left-field grandstand. Because the grandstand was empty, we could easily see through the aluminum lattice to the outfield, where players from both teams were taking advantage of the slow pace during batting practice to catch up with old friends. This was the first meeting of the year between the visiting Legends and the Winter Haven Super Sox, which made it a night for reunions.

Blue's face was smooth and boyish. As long as he kept his hat on and his hairline hidden, he didn't look anywhere near forty years old, his actual age. Unless you were very close, you weren't likely to notice the gray specks in his mustache, either.

Twenty years ago, Blue was the streak that heralded the arrival of the Oakland A's. Recalled in September 1970, Blue pitched a one-hitter in his first start of the year and a no-hitter three starts later against the first-place Twins. Nineteen seventy-one, Blue's first full season in Oakland, was the year the A's set out on their spectacular run of five straight American League West titles sandwiched around three World Series victories. Blue turned twenty-two that summer, won twenty-four games, lost eight, finished with a 1.82 ERA, and held opposing hitters to a batting average of .189. He was the starting pitcher in the All-Star Game and won the American League Cy Young Award *and* was named Most Valuable Player.

Somehow, Blue's career never again achieved the clarity of that first magical summer. For every achievement that followed, there was always a corresponding qualifier. In 1972, Blue held out for more money and didn't get it. After missing the first month of the season, he won just six games all year and was banished to the bull pen for the play-offs and the World Series. Blue had always been cocky; now it didn't wear so well. Putting "Vida" on the back of his game shirt was fine as long as he was winning, but it looked pretty silly on a mop-up man.

Then Blue came back. Over the next four years, a period corresponding with the flowering of the A's dynasty, Blue won seventy-seven games. Together with starters Ken Holtzman and Catfish Hunter, and reliever Rollie Fingers, Blue was a mainstay on the best staff in baseball. But eventually the A's reign came to an end. Left with a team that was growing old and fearful of the consequences of free agency, Charley Finley did his best to dismantle the A's before it was too late to recoup any value. By 1977, only Blue remained; the others had all been traded, sold, or lost to free agency. The once powerful A's fell to last place that year and Blue lost more games (nineteen) than any other pitcher in the American League.

In 1978 Blue was traded across the bay to the lowly Giants in exchange for *seven* players and three hundred ninety thousand dollars cash. Once again, he rebounded to top form. His first year in the National League, Blue won eighteen games and again was selected as starting pitcher for the All-Star Game, becoming the only pitcher ever to start for both leagues.

Blue would be eligible for the Hall of Fame in 1991, but there were many reasons why he'd never be elected. Some of them had to do with his performance on the field. After 1978, Blue never really shone again. Somewhere in his early thirties, when he should have been reaching his prime, Blue slipped from staff ace to workhorse to third or fourth starter. When he retired in 1986, he left a statistical record that was impressive but not quite spectacular: three twenty-win seasons, two hundred nine career wins, two thousand one hundred seventy-five strikeouts. If Blue were a high school student applying to Harvard, he'd probably be wait-listed.

But there was another reason why Blue would never be a strong candidate for baseball immortality, and it had nothing to do with baseball. On October 17, 1983, Blue pled guilty to a charge of possession of three grams of cocaine. He was sentenced to one year in prison and fined five thousand dollars. Most of the prison term was suspended but not all of it. Blue wound up serving three months at the Federal Correctional Institute in Fort Worth, Texas.

A lot of athletes got mixed up with drugs during the eighties, but Blue's case stood out. Not only did he admit to frequent cocaine use while with the Kansas City Royals during the 1982 and '83 seasons, he also admitted buying cocaine for others, introducing teammates to his supplier, and exposing a teenage batboy to cocaine by inviting him to a party in his apartment, a transgression which Commissioner Bowie Kuhn found particularly galling.

Besides Blue, three other Royals were sentenced to prison at the same time: Willie Wilson, Jerry Martin, and Willie Aikens. Two years later, during the trial of former Phillies clubhouse caterer and accused drug dealer Curtis Strong, part two of baseball's drug scandal erupted. Among those implicated in court testimony then as having used cocaine were Bernie Carbo, Joaquín Andújar, Al Holland, and Lee Lacy, all of whom, together with Blue, Martin, and Aikens, were back playing baseball in the senior league this winter. Still another reported cocaine user, J. R. Richard, tried out for the Legends but failed to make the team.

I thought it had to be more than mere coincidence—the fact that so may ex–drug users, not to mention recovering alcoholics, had found their way into the senior league. Some, like Ron Dunn of Winter Haven, who had given up drinking, seemed to be dealing from a position of strength. Dunn's life was in better shape now than it had been in years; for him, it was a challenge to see if he could play the game sober. But others, I suspected, were still drifting.

Blue had never had a job in his life that was not in some way related to baseball, not even a paper route. He said he was "sitting up in Lake Tahoe in two feet of snow" when he first talked to Jim Morley. "Of course being in Florida sounded great," he said. "I didn't even hesitate to give him a verbal commitment."

Now that he was here, Blue was clearly enjoying himself. The surliness (it was a put-on, I decided) disappeared as he rhapsodized about the pleasures of being back in uniform. "This is the reincarnation for a lot of us," he said. "I mean, they had to turn guys away. Even though the conditions are not the best in the world, it's *baseball*, that's the big kicker. You still enjoy the smell, the camaraderie. I'm still a baseball player at heart, and this will always be my true love."

No one would deny him that pleasure. On the other hand, Blue was a middle-aged man now. Whatever his passion for the game, he had come to the end of the road. But Blue didn't see it that way. There was one thing he had wanted to get straight before he signed a senior-league contract. "What contractual restrictions would there be," Blue asked Morley, "if a guy came down here, did well, and wanted to go back to the big leagues?" Morley assured him there were none.

So here was Blue, forty years old, three seasons removed from the game and still dreaming of a comeback. He even had a plan, a way to make it happen.

"Well, what the hell, I still think I could go pitch in the major leagues. You never know. I was thinking in terms of—I mean, this is a farfetched idea, but I'm one of those guys that leaves all doors open—the possibility of a strike. 'Would you cross a picket line, would you go against the current Major League Baseball Players Association?' Hell, yes. I love baseball, and they would just have to understand that."

EVER SINCE THE CHANGE AT THE TOP, THE SUPER SOX HAD BEEN playing like world-beaters, sort of like their spiritual parents, the Red Sox, in July. They swept the weekend series in Bradenton, lifting their record to within two games of .500, and now they had the lowly Legends to look forward to for the next couple of days. If Bill Lee was sore about his demotion, you wouldn't know it from the way he was pitching. Yesterday he came on in relief of Ferguson Jenkins and picked up his league-leading third save.

Even so, it was the hitters who were leading the parade, especially Pete LaCock, batting .450 with an obscene on-base average of roughly 60 percent, and Cecil Cooper, who went seven-for-nine in Bradenton, including a homer, a double, three runs batted in, and five runs scored, not to mention five walks and a stolen base.

Not surprisingly, the Sox seemed happy and loose when I stopped by their clubhouse after talking to Blue. Bernie Carbo, a changed man absent the self-pity that was so evident the other night, was in the trainer's room, neck-deep in a whirlpool bath. Actually there were two whirlpools, one scalding, the other near freezing, and Carbo kept switching back and forth between them. From what little I knew of Carbo's temperament already, I didn't need any neon sign to point out the obvious symbolism.

I decided to check in with Cooper. Since he retired from baseball in 1987, the former five-time all-star for the Brewers was working as a player agent. I asked him, "Do you like doing that?"

"Yep," he said. He had a full black beard and wore tinted glasses with steel rims. "Better than baseball."

"So what are you doing here?"

"Oh, I think it needs a little support. I don't want to say I'm having fun, a blast. I'd be lying. But I don't want to say I'm *not* having fun. So far it's been all right."

Cooper shrugged his shoulders.

"I'm playing baseball," he said, the same way he might have said, "I'm getting dressed" or "I'm eating dinner."

Cooper's attitude was unique. Without exception, all the other ballplayers I'd talked to were passionate about playing again, in some cases pathetically so. But Cooper sounded absolutely indifferent.

"I don't want to say there's no fun involved," he said. "You get a nice relationship with some of these guys, your teammates. You enjoy being with them, having fun, laughing. I mean, *that's* fun. But when I'm on the field, it's a job. That's the way I look at it. It didn't start out that way. It was fun when I was a kid, jumping around and bouncing and ripping and running. It was fun then. But once I got into it, and I'd been in the league five, six, eight years, then I knew. It's a job. It's a business.

"I'll tell you why I think I was able to keep it in that perspective. I never let baseball run my life, understand what I'm saying? I never lived, ate, slept, took it home with me, none of that stuff. I got to the point where I could separate it. It's a profession—*it's what I do*—and that's it. That's why I never missed it when I left. And basically I came here to try to help [the senior league], maybe put a name to it or give it some credibility, 'cause I know what it's gonna mean to a lot of people. Other people."

"You mean jobs."

"Yeah, sure. I want to do well, we all want to do well. But my main motivation is to help other people make this thing work. I see a lot of guys—maybe some guys in this very room right here—guys that they finish, they don't have nothing from playing in the major leagues."

Cooper's only clients so far were minor leaguers, although the agency he worked for represented Wade Boggs, Jody Reed, and John Franco. "I'm growing to the point where I can do major-league contracts," he said. "It's the business world. You gotta outthink the other guy and outmaneuver him. That can be a challenge.

"This I can only do for a little while longer," he said, and he flicked his head, a gesture that took in the locker room, the playing field, and the game itself. "But that I can do for a long time."

TONIGHT WAS DOLLAR NIGHT AT CHAIN O' LAKES PARK. ALL tickets—normally three dollars to six dollars—were on sale for the bargain price of one dollar per seat, first come, first served. The Super Sox wouldn't be trying this sort of thing if they weren't having a hard time attracting customers, and boy were they ever. Attendance to date was averaging five hundred eighty souls a game. Unless things improved, the Sox wouldn't raise enough cash in a whole season's worth of ticket sales to meet even one biweekly payroll.

Winter Haven, population twenty-two thousand, was the second smallest market in the league after St. Lucie. Unlike St. Lucie, it was unstrategically located in the center of the state, exactly seventy-five miles from either coast. A lot of old people lived in Winter Haven, not just retirees but people who had actually lived in Florida all their lives, a species not known to inhabit the coasts since the days of Ponce de León.

Ever since opening day, league officials had spoken hopefully about the imminent arrival of the snowbirds, northern tourists who were being counted on to set senior-league turnstiles spinning as soon as they arrived. But none of that had much relevance for Winter Haven. With the exception of Orlando, which, of course, had Disney World, snowbirds were a coastal phenomenon. The only tourists who came to Winter Haven were Red Sox fans, and they only came in March to see the Red Sox. Then the place was so full of New Englanders that the Boston *Globe* and the Boston *Herald* were available in coin boxes all over town. Owner Mitch Maxwell was banking on the Red Sox connection when he chose to locate his team here, but so far it looked as if it was going to take more than the return of Bill Lee and Bernie Carbo to draw the locals out of their trailer homes.

The killer was, Maxwell could have had Fort Myers. Fort Myers was among the fastest-growing communities in Florida and *the* hottest real estate market. Like Winter Haven, Fort Myers had its own newspaper. Unlike Winter Haven, Fort Myers also had three network-affiliated television stations, all of which sent cameras to the game every night and showed Sun Sox clips on the 11:00 news. Fort Myers had Sanibel and Captiva, islands with beaches where thousands of snowbirds landed every winter. Even now, before the snowbirds' migration, attendance in Fort Myers was running three times what it was here.

But Maxwell, when he visited Fort Myers, didn't like the look of Terry Park. He didn't see the excellent lease the city was prepared to offer, including full control of concessions. He saw only that it had fallen into disrepair after the Royals left town and was badly in need of a paint job. Now Chain O' Lakes Park, ah, here was a baseball palace. The grass was immaculate, the stands freshly painted in a pleasing blue and red. And the light— maybe it was the reflection from nearby Lake Lulu—the light was magical. Maxwell, it happened, was a man who made his fortune in the theater. He produced off-Broadway plays in New York, he bought old theaters and lovingly renovated them. He fell in love with Chain O' Lakes Park from the moment he laid eyes on it. It was so . . . so *right*. "It's like they say in the movies," Maxwell once said. "There's magic time here sometimes." What did he care about demographics if he could stage his production on a fantasy movie set?

"Nice night, huh?" Maxwell said when he sat down next

to me in the open-air press box. "The moon is great." It was. It looked like an orange helium balloon tied to the right-field wall.

Maxwell was dressed for cool weather in a two-piece blue-denim suit, under which he wore the kind of blue shirt that used to be called a work shirt and was no doubt the height of hip when Maxwell was at Tufts in the early seventies. Maxwell was a big man with a solid jaw, an enormous chin, sleepy, condescending eyes, and a hairline like a convertible top in the down position. His glasses were horn-rimmed.

"So," I said, raising the obvious question, "are you worried about your attendance?"

Maxwell let out a loud, exasperated sigh that was partly to blow off steam, then he pounced. "Quite frankly, I think it's a stupid question. I'm sorry to say that, but I think it's a *stupid question.* I don't think attendance is really the issue in the viability of the league *five games into the season.* Opening night I had fourteen hundred people here. I was down nine-nothing in the eighth inning and I scored a run, and the fans stood up and they clapped. To me, that answered all my questions about attendance. Because if the product's good, the people will come. If the product's bad, they won't. It's not a question of how many people we have in the ballpark today or tomorrow or December fifteenth. It's how many people we have in the ballpark by the end of the year. I've come to the conclusion very quickly that the league is going to be a huge success."

I wrote down what he said.

"I don't want you to think I'm crazy or anything, 'cause I'm not. I'm a very sane guy. I have a wife and kids. I've worked hard. But the question about attendance is ridiculous. It's putting an idea in people's minds that we're going to fail. Cynicism is tiring after a while. The [owners] that put up a million dollars apiece, we don't want to hear that people are skeptical. I heard people who were skeptical in July—'Will the league really be financed?' Well, it is. 'Will the players really come?' We said yes. They did. 'Will the quality of the game be any good?' We said yes. It is. The public has no right to judge us for an idea we believe in. All the public has a right to do is judge the product, and the public that isn't coming are idiots. They're scumbags, quite frankly, 'cause they're sitting home judging something they don't even know what it is! That's absurd, that's just absurd. It's what's wrong with this country, also. What's wrong with this country is everybody's a wiseass."

Maxwell was angry, but in such a way that seemed to bring him pleasure. He was like an actor enamored of his own performance in a passionate role. The first play he ever produced was a college production of *Man of La Mancha* at the Great Neck Summer Theater after freshman year. He made six thousand dollars. The next summer he returned with a bigger cast and a more ambitious production and nobody came to see the show for a week. He thought of closing down. But his father convinced him to stick with it, and when he counted his profits at the end of the summer he'd made twenty-seven thousand dollars. Maxwell knew what it was like to open in front of an empty house. He also knew that, with time, an empty house can sometimes become a full house. So what if the senior league hadn't exactly opened to rave reviews? Okay, so he was disappointed. But discouraged? No way.

"I mean, what in life takes off in six days? You gotta be an idiot to assume that you're gonna open the doors and people are gonna come. This isn't the movies. It's not a show, you don't know how it finishes, you can't say it's the greatest finale that ever was. You can't hype baseball. It's gotta grow, it's gotta become part of the fabric of life. It's a new idea, and new ideas take time. It takes nurturing, just like a child takes nurturing."

Reaching now, Maxwell finally hit upon the metaphor that pleased him most. "This is a *relationship* between our potential constituents and the league," he said with apparent self-satisfaction, and then he explained: "It's just like any other relationship. If I meet a woman and I say to her, 'Hey, let's fuck,' I mean, she may say, 'Yes, I'm interested, but give me six or seven days,' you know? And if I say to the public, 'Come to my ball game,' they say, 'Yeah, I'm interested but I've got something else on Tuesday and something on Thursday.' As long as they're *interested.*

"The point is, you turn things around if you believe in them. And if your belief is wrong, then at least you tried. The process in life is as important as the outcome. Otherwise you're living in the eighties and all you care about is the bottom line. The bottom line is not always winning."

That said, might not a reasonable person wonder why Bill Lee was fired when the season was only one week old?

"Quite frankly," he began, in the time-honored way of those who have no intention of being frank at all, "quite frankly I think the league turned out to be much more competitive than I ever thought it would be. I thought it would be good baseball, and exciting baseball, but I never thought it would be on the level of the major leagues—cutthroat, trades, scouting, protests, and all that. So I met Bill Lee and I thought he would be the perfect spirit for this league and the perfect guy to put together a club. And he did, he put together a good club for me. But Bill was a little overwhelmed with playing, managing, pitching so we brought in Ed Nottle to help us.

"But I think Bill Lee is a fantastic person. You won't meet anybody smarter than Bill Lee, or more sensitive or more humane than Bill Lee. I'm very happy that I met Bill Lee and I'm very happy that he's involved in our club. The world needs more people like that and less people like Donald Trump."

In the stands beneath us, the seats were filling up fast. Tonight's attendance would come to two thousand one hundred thirteen, raising the Sox average by 30 percent in one game. George Thorogood, lead singer of the Destroyers, sang the national anthem (and afterward told Bill Lee that *The Wrong Stuff* was "the best book I ever read"). Then the game began. It wasn't exactly a "Little Shop of Horrors" (one of Maxwell's plays), and Winter Haven was by no means "Bad to the Bone" (one of Thorogood's hits), but in the end, the Super Sox lost, 4–2. Nottle's winning streak was over.

Or was it? Don Cooper, the winning pitcher for the Legends, enjoyed his best outing of the year: seven innings pitched, six hits, one run, one earned, one walk, four strikeouts. Anyone who saw him pitch might well have been inspired, as Maxwell was, to check his listing in *The Baseball Encyclopedia*. If so, they would have seen that he pitched for the Twins, the Blue Jays, and the Yankees during his brief major-league sojourn, that he retired in 1985 with one career win, six losses, and an ERA of 5.25, that he was a native of New York City. They might even have noticed the one fact about Don Cooper that particularly interested Maxwell: his birthday.

Earlier, Maxwell had spoken regretfully about how damn serious everybody in the senior league had turned out to be, what with "trades, scouting, protests, and all that." But Maxwell was learning. Tomorrow he would file a protest of his own.

BRADENTON, ST. PETERSBURG • November 14

WHY COME BACK? YOU GOT OUT, YOU DEALT WITH THAT. YOU FOUND a new way, maybe something else you were almost as good at. You added years, you put on pounds, you lost steps to first base and feet off your fastball. You *settled down.* So why on earth would you ever come back?"

"I've always loved playing baseball," said Toby Harrah.

For some of them that was the whole thing, love. I spoke to Harrah while he sat on a stool in front of his locker in the visitors' clubhouse in Bradenton. There was a window above his shoulder that looked out over left field and let in sunlight and a breeze. It was the time between the end of batting practice and the start of the game, when you were dressed and loose and there was nothing left to do but wait for the game to begin.

Harrah looked like an old sailor, back in New Bedford after two years at sea on a whaling ship. His skin was tan like tanned leather, of a color and texture that by now was probably permanent. He had bright, beady eyes from which wrinkles fanned out like tiny ropes, what comes from a lifetime of squinting in the sun. He wore a reddish beard, meticulously trimmed. When I asked him where he was from, he said, in a high-pitched drawl, "Fort Worth, Texas," the city *and* the state, the way they do in Texas.

When Harrah retired in 1986, he was the last remaining player to have once worn the uniform of the Washington Senators. He spent the next two years as manager of the Rangers' AAA farm club at Oklahoma City, then rejoined the big-league club in 1989 as hitting instructor. Harrah had no illusions about making a comeback—"that's in my past." He just wanted to play again, and since he was on vacation all winter anyway, there was no reason why he couldn't. "I'm enjoying this," he said. "I never thought I was gonna get a second chance. It's been *fun.* Always has been fun playing baseball."

Though he'd hardly swung a bat in three years and hadn't fielded any ground balls, Harrah looked sharp. He was hitting .400 (with a .571 on-base percentage, twelve walks, and one strikeout), leading the team in runs batted in, and—what impressed me most—making the plays at third base. I thought I knew from softball what it felt like to make the big play at third—first the lunging backhand stab, then the hard throw all the way across the diamond. I told him that, in my opinion, that was the most fun you could have playing baseball, more fun even than hitting.

Harrah heard me out and chuckled softly. "Oh, yeah, that's fun to do that. But it's *all* fun, you know. Charging the ball and bunt plays and one-hopper double-play balls and catching the ball and throwing it and hitting it. It's fun doing all those things. It's just fun to be playing baseball again."

Then there was Rollie Fingers, Harrah's teammate on the Tropics, whose locker was around the corner. Fingers was having fun, too, but that wasn't the reason he was here. "Well," he said, hedging a little when I asked him what *was* the reason, "money." Then he laughed staccatolike: "hah-hah-hah!"

Rollie Fingers, perhaps the greatest relief pitcher of all time, first in career saves with three hundred forty-one and headed for the Hall of Fame, was broke. "I filed bankruptcy, oh, about seven, eight months ago," he said, "Chapter seven bankruptcy. I trusted friends and things didn't work out. Got in a couple of scams. It completely wiped me out. So I'm starting all over. If it wasn't for that I probably wouldn't be down here. The pay for three months is pretty good." Fingers was making thirteen thousand a month, near the top of the scale.

Prior to this winter, Fingers was living in San Diego. He had a job as a salesman for a communications company. It was phone work, mostly, keeping up with clients, and he could do that from Florida as well as anyplace else. "I made sure it was okay with my boss to come down here and still do my work and he said, 'No problem.' If it had affected my job I wouldn't have come."

But having come, he was glad to be here. Already he'd lost twenty pounds, which brought him down to two fifteen. That was still twenty-five pounds more than he played with—and a lot to be carrying around, even on a six-four frame—but, he said, "I feel a lot better." He was splitting time in the bull pen with Al Hrabosky, the other half of a lefty-righty combo that would have been awesome, say, in 1975 but was struggling in 1989 with a combined earned run average of 10.29 and only three saves.

"Some of these guys still swing the bat pretty good," Fingers said by way of explanation. "If you haven't picked up a ball for four years, you're not sure where you're gonna throw the ball or how hard you're gonna throw it, or if the breaking ball's gonna break. You gotta change speeds a little bit more down here. I'm more or less trying to finesse the ball instead of trying to blow it by anybody."

I couldn't help it—I had to ask him how much money he *used* to have, before it all disappeared. It was probably a rude question, but Fingers didn't blink. "Oh, I had a financial statement of, oh, two or three million dollars. I lost *everything*. I lost three houses, I lost some horses, I lost some land, investments, cash, cars. You name it, I lost it. You know, you live and learn. It was definitely a hard learning experience."

"So what are you doing with your paycheck now?"

"My check? I'm trying to save every dime I can. Oh, *yeah* [laughing]. I don't own a house right now so that's the first thing on my list, to save enough money to where I can get into a home 'cause I hate paying rent." Fingers laughed again and shook his head. The flesh on his face trembled but his mustache—curled and waxed and perfect as ever—stayed stiff as a bone. "There's no future in paying rent."

RATHER THAN WATCH THE WHOLE GAME, I DROVE BACK TO ST. PETersburg where tonight the Pelicans were playing the Fort Myers Sun Sox. I wanted to talk to Amos Otis, who, over the course of nine games to start the season, had accumulated a set of statistics that had to be a typographical error but wasn't: a .444 batting average (fourth in the league), nine homers (first; four others were tied for second with three), and twenty-six runs batted in (also first; two others were tied for second with fifteen). Over the weekend in St. Lucie, Otis had hit five homers, including three three-run blasts in a row, which had to be some kind of record. If he could keep up his current pace—impossible, I know, but what the hell—he'd finish the seventy-two-game schedule with sixty-five homers and one hundred eighty-seven RBIs.

"I been hot," Otis said, relaxing in the dugout while his teammates took batting practice, "but I ain't never been on fire like this." He had a sheepish smile on his face, like he'd just won the lottery or something. His pleasure seemed to come less from a sense of his own accomplishment than from the knowledge that he'd been smiled upon by Fortune. "Seem like, instead of getting base hits, I'm getting home runs. Every swing is a home run, almost. It's unbelievable. I been lucky. Like my parents used to say, 'It's better to be a little bit lucky than good all the time.' "

Before this winter, Otis hadn't played baseball for five years. Since 1988 he'd been the hitting instructor for the San Diego Padres, a job, like Harrah's, that afforded him an occasional opportunity to step into the cage and take a few cuts. When he came to Florida he'd hit so much the first week he'd hurt his wrists. Since then, he'd given up taking batting practice altogether. He was doing just fine without it, thanks. "When I was in the major leagues I used to take it all the time," he said. "But since I been down here, I stopped taking it and I seemed to get hot. I'm superstitious. I'll wait 'til I go o-four again."

Otis was from Mobile, Alabama, "Hank Aaron's town." He came up with the Mets in 1967 when he was twenty years old and was traded two years later to the Royals. For eleven years, beginning in 1975, the Royals never finished worse than second in the American League West, and for most of that period Otis was the right fielder. He won three Gold Gloves, hit for a decent average with good power, and had outstanding speed. But by the time the Royals finally won it all in 1985, Otis was gone. His last year was 1984 with the Pirates.

"When I retired five years ago the skills were beginning to diminish a little bit," he said. "When I hit the fastball, it was only getting to the warning track. I started fouling them off a lot. I always prided myself on being a good breaking-ball hitter; whenever somebody made a mistake, I very seldom missed it. All of a sudden I kept missing them. I hit change-ups pretty good, and I started swinging right through the guys who threw change-ups. So I knew I was starting to go down."

The year he retired, Otis batted .165 in forty games, an embarrassment. And therein lay the reason why Otis seized the opportunity to come back. It wasn't about love, like it was for Harrah. And it wasn't about money, like it was for Fingers. For Otis, it was about pride and about honor, about leaving on your own terms.

"I'm here for that disastrous year I had in 1984," he said. "That's my incentive right there, to come back and try to go out on top. I had a real bad year that year. It's been like a thorn in my side for five years. People always seem to remember the last thing you do and that last year was *bad.* I'm hoping to carry on the way I am right now, have a good season. And then I can go out like I want to go out."

POMPANO BEACH · *November 15*

Pompano Beach (THE NAME COMES FROM THE FISH) USED TO BE THE spring-training home of the Washington Senators. Back in the sixties, Frank Howard hit so many balls out of Pompano Municipal Stadium that a net was raised above the fence in left field. The net stayed, but the Senators' successors, the Texas Rangers, packed up several years ago and moved to Port Charlotte.

This morning I reversed the migration. From St. Petersburg I drove south on I-75 past Port Charlotte and Fort Myers to Naples and the start of the Everglades Parkway, better known as Alligator Alley. It was mostly two-lane blacktop for the next two hours, through Big Cypress Swamp, past signs that read "Panther Crossing," all the way across the peninsula to Fort Lauderdale on the Atlantic coast, then north on I-95 to Pompano Beach.

I found the ballpark—home of the Gold Coast Suns—out by the airport. It had a press box that made you understand why they called them boxes. Raised up on stilts, accessible only by a steep set of stairs (more like a ladder), too narrow inside to accommodate two-way traffic, and absolutely the best seat in the house. You looked almost straight down on the field; the home-plate umpire should have had such a view. Once, in the spirit of modernization, an air conditioner had been installed. I never saw it used all season. When you propped open the window there was nothing between you and the action and always a cool, salt breeze blowing in from the east.

Gold Coast was one of the senior league's conceptual teams, in a category with Winter Haven (old Red Sox), Bradenton (Pirates), and St. Lucie (famous names). Hoping to build a following among Hispanics in Miami—where they had scheduled one-quarter of their home games—the Suns packed their roster with natives of Central America and the Caribbean: Puerto Rican Ed Figueroa; Panamanian Rennie Stennett; Dominicans Rafael Landestoy, Joaquín Andújar, and Jesus de la Rosa; and Cubans

Bert Campaneris, Paul Casanova, Orlando Gonzalez, Bobby Ramos, Pedro Ramos, and Luis Tiant. So far, the Suns were drawing fairly well, at least by senior-league standards, so maybe the concept had merit. On the other hand, they'd only won two games.

The Suns' main attraction—and biggest mystery—was their manager, Earl Weaver. On a bright October afternoon eight years earlier, I had sat in the last row of the upper deck at Baltimore's Municipal Stadium and watched the Brewers beat the Orioles in a one-game play-off for the American League East division championship. After fifteen seasons as manager—during which his O's won six division titles, four American League pennants, and one World Series—Weaver was calling it quits. Even though Baltimore lost that day, everyone in the sellout crowd stood and cheered. The ovation lasted until Weaver came back out on the field in his undershirt and tearfully waved good-bye.

That was 1982. Less than three years later, partway through the 1985 season, the Orioles fired Joe Altobelli and gave Weaver his old job back. Okay, so he was only fifty-five. It's not as if he was the first man who'd ever changed his mind about retirement. But he came to regret it. The Orioles played .500 ball through the end of '85, then fell to last place with a record of seventy-three and eighty-nine in '86. It was by far the most difficult season of Weaver's long career, and it took a toll. As soon as it was over he beat a fast retreat to his country-club home in Hialeah, vowing never again to return to baseball.

So what was Weaver doing here? I found him in a characteristic pose: standing between the dugout and the cage, hands buried deep in his back pockets, watching batting practice with narrow, critical eyes. Standing nearby—also in a blue-and-orange Suns uniform, also white-haired—was Bill Hecht, otherwise known as Speedy. Speedy (who wasn't anymore) was one of Weaver's golf buddies. He had two jobs with the Suns: coaching first base and driving Weaver to the park every day, fifty minutes to Pompano and twenty-five minutes to Miami. The chauffeur was one way Russ Berrie, owner of the Suns, had tried to make it easy for Weaver to come back. Paying him the maximum salary of forty-five thousand dollars for three months' work was another way. Still, you wondered why Weaver was here. If he didn't want to manage the Orioles, why would he want to manage the Suns?

I asked him, "How's it going?"

"Well, it was great right up until the fucking season started and we go two and eight," Weaver said, speaking in the raspy voice of a lifetime chain smoker. "I was enjoying it tremendously until we started losing, and losing just ain't no fun. Our defense hasn't been good and the pitching hasn't been what I expected, *or* the opposition hitting has been better than what I expected. We've hit the ball, we've looked great at times—but you gotta win, it's gotta be competitive. It's not just fun, it's not just games."

Weaver was right about that. The news from St. Lucie that afternoon was that Legends manager Graig Nettles was about to get the ax. Here we were only two weeks into the season and already two managers of losing teams were going or gone. I wondered, Was Weaver worried about *his* job?

"I'm sure there's gonna be ownership pressures but at this stage of my life, I don't care. I'm financially set. The owners all want to win. But you see, you want to win yourself. When you're losing that's aggravating. It's just not any good. You can forget about the owner because for me to lose is terrible."

Weaver spent twenty years in the minor leagues, hanging around long past the point when it would have made more sense for him to quit. It wasn't until he finally gave up trying to make it as a second baseman and got into managing that he even progressed beyond AA. In a lot of ways—what with the old parks, the crummy lights, the small crowds, and the cramped dressing rooms—managing in the senior league was like going back to the minor leagues all over again, the main difference being that this time around Weaver was almost sixty years old. But evidently Weaver didn't see it that way. Not even the prospect of riding the buses again seemed to worry him.

"The travel shouldn't be no problem at all," he said. "I guess the longest trip is Bradenton at five hours—like a trip from Baltimore to the West Coast—but that's the longest one. The other ones are two and a half hours. The buses have VCRs. You see a movie and you're done. But we got our first long road trip coming up. I *call* it long. I'll spend two days at home for Thanksgiving, then go to Bradenton, then it's six days. I'll see how that six-dayer goes.

"I *will* tell you this, though. We had one night game on the road already and that seemed like it was a week long, waiting to go to the ballpark. That's the one thing. It's the only thing so far that was distasteful."

"What town were you in?"

"Fort Myers. It don't make no difference what town. I'd rather be in Fort Myers than New York or Chicago or Detroit, there ain't no doubt about that. The thing is, it's a long day—the same old thing. I'll have to find something to occupy my time on the road."

Pompano Stadium was lovely in the twilight—the sun low in the sky, the clouds puffed up with pink light and edged in orange, the infield clay a ruddier orange than the clouds, the grass a summer green (in November!). I felt like I was standing in a Maxfield Parrish illustration. After a while, the Orlando players started drifting onto the field. Men who hadn't seen each other in years greeted one another as if it were their high school reunion. "Gates!" Weaver shouted suddenly. "Whattaya say, Gates! Oh, I can see you coming out of that Tiger Stadium dugout!" The two old antagonists embraced and moved away out of earshot.

I T WAS BABY-BOOMER NOSTALGIA NIGHT IN SOUTH FLORIDA. THE choice was between Keith Richards (forty-six years old), Mick Jagger (also forty-six), and the rest of the Rolling Stones in concert at the Orange Bowl in Miami; or Bert Campaneris (forty-seven), Paul Blair (forty-five), and Mike Kekich (forty-four) of the Suns in a game against the Juice at Pompano Stadium. The Stones sold out. The Suns sold eight hundred forty-five tickets.

You remember Mike Kekich. He was the one who traded his wife, his two daughters, the house he was renting in Franklin Lakes, New Jersey, and his dog, even up to Fritz Peterson for Peterson's wife, Peterson's two sons, Peterson's house in Mahwah, New Jersey, and Peterson's dog. "It wasn't a wife swap," Kekich told the New York Times when the news broke during Yankee spring training in 1973. "It was a life swap."

Kekich and Peterson, both left-handed starting pitchers for the Yankees, had been close friends for years, but after the trade things were never quite the same. Someone was bound to get hurt, and it turned out to be Kekich, who lasted only two months with Marilyn Peterson. "Love is funny," he said at the time. "It can build fast but it can wear on you, too."

Kekich had no luck tonight either, pitching against the Juice. He gave up five runs on four hits through an inning and a third, and when Weaver took him out of the game, he cursed the umpire all the way to the dugout. Afterward, I didn't have the heart to ask him about Marilyn. Besides, the game produced a hero of note. Pete Falcone, looking like the Falcone of old, won his third straight without a loss—a complete-game, three-hit shutout. Never a hard thrower, Falcone had always relied on sharp control, good movement, and a willingness to work in the top half of the strike zone, where mistakes can be disastrous. Against the Suns, typically, almost all his outs were strikeouts (seven) and pop-ups (fifteen). Bill Madlock, playing first base, registered just four putouts—two in the first and two in the ninth—and didn't have a single ground ball hit his way all night.

Falcone was another mystery. In 1984, after a ten-year career, he turned down a contract offer from the Braves and did what few major-league players have ever done and fewer fans would ever be able to understand. At age thirty-one, he retired voluntarily from baseball. "The game is fun," he said, speaking softly in his native Brooklyn accent. "The life itself is a hard life. You pay a price to play pro ball. But with this thing starting up, it kind of got my juices flowing."

After four years away from the game, Falcone decided that before he was absolutely too old, he wanted to give it one more shot. Pitching in the senior league had been fun so far, but it wasn't his goal. His goal was to return to the big leagues.

What separated Falcone from all the other Don Quixotes in the senior league was the fact that last June he had been signed to a minor-league contract by the Dodgers and pitched sixty-five innings with their AA affiliate in San Antonio. He knew that the only way he was going to be invited to spring training—and have a chance to win a big-league job—was if he pitched brilliantly all winter, and even then he knew it was a long shot. It had been a struggle to get in shape after four years, he admitted, "because you knew there was gonna be a letdown. But I had nothing to lose. I still don't. Just the fact that I got a minor-league contract from the Dodgers is a miracle to me. I was not Dodger property, and that's a hard organization to get into. They're very close to their own people. Now all I need is another miracle."

After the game against the Suns, anything seemed possible.

Falcone was definitely pleased, but in his heart he knew he hadn't really been tested. "I had good command tonight," he said. "I had good movement and I had good breaking pitches— tonight I had it going. But I don't know how I'd do against big-league hitters. I don't know how I would have done if I had faced the Reds or the Giants. I don't know. I might never know. I could easily say, 'Yeah, I pitched a shutout tonight, I could pitch in the big leagues,' you know? But you don't know. You *don't really know*."

THERE WAS NEWS TODAY FROM THE LEAGUE OFFICE. COMMISSIONER Curt Flood, acting on a formal protest filed by Winter Haven Super Sox owner Mitch Maxwell, found in favor of the Super Sox. It was determined that Don Cooper, according to *The Baseball Encyclopedia*, was born on February 15, 1957. According to *Total Baseball*, Cooper was born on January 15, 1957. In either case, Cooper was thirty-two years old. The league minimum for pitchers was thirty-five years old. Therefore, in accordance with Rule 2.6 of the league bylaws, Flood reversed what had been a 4–2 win by the Legends on November 13 and declared the Super Sox the winners by forfeit. So ended the senior-league career of Don Cooper.

POMPANO BEACH • *November 16*

TAYLOR DUNCAN HAD A BAD DAY YESTERDAY. IT WASN'T JUST THAT he didn't get a hit—*no one* got any hits except Joe Hicks, who had two, and Derrel Thomas. It was the awful time he had at third base. Although he was credited with only one error by the official scorer, Duncan was burned at the hot corner all night long. So as soon as he came out of the locker room for infield practice, Paul Blair made a polite introduction. "This is a glove," he said. "You use it to catch the ball."

Duncan smiled bravely while his teammates guffawed. It was all out in the open now and just as quickly forgotten. Today was another day.

Only doctors were allowed to dispense that kind of medicine

on a ball club and Blair certainly qualified. He played seventeen years, mostly with the Orioles, and won nine Gold Gloves as the premier center fielder in the American League. Blair led a charmed career in the company of winners. He appeared in fifty-three postseason games for the Orioles and the Yankees, went to six World Series, and was on the winning side four times. Back in center yesterday, ten years removed from the game, Blair effortlessly ran down a monster drive by Ike Blessitt in the first that should have been a three-run triple but instead was just a long sacrifice fly—and afterward he said his legs had been killing him.

"I done played three years in the minors and seventeen in the majors and I never had a problem with my legs," Blair said. "Never had a pulled muscle my entire career. I'm down here and I have a tear in my left knee and pulled muscle in my right leg."

"Isn't that because you're older now?"

"That's the outfield. When I came down here I was in great shape. I can still run now, but out there it's like running in sand. Can't do nothing. It kills your legs."

Blair wasn't even thinking about playing when he heard about the senior league. He wanted to manage. Ever since former Dodgers general manager Al Campanis told Ted Koppel on "Nightline" that blacks didn't have "the necessities" to manage in the big leagues, Blair had wanted an opportunity to prove him wrong. "Al Campanis has thrown a challenge out there," Blair said. "I like to meet challenges, that's all. I don't blame baseball. If I'm an owner, and I hire somebody to run my ball club, it's going to be somebody I've mingled with because I'm gonna be more comfortable with him. We got all white owners, so it's logical they're gonna hire white managers. That's just part of life that you have to accept. But I have no problem with working my way to the top. I'll go down to the minor leagues, I have no problem with that. If I can't do the job, I'll go on back home and they won't have another bitch out of me."

The news today from St. Lucie was that Bobby Bonds had been promoted to replace the fired Graig Nettles as manager of the Legends. He joined Bobby Tolan in St. Petersburg and Gates Brown in Orlando, making three black managers in the senior league, plus Curt Flood, a black commissioner. "It's a great start," Blair said. Then he added sarcastically, "It's a great opportunity to show that we as blacks can handle decision-making positions," and he laughed. "I'll say this. Hank Aaron, Willie Mays, Ernie Banks, when they retired, if they wanted to manage, they coulda got a job. There's no question in my mind. I think too many of them just walked away from the game. We've had opportunities and we haven't taken advantage, so you can't put it all on the owners."

"How long has it been since you caught up with a fly ball like you did yesterday?"

"Since 1980. Hah! That was a heck of a long time ago. When I hung 'em up, that was it. I wasn't playing no softball, no nothing. After you play at the major-league level, who wants to play softball? Not me. But I don't think I lost too much out there. I can still get a good jump. I don't know, it just seems like the same as when I played. I run after a ball, and when I first take off I say, 'Well, I probably don't have a chance at this ball,' and then I'll get to running and I'll look again and something inside me makes me go a little faster and I wind up getting there. I don't know what it is." Blair paused, and when he spoke again he almost whispered. "That is *more fun* to me. It's really satisfying to say, 'Hey, at forty-five I can still go out there and get it! Don't hit it to center!' That is a *nice* feeling."

AH, YES, IT WAS A GREAT NIGHT FOR A BALL GAME. BALMY TEMPERatures, clear skies, a gentle sea breeze blowing in from right— and lots of empty seats for the fans to spread themselves around in. The game was supposed to start at 2:05 but was moved back to 7:05 when the Suns' front office decided at the last minute not to try to play any more day games in the middle of the week; they just weren't getting the crowds. So Chuck Malkus, the PR man, had personally called all of the Suns' season-ticket holders. Naturally, he'd missed a few; some showed up at the ballpark five hours early and had to be sent home. You could hardly blame them for not coming back. In any case, I sat in the press box at 6:45 and counted three times as many people milling around the softball diamonds beyond the fence in left as there were inside the ballpark.

"I'm not even gonna use the microphone tonight," the PA announcer said glumly. "I'm just gonna stick my head out the window and tell everybody what's happening."

The official attendance—which was never announced and had to be asked for—was two hundred fifty-four, a new record low for the senior league. As it happened, the lucky few who were in the stands witnessed a performance they will never forget. Only it wasn't baseball, exactly. It was more like professional wrestling—Barry "Don't Show Me Up" Shulman against the tag team of Bobby "Don't Make Me Swing" Molinaro and Earl "You Got It in for Me" Weaver.

Bob Galasso, the Juice's starting pitcher, was wild from the start. He walked the first two batters he faced—setting up a run-scoring single by George Hendrick—and walked two more in the second. So when Bobby Molinaro came to the plate with two out and nobody on in the third, he knew enough to look for his pitch. Galasso's first offering was a fastball. It might have been low, it might have been inside—in any case, Molinaro didn't swing. Barry Shulman, the home-plate umpire, called strike one.

You can't argue balls and strikes and expect to get away with it. In the senior league, as in the major leagues, that's grounds for an automatic ejection. In practice, mild protests are ignored; as long as you don't raise your voice or turn and face the umpire, you're usually okay. But show up the man in blue and you're gone.

As soon as Shulman's right arm went up, Molinaro's face turned red and his neck swelled. "It was three inches off the ground!" he screamed, loud enough to be heard in the press box.

Here, accounts vary. Shulman said later that he told Molinaro, "If the next one's in the same place you better swing at it, because it's gonna be a strike again."

Molinaro begged to differ. He said later what he heard was "You better swing at the next one," and of course that set him off. "I never heard an umpire in twenty years I played ever tell me, 'You better swing at the next pitch,' " Molinaro said indignantly after the game was over.

Now Molinaro was *really* mad. He stuck his face in Shulman's: "WHATTAYA MEAN I GOTTA SWING AT THE NEXT ONE?!" Then he turned toward the dugout, just like a little kid calling for help from his big brother. "Hey Earl!" he whined. "He told me I gotta swing at the next pitch!"

That's all Earl needed to hear. Eleven days earlier, after an argument with the same Barry Shulman over a check-swing called strike, Weaver had entered the senior-league record book as the first manager ever to be ejected. Not that anyone was surprised. Weaver was tossed out of games, on average, once a month during his major-league career. Why should he change now? He rocketed out of the dugout—head down, arms pumping—and went straight for Shulman.

What little noise two hundred fifty-four people are capable of making, they began to make as soon as they saw Weaver. So I can't be sure what was said. The following exchange is from Shulman's report to the league office.

WEAVER: "Why are you always in trouble?"
SHULMAN: "I'm only in trouble when you come out."
WEAVER: "Why are you here five games in a row?"
SHULMAN: "I don't know."
WEAVER: "You have it in for me!"
SHULMAN: "You're not important enough in the scope of my life for me to think about having it in for you."
WEAVER: "You know you have a bad heart and He [pointing upward] knows you do, too."
SHULMAN: "I'm not going to stand here and argue balls and strikes."
WEAVER: [Walking back toward the dugout] "You're bad, you're a loser, I'll bet you're a failure in business!"

For a while, it looked like that would be the end of it. Molinaro struck out (Shulman *did* call the next pitch a strike), the two teams changed sides, and the crowd quieted down. But before Ed Figueroa could finish warming up, Weaver started in again. This time I heard him.

"You been a failure at everything you ever did!" Weaver called from the dugout.

"I'm not gonna take this from you all night!" Shulman called back.

At that point Weaver charged back on the field, the crowd commenced to roar, and again I lost the sound track. It didn't matter. What followed was pure slapstick, like a scene in a silent film.

Weaver went full speed right at Shulman, jammed on the brakes at the last instant, and deftly twirled his cap one hundred eighty degrees. It was a classic manager's sequence, one Weaver helped immortalize, and it momentarily gave him the upper hand.

"This was like after five minutes of bullshit, excuse the expression," Shulman later explained. "So I turned *my* hat around. I said, 'Now what is this supposed to prove?'"

Weaver looked stunned, but he quickly recovered. He snatched the hat off Shulman's head, took two long punter's strides, and gave it the boot. Lousy hang time but very effective. Shulman had seen enough. With energy equal to the task of committing the act literally, he wound up, leaned back, and threw Weaver out of the game.

Weaver eventually left the field, but not before he picked up Shulman's hat—which had been lying in the grass—squeezed it and twisted it until the sweat dripped out, and Frisbeed it into the stands.

Shulman stood there helpless, prohibited by the demands of professional dignity from continuing without his hat. After what seemed like several minutes, a tiny ball of wadded-up black fabric came flying out of the stands and landed in the clay by the on-deck circle, halfway between Shulman and the Suns' dugout. Shulman made no effort to pick it up. Instead he folded his arms and stared into the dugout. Did he really expect the hat to be handed to him?

No one moved. The confrontation had reached a stalemate.

The third-base umpire tried offering Shulman *his* hat. Shulman shook his head. The first-base umpire told him, "You don't need a hat!" Shulman didn't budge. Finally Al Oren, the Suns' assistant equipment manager, came out of the dugout, picked up Shulman's hat, took a step in his direction, and threw it at him. This time the wind picked it up, and when the hat landed it was no closer than it had been before.

At this point I was afraid we were going to be here all night. But Shulman must have decided that this latest insult was unintended. Moving briskly and with all the dignity he could muster, Shulman retrieved his hat, brushed it off, and put it back on his head. José Cruz stepped into the batter's box, and the game recommenced.

Afterward, I followed the other reporters into the manager's office. Weaver was there all by himself, sitting on a stool in white undershorts and baseball hose gartered at the knee, sipping what may or may not have been his first beer of the night. The Suns had won, 3–1—only their third win of the season—but no one wanted to talk about that.

"That guy is something," Weaver said. He sounded tired. "He is *really something*. That's nine out of twelve games we've had him. He told Molinaro he better swing at the next pitch. Of course, he'll deny it. Now that's nothing for an umpire to say. I'm here to see that we get a fair shake, that's just about all that a manager can do. When he does that to one of your players, what are you gonna do? You pick your players, and then you better stand up for them. If you don't stand up for your players, you're lost.

"We've played twelve ball games, and there's been *one* argument on the other side. They get a lot of 'em right, you know, but the ones they get wrong, every one of 'em has gone against us. Well, I guess it'll go on all year."

Somebody asked Weaver if he had ever removed an umpire's hat before.

"Nope. I'm telling you, ninety-six times in the major leagues"—Weaver was thrown out of ninety-*one* games, according to *Total Baseball*—"over an eighteen-year period, that's about six a year. Every one of them was impromptu, every one of them. Whatever happens, happens."

After the reporters left, Weaver—still in his underwear, still working on a beer—lit a cigarette. He leaned over and propped his elbows on his thighs. From where he sat, he could see through the door into the players' locker room.

Paul Blair caught his eye. "Earl," he said, "you're in the wrong sport. You shoulda been a placekicker."

Blair laughed, and Weaver smiled wearily. Then the outer door next to Weaver's office opened halfway and Bill Madlock poked his head in.

"Where's Earl?" Madlock asked, grinning widely. Then he saw him. "Earl, you're gonna have a heart attack in the fucking senior league!"

Weaver raised his head. "That ain't funny 'cause you're fucking right."

THE SEASON WAS LESS THAN THREE WEEKS OLD, BUT ALREADY IT WAS obvious which were the two teams to beat: the Pelicans, with their powerful, young lineup, made up mostly of names you probably never heard of, and the Tropics, who had speed to burn (twenty-two steals, twenty-two attempts) and so made everybody else look old and slow. Both led their respective divisions: the Pelicans in the north with a record of nine and three and the Tropics in the south with a record of ten and two. This weekend, they would be meeting for the first time in a three-game series at Al Lang Stadium.

For reasons that went beyond the won-lost records of the respective teams, league officials viewed this weekend as an important test. A respectable gate would be an indication that fans were willing to pay to see good baseball, an assumption the owners had held to all along. The senior league was never meant to be a round of meaningless exhibitions, the sort where old-timers dress up for three innings and parade themselves in front of the fans like so many animated artifacts. Instead it was designed to approximate the real thing, with big-league rules, a big-league schedule, and big-league competition. In order for the concept to work, the league had to attract fans who cared whether their team won or lost, not just one-shots who came out on a whim to gape at Rollie Fingers. If such fans existed in St. Petersburg, they'd be here this weekend for the series with West Palm Beach.

The Pelicans had made a big trade earlier in the week. They sent outfielders Bake McBride and Jerry Martin, catcher Mark Corey, and pitcher Gerry Pirtle to the Orlando Juice for outfielder Ken Landreaux, who became their new center fielder. Landreaux was the youngest position player in the league. He would not turn thirty-five until December 22, only nine days before the deadline for eligibility. Landreaux's eleven-year major-league career ended abruptly in 1987 when his batting average dipped to .203 and the Dodgers let him go. Even now, Landreaux seemed stunned by his sudden fall. He'd spent the last two years in the minor leagues—first at Rochester and then at

Albuquerque, a Dodgers farm team—hoping to be called back up. But lately the dream was receding. The good news this winter was that the Dodgers had offered him a new contract. The bad news was that it was for AA, one step *down* from Albuquerque.

"This past year has been tough for me," Landreaux said softly. "I been away from my family, trying to keep my head above water. It's been real shaky."

Shaky or not, Landreaux's presence solidified an already potent Pelicans' lineup, adding speed, defense, and a .300 batting average without having to give up any everyday players. Tonight, Landreaux was one of four Pelicans to collect three hits off Tropics starter Ray Burris and two relievers. He was also involved in the key play of the night, one which probably saved the game for the Pelicans.

The Tropics were batting with two outs in the seventh inning, down 8–6. With Tito Landrum on second base and Luis Pujols on first, Mickey Rivers hit a sinking line drive to center that Landreaux charged and appeared to pick cleanly off the top of the grass for out number three. The ump called Rivers out. But was he? Manager Dick Williams demanded an appeal, the call was overruled, and Rivers was awarded first base. Now the question became what to do about Pujols, who was standing on third base, and Landrum, who had scored. The decision by crew chief Bill Deegan, a major-league veteran, was to send Pujols back to second and Landrum back to third, erasing the Tropics' run.

There followed a performance by Williams to rival Earl Weaver's of the night before (although this time Williams was the only one to turn his hat around). After ten minutes, Williams was ejected; after *twenty-three* minutes—during which time the crowd of one thousand two hundred sixty-five (a decent turnout on a cool night) grew restless, and some went home—Williams finally left the field. When play resumed, Mark Wagner grounded out to first base and the inning was over.

St. Pete scored three more runs in the eighth to pad their lead, making the score 11–6. In the top of the ninth, West Palm rallied for four of its own on back-to-back doubles by Toby Harrah and Ron Washington but came up one short when Jerry White flied out to end the game.

As anyone who ever played for him could attest to, Dick Williams was a man with a temper. Yet he was no fool, and he knew where his bread was buttered. For fourteen years he had bellied up to the trough as a spokesman for Miller beer. In fact, were it not for the senior league, Williams at this very moment would have been somewhere in the Caribbean on a promotional gig, retelling the same old stories and drinking Miller Lite. Ever since he got involved with the senior league—and Williams was there at the beginning at the press conference in May—he was regarded as one of the league's most valuable assets, a guaranteed gee-whiz promoter who always could be counted on to say the right thing.

But not tonight. Tonight Williams was livid. Any thoughts the press may have had of asking him what he thought about the umps were erased as soon as we laid eyes on him, storming around the clubhouse like a crazed dervish. Red veins burst in his cheeks and his big silver mustache rode his lip like a cowboy on a bull. I don't know who was more afraid, us or his own players.

"Ask me about those fucking umpires!" he demanded when he saw that we shrank from him. "They don't want us to say anything bad about the umpires, I even got a directive! FUCK THE UMPIRES!! I tell you it's a fucking disgrace to have umpires like that in this league! We're busting our ass! Sometimes we may not look good, but we're trying! That's incompetency! You can take every one of those cocksuckers out there and shove 'em right in the shithouse! And you can quote me! That's with one 't' and an 'i'! That's all I have to say about the whole fucking game! FUCK THE UMPIRES!!!"

ST. PETERSBURG · November 18

PART OF WHAT MADE YOU A BALLPLAYER WAS BEING ABLE TO PUT ON polyester stretch pants with no belt and *not* have them look like pajamas. When Don Sider, co-owner of the Tropics, put on baseball pants and a shirt the next day to take batting practice with his team, he looked as if he was ready for bed. He wore nerdy, black-rimmed glasses, a hat pulled down low on his head, and a permanent grin that made you wonder what terrific news he'd just received. But there was no news, just the supercharged pleasure he got all the time from being on a baseball diamond with real baseball players. It was the grin, even more than the way he wore his pants, that set Sider apart from the true professionals with their practiced nonchalance.

"Why can't I get any lift?" Sider was having a tough time in the cage. A steady stream of dribblers left his bat and rolled lazily across the infield.

"Tuck in your front shoulder." This from Lee Lacy, offered casually but seized on by Sider as if it were the Word. *Tuck in your front shoulder.* He did as he was told and was able to hit the next pitch in the air all the way to the lip of the outfield grass. More happy now than ever, Sider ran all the way around the bases.

"I like baseball," Sider said when we sat down in the dugout to talk. "I *love* baseball."

Sider was a lawyer and a CPA, originally from Chicago but practicing now in Boca Raton. He did estate planning, probate trusts, business law, contracts, all horrible, crusty, indoor stuff that was probably why he was so passionate about baseball. He was thirty-four years old, and so like Jim Morley, Mike Graham (owner of the Fort Myers franchise), Joe Sprung (St. Lucie), and Rick Horrow (president of the league), ineligible to play in the senior league except as a catcher. Strange, in the big leagues, the players were all kids and the owners were old men. Here it was just the opposite.

For the guys like Sider, owning a baseball team was a fantasy on a par with the life-after-death fantasy the players were experiencing. The senior league's thirtysomething contingent were all self-made men, middle-class kids who had come of age in the eighties, made a lot of money in one of the professions, and hence had come to view the world as a kind of playground where energy and imagination made dreams come true. Some guys went to fantasy camps, other guys played Rotisserie baseball. These guys bought their own damn teams.

"I never knew what Rotisserie baseball was until I heard someone explain it to me two weeks ago," said Sider of the popular game in which contestants put together their own teams of major-league players and compete with one another in various statistical categories. "I never did that. That stuff's dumb. If it's not real baseball, then it's dumb. I'm interested in this because it's real, not because it's an opportunity to be a GM and make trades and choose players and then follow them and see what their averages are. Talking to Dick Williams about whether we're gonna send this guy down or bring in a new catcher, that's not exciting to me 'cause you're playing with people's lives and I don't really like that part. But having breakfast this morning with Ron Washington and Toby Harrah, that was great for me, talking to them about their lives and how they view the game, that was a big thrill. And then going out here today and taking grounders at third or fly balls in right, getting in the batting cage and taking five or ten cuts, to me that's the best. That's where I'm getting all my thrills from—the association with the players."

Just then a child, who had leaned around the corner of the dugout to see what was going on, handed Sider a pen and a scorecard and asked him for his autograph. Sider signed without flinching. Didn't he feel just a little bit foolish, I wondered. I didn't mean the autograph so much as invading the players' territory on the field.

Sider looked puzzled. "Not at all. I'm a decent ballplayer. I feel good, and they make me feel good. They razz me. Dick used to say, 'Make sure you put on a helmet when you go out there.' Then after a few days he said, 'I apologize for saying that to you, I didn't realize you'd be able to handle it.' I sat on the bench for an exhibition game and Billy Williams came over and said, '[You sit on the bench during] a game when I'm umpiring, you're outta here.' I thought he was serious, I couldn't tell. So I called the league and asked if it was okay, and they said, 'No, you can't.' Otherwise I woulda been. So I sit above the dugout on our side and scream my lungs out."

Sider acknowledged that owning a team was "a big investment" for him and not necessarily a good one. "This is a once-in-a-lifetime opportunity to live out a fantasy," he said, "but it's crazy from a business point of view. This year was an impossible year to make money. We're hoping to get by without losing a bundle because there was no time to plan. You know what? Crowds are gonna double because the population increases in the next thirty days (snowbirds, again), and they're gonna maybe double on top of that because of the additional interest in the game, and the additional press that we're gonna get, and the reduction in competition from college football and the NFL. So I'm not worried about crowds."

In the first inning of the middle game of the series, Lenny Randle made an acrobatic play at second base. It came when Toby Harrah hit a hard shot straight up the middle that pitcher Milt Wilcox deflected but couldn't handle. The ball skidded to the right side of the infield. Randle, who had broken to his right at the crack of the bat, abruptly changed directions, scooped up the ball, and made a shovel toss to Dave Rajsich at first just in time to catch Harrah. It was the sort of graceful play major-league second basemen make all the time. But seeing it made me realize how few like it I'd seen over the last three weeks.

There was a lot of speculation about where to put the senior league in the hierarchy of baseball. Was it the equivalent of college ball? AAA? Willie Aikens came to the senior league from the Mexican League, and he thought the two were comparable, with some players good enough to be in the big leagues and others who probably wouldn't make it at any level in pro ball. That said, most of the games, most of the time, looked to me like the real thing. Obviously, no one in the senior league could run as fast as Rickey Henderson, but then no one could make the throw from short like Shawon Dunston, either. The weaknesses were relative and tended to cancel each other out. The balance of the game was largely preserved.

Triples, rare in any league, were a case in point. With so few speedsters in the senior league, you wouldn't expect to see many triples at all. In fact, senior leaguers ended up hitting one hundred fifty-four triples for the season, or 2.5 percent of all hits, exactly the same percentage as were hit in the major leagues in 1988 and almost the same as in the two other years I looked at, 1978 (2.9) and 1968 (2.7). The hitters were slower but so were the outfielders, and the outfielders couldn't throw as well, either. Again, not that you were likely to notice.

"You can't tell the difference, you just can't," Mitch Maxwell insisted. "You put a twenty-five-year-old girl in a bathing suit next to a forty-year-old woman, she looks better. If you put forty-year-old women next to forty-year-old women, they all look pretty good, the good ones, you know?"

Still, defense generally and infield play in particular were the areas where players tended to show their age. A hard-hit ball in the senior league jumped off the bat as violently as a hard-hit ball in the big leagues, and when it did, infielders were sometimes slow to react. Baseball is a game of sharp angles and straight lines, until a ball comes skidding through the infield at fifty miles per hour. Then anything can happen, and it takes not only quick reflexes but confidence to stay with the ball and make the play. In the senior league, you saw too many ground balls pass through the wickets and not enough plays like Randle's at second, with its midcourse correction and improvised solution.

Tonight's crowd was down slightly from last night, only one thousand fifty-five, attributable partly to more cold weather and partly to a scheduling mix-up that left some thinking the game was supposed to start at 1:00. Morley tried to apologize by offering everyone in attendance two free grandstand tickets to a future game. Those who were here saw Wilcox come within two outs of pitching his first complete game since he was with the Tigers in 1983 as the Pelicans won for the second time, 7–4. Wilcox, who was the first pitcher to learn the split-finger fastball from then Tigers pitching coach Roger Craig, looked the same as he always had, not overpowering, not many strikeouts, and not many hard-hit balls.

"I try to get 'em to hit my pitches," he said after the game, standing with his grade-school-age son on the edge of the darkened field. "That's all I try to do—get 'em to hit the ball, get ahead of the batters, don't give 'em too good of a pitch to hit. My sinker's starting to work real well."

Wilcox started thirty-three games with the world champion Tigers in 1984—thirty-five counting the play-offs and the World Series—and never had a complete game. I asked him if he was sorry not to get one tonight.

"Complete games are not important," he said. "Wins are."

Of course, how silly of me. Obviously, Wilcox's sinker wasn't the only part of his game that was starting to come around. His clichés were looking good, too.

ST. PETERSBURG · November 19

ONLY THREE PLAYERS IN THE SENIOR LEAGUE HAD SPENT TIME LAST summer in the majors and all three were Tropics: pitchers Tim Stoddard and Paul Mirabella, who saw limited action with Cleveland and Milwaukee, respectively, and shortstop Ron Washington, who hit one double in seven at-bats with Houston. Last week, Washington became the first player to re-sign with a major-league organization when he accepted a AAA contract offer from the Texas Rangers. In signing Washington, the Rangers acted on the recommendation of their hitting instructor and sometime scout Toby Harrah, who'd been watching Washington closely all season from over at third base.

Washington, a twenty-year pro, was the second graduate of the Royals Baseball Academy (after Frank White) to make it to the big leagues. He came up with the Dodgers in 1977 but it was not until 1982, his twelfth year, that he spent his first full season in the majors with the Twins. Washington was an adequate fielder with an adequate bat and good speed, qualities that led him to be pegged early on as a utility player. During the course of his career, he had played for six different organizations (the Rangers would be the seventh) and appeared at every position except pitcher and catcher. Last summer, at age thirty-seven, Washington had played mostly for Houston's AAA farm team, the Tucson Toros. John Henry, owner of the Toros and co-owner of the Tropics, said he had expected Washington to be called up in September when the Astros were fighting the Giants for the division title. Instead, Washington was released when the season ended and this winter was a free agent.

Harrah was not the only scout following the action in Florida this winter. Yet he said he thought most of the players who wanted to use the senior league as a springboard for returning to the majors were going to be disappointed. "If you come down here and play well, there's a chance," he said, "but if you don't play well . . ." Harrah shrugged his shoulders.

Washington had played well. He was batting .391, was among the league leaders in homers, runs batted in, and stolen bases, and was a solid defensive player at the one position where most teams were vulnerable. His performance had earned him one more shot at the big leagues, and Washington was determined to make the most of it.

"It's a minor-league contract," Washington said. His face was hawkish and angular and was the only place the years showed. The rest of his body was like a twenty-year-old's. "But I'm going to big-league camp. It don't matter as far as I'm concerned. *I'm going to Arlington, Texas.*"

In today's final game of the series, Washington pushed his

average closer to .400 with two doubles and added an RBI and two runs scored as the Tropics won easily, 5–1. The game featured another fine pitching performance, this time by Tropics starter (and Dartmouth lawyer) Pete Broberg, who held the Pelicans to three hits with help from reliever Al Hrabosky.

For Jim Morley, fan, it was a terrific weekend. His Pelicans had won two out of three and were tied now with the Tropics for the best record in the league. All three games had been well played. But Jim Morley, businessman, was worried. Attendance for the entire series had totaled just over three thousand fans. Not good, not good at all. In exactly twelve days, Morley had a payroll to meet. He would need one hundred thousand dollars. Morley had been squeezed before, but this time he couldn't very well fall back on American Express. As far as he knew, ballplayers didn't take plastic.

ORLANDO · *November 20*

"**What the hell's going on in this league?!**"

Earl Weaver was steamed, never mind that his Suns had just won a game for what was only the fifth time all year. It had been a terrific game, even he admitted that. They'd fought back from a 5–1 deficit, tied it in the eighth, held on in the ninth, and won in the eleventh—on the road, no less. "Great game, everybody," Earl yelled to his troops when he met them in the locker room. "Great game, *everybody!*"

But damn if it hadn't happened again. For the third time in this young season, Weaver got himself tangled in a silly fight with a trigger-happy umpire and was ejected. And this time he wasn't taking it calmly, not at all.

"I don't wanna go out of the dugout," he said almost pleadingly. Around him his players were balancing paper plates on their laps, filled with the bounty of the postgame spread. Only Weaver had no appetite. "I don't wanna argue with anyone. But I know this! If it keeps up, if there's two more times like this or one more time like this, I'm gonna resign and to hell with it. 'Cause I'm not here to be embarrassed by amateur umpires. *I'm not here to be embarrassed by amateur umpires!*"

Normally it was a two-hour drive to Orlando. Tonight it took a little longer. First I got stuck in rush-hour traffic, then I got lost downtown trying to save a quarter by avoiding the tollway. By the time I arrived at Terry Park the sun was long gone. The damp night air hit me as soon as I opened the car door. I wore a heavy gray sweatshirt under a jean jacket and still I was cold. I wished I'd brought a hat.

The park felt that much colder inside for being nearly empty. Maybe Ben Kaufman, the Juice marketing director, was right; maybe all the sports fans in town *had* stayed home to watch the Broncos and the Redskins on "Monday Night Football." But it was obvious that the Juice's problems went well beyond competition from TV. As of this evening, they were averaging five hundred twenty-two fans per game, last in the league. Tonight, when all were counted, they would number less than three hundred.

With so many seats to choose from, there wasn't much point in hiding in the press box. Besides, it was windy up there. So I bought a cup of coffee and moved down to field level, where I found a front-row seat right behind the Juice's on-deck circle. As it happened, it was the best game I'd seen all year. Both starting pitchers were chased early—the Suns' Ed Figueroa after three, the Juice's Pete Falcone in the fifth—but tonight the bull pens were up to the task. Orlando made it to the eighth inning holding on to a 5–3 lead. Then Weaver squared off against Gates Brown in a classic managerial duel.

In the bottom of the eighth, Juice reliever Roy Branch retired leadoff hitter Rennie Stennett on a fly ball to center. But he walked pinch hitter Bobby Molinaro and gave up a single to Derrel Thomas, which put the tying runs on base. Weaver, playing the percentages, sent lefty Glenn Gulliver to the on-deck circle to pinch-hit for Bobby Ramos. When Brown brought in lefty Jamie Easterly, Weaver called Gulliver back to the bench and sent out righty Joe Hicks instead. Hicks singled, scoring Molinaro to make it 5–4. With the tying run on third and only one out, Brown went to his bull pen ace, Doug Corbett. Corbett already had three saves in six appearances and had not allowed a run, but Bert Campaneris slapped his first pitch for a single and that tied the score. Corbett gave up another single to the next batter, Rafael Landestoy, but was able to escape with no further damage when George Hendrick bounced into a double play.

Orlando threatened in the bottom of the ninth against Joe Decker, who was working his sixth inning in relief. With one out, José Cruz singled, then took third on a single by Tom Paciorek and a throwing error by Campaneris. That brought up Jerry Martin, recently acquired from the Pelicans. Martin hit a fly ball which Molinaro caught for out number two. Cruz tagged, but Molinaro's long throw from center field was right where it had to be to complete the double play. And with that the game went into extra innings.

By now the evening had begun to take on some of the qualities of a dream. Dreams are private; I saw nothing except what was taking place on the field and so felt like I was the only witness. Dreams are silent; except for occasional outbursts, the only sounds I heard were the ones made by bats and balls. By the time Hicks singled again in the twelfth inning, this time to drive in the winning run, there were more players on the field than fans in the stands. And that's not counting Weaver, who was cooling his jets in the clubhouse.

It happened in the bottom of the eleventh when, with two outs, Cliff Johnson looked at strike three—"outside and low," Johnson said later, "terrible call." Weaver thought so. Johnson was the third out of the inning and left a runner stranded on second base. For all Weaver knew, that call had cost him the game. He was out of the dugout in a flash.

"You proud of yourself, you idiot? You *proud* of yourself, you idiot?" Since Weaver was arguing balls and strikes, the ump gave him the hook almost instantly. The Juice players ran straight for the dugout, the Suns headed out to take their positions, and the PA man cut to the between-innings musical selection:

> I'm so excited,
> And I just can't hide it!
> I'm about to lose control and I think I like it!

The music was too loud. Weaver was still out there giving hell to the ump, but no one could hear what he was saying. So a couple of fans turned and yelled at the PA announcer to cut the music. I didn't think he would but he did. Then the fans joined in the fight:

"I'M AN ORLANDO FAN AND HE'S RIGHT, BLUE!"

"I'LL BUY YOU A DRINK, EARL!"

Weaver hung on until he was so hoarse he could hardly be heard, then he hung on a little longer before he finally left the field.

"I don't know why he threw me out," he said in the locker room after the game was over. "You go out to get your ballplayer out of the goddarn argument so he don't get thrown out. *Aaaagh,* now he can tell his kids he threw Earl Weaver out, that's all they want to do in this league. They been watching me on television and saying to themselves, 'If I ever get a shot at him I'm gonna throw him out,' and that's what they're doing. That's *exactly* what they're doing. And it shows. Sometimes I honestly believe that they make a call just to get me out of the dugout. That's not why I'm here. I'm here to manage a ball club. That's all I have to say."

FORT MYERS • *November 21*

IT WAS THE TIME BEFORE THE GAME, AFTER BATTING PRACTICE. THE Terry Park grounds crew was tending to the infield, raking the orange clay, laying down the chalk. The sky was already black. "May I have your attention," came the voice through the loud-speakers mounted in the steel rafters, under the tin roof. "Curt Flood, the commissioner of the Senior Professional Baseball Association, will be available to sign autographs by the concession stand behind home plate."

Curt Flood—a somber, middle-aged man in a dark suit and tie, slight of build, with a widow's peak that was fast losing its point— stood waiting quietly with his hands crossed beneath his belt until a table and chair were brought to him, then sat down and went to work.

"You look like you could still play, Curt," said a man his age, handing over a scorecard and a pen.

"You can't see my legs."

"Is that what it takes?"

Next came a younger man, himself barely old enough to re- member, pushing ahead a child who couldn't possibly have had any idea who this man was. "Shake his hand," said the father. "Shake Mr. Flood's hand."

"Sign my ball, please," asked another, handing over an official senior-league ball with Commissioner Flood's signature already on it.

"I stayed up for weeks signing all these balls," Flood joked. "Now you want me to sign it again?" While the supplicants laughed, Flood signed—a big, flowing C, a dashing, continental F, there between the stitches in the space reserved for super-stars.

I had witnessed scenes like this before, and I still found them jarring. Curt Flood, the man who would not be traded against his will, who challenged baseball's reserve clause and lost, who disappeared from public view for the better part of two decades, who was rescued from the shadows by the senior league and thrust back into the limelight—as commissioner, no less—now routinely throwing out first pitches and signing autographs for adoring fans. In the world of baseball, this was a development as unexpected as the fall of the Berlin Wall.

Flood belonged to the first generation of black ballplayers who followed Jackie Robinson into the big leagues. He was signed by the Reds in 1956, eighteen years old, only five-nine, and way too skinny, an outfielder who covered a lot of ground and hit for a high average but lacked power. Flood grew up in an all-black section of Oakland (Frank Robinson and Vada Pinson were his high school teammates), sheltered almost entirely from contact with the other race. His first real encounter with bald white hatred came during his first spring training, when he tried to register at the Floridian Hotel in Tampa. In his book, *The Way It Is*, Flood later recalled how the desk clerk looked at him "whitely" before summoning a porter, who showed Flood to the back door. Flood's reservation was at Ma Felder's, a boarding-house across town.

At High Point–Thomasville and all around the Class B Carolina League, Flood was dealt the full deck of racial indignities. He was taunted and baited by fans, isolated from his white team-mates, and made either to wait in the bus or slink around back to the kitchen whenever the team stopped for meals on the road. One day during Flood's second pro season with Savannah, be-tween games of a doubleheader in Danville, Virginia, all the players tossed their sweaty uniforms on the floor. Then, while

Flood watched, the clubhouse boy poked around in the pile with a trash picker and removed Flood's shirt and pants. They had to be sent to the colored laundry.

Flood was traded to the Cardinals organization in 1957. The following year he made the big club as the starting center fielder, a position he kept for the next twelve seasons. Over that span, Flood won seven Gold Gloves, appeared in three All-Star Games, and played a key role on three World Series teams in the sixties.

"He was a very unselfish player," said Dal Maxvill, a former teammate, now the Cardinals' general manager. "He hit behind Lou Brock, so he was taking all the time so that Brock could steal a base. Once Brock got to second base, he was always giving himself up going the other way, trying to move him to third so that Roger Maris and Orlando Cepeda would have a shot at driving him in. He was a smart outfielder, a smart base runner, really a complete player for many years."

Success in baseball brought Flood wealth and status. Ultimately he became one of the best-paid players on the richest, most glamorous team of his era. By 1969 he was earning ninety thousand dollars a year, an unprecedented sum for a player who was neither a home-run hitter nor a twenty-game winner.

Then Flood was traded to the Philadelphia Phillies, a losing team in a city not known for its hospitality to black athletes. "Player trades are commonplace," Flood wrote in his book. "The unusual aspect of this one was that I refused to accept it." By saying no, Flood gave up fame, riches, respect, everything he had achieved since the dark early days of his career. He became a "nigger" again.

To Marvin Miller, who came to baseball as head of the Players Association in 1966 from the United Steelworkers Union, the reserve clause was simply "the most outrageous thing I ever saw." What was known as the reserve clause was really an interlocking system of standard agreements, the upshot of which, in 1969, was that no team could offer employment to a player under contract to another team, and that every player was required to sign a contract that included an option on the following year. In other words, from the moment a player signed his first contract, he lost the right to choose where he wanted to work, forever.

The legal precedents for challenging the reserve clause on antitrust grounds were not encouraging to Flood. In 1922 the U.S.

Supreme Court ruled that baseball was not subject to federal antitrust legislation. In 1949 a federal court of appeals ruled in favor of New York Giants outfielder Danny Gardella, who was blacklisted after he jumped to the Mexican League. But Gardella agreed to a cash settlement in exchange for dropping the case. And in 1953, in a case brought by George Toolson, a pitcher in the Yankee organization who refused a minor-league assignment, the Supreme Court upheld its 1922 decision, with reservations. The court urged that the issue be resolved through legislation.

In October 1969, Flood met with Miller and Dick Moss, the players' counsel, in the coffee shop of the Summit Hotel in New York. Miller laid it out for him, told him about the precedents, warned him that he should expect to lose, that he might well be turning his back for good on organized baseball. Miller remembered, "I said, 'I don't know what you feel your future is. Does it have anything to do with baseball? Minor-league managing, major-league managing, coaching? These are very vindictive people. Once this is filed, you're at an end. There's no future there. You're going to wipe it out.' I said, 'I don't want to know, but if there's something in your personal life that you don't want exposed to the press, whatever, it's going to come out.' And on and on like this, enough to scare fourteen people, and I didn't scare him."

History records the fact of Flood's refusal, his willingness to take a stand, his determination in seeing the fight through to the end. Really, that's all that matters. If then we wonder *why* he did what he did, it's only because we're curious.

Was Flood a martyr? Ask that and you have to ask, What was he giving up? And that, Miller suggested, was not an easy question.

"It's true he'd been an outstanding center fielder for some years," Miller said. "Some signs of slippage, past year or so. I watched that 1968 World Series, seventh game. You know, it all came back in a flood, a rush. Was that an ordinary error? Really a strange error for a great, great center fielder. He came in on the ball and it was about fifteen feet over his head. Could happen to anybody, you never know. There was sun, there was tension, I'm sure. Who knows? I knew he was thirty-one, thirty-two. While that's very, very young in anything, and may be young today in baseball, it wasn't young then. In your thirties, they began looking at you in those days."

Some who knew Flood at the time hint at developments more ominous. He was drinking heavily, to the point, some said, where he was incapable of saying no. The alcohol was affecting his health. He may well have wondered how much longer he could continue in his profession.

"I think he showed a tremendous amount of courage, no matter what," said Miller. "He's certainly not a fearful man. What I don't know is what his own inner feelings about continuing his career as a player really were. I just don't know that. I don't know if he had questions about himself, or questions about that life. I have suspicions that he did."

Flood, represented by Arthur Goldberg, filed suit against Commissioner Bowie Kuhn, the presidents of both leagues, and the twenty-four owners. He sought changes in baseball's reserve clause and one million four hundred thousand dollars in damages. Coverage of the trial spilled out of the sports pages and became a national news story. The following is from an account in the June 1, 1970, issue of *Newsweek*:

"Curt Flood, nattily dressed in a blue, double-breasted suit, was the first witness called to the stand. Mumbling his answers and rubbing his hands, Flood seemed to have lost much of the aplomb that helped him earn $90,000 last season for playing baseball for the St. Louis Cardinals. After repeatedly asking the witness to speak more distinctly, presiding Judge Irving Ben Cooper chided gently, 'You're not finding this as easy as getting up to bat.'

" 'No, sir,' replied Flood."

"We were in a large courtroom," Flood recalled nearly two decades after the fact, "and I was trying very, very hard to appear not to be nervous, but of course the world is watching you. I was scared to death, very simply. And he kept interrupting me. That really got me flustered. He kept saying, 'Speak up.' He wanted me to enunciate so the people way in the back could hear me. And I just couldn't find myself able to do that. Just when I would get my train of thought together he would interrupt me and I would lose it. I was very nervous, very uptight. I was afraid I would say all the wrong things. I guess that they were looking for a Sidney Poitier playing me. I was me playing me."

As the case made its way up through the courts on appeal, Flood was running out of money. He earned no income at all from baseball in 1970, and what other business interests he had in St. Louis were failing. So when Bob Short of the Washington Senators called, Flood listened. Short had acquired Flood's contract from the Phillies. Would he consider playing again?

Flood flew to Washington from Copenhagen, where he was visiting friends. After Goldberg gave the go-ahead, Flood signed a one-year contract with the Senators for one hundred ten thousand dollars. The contract contained the reserve clause.

From the beginning, Flood struggled, both professionally and personally. In thirteen games with the Senators, he came to bat thirty-five times and got only seven hits, all singles. "During that time I was getting all kinds of freaky letters," Flood said. "People thought I was trying to destroy baseball. I was an ingrate. I was a spoiled brat. I was making all this money and I wouldn't shut up. Threats in the mail, on the telephone, threats against my children. I ignored all that as long as I could 'til one day we flew into New York. It was Yankee Stadium. And there was a black funeral wreath in my locker. Whoever it was had to have some clout to drag this funeral wreath in and put it in my locker. Scared the shit out of me."

Flood had seen enough. When the team got back to Washington, he packed his bags, dashed off a telegram to Short—"I tried. A year and a half [out of baseball] is too much. Very serious personal problems mounting every day. Thank you for your confidence and understanding"—and was gone, to Lisbon first, then to Barcelona and from there by ferry to Majorca.

He bought a red sports car to drive around the island and a bar called the Rustic Inn. The Rustic was at the end of a dead-end street. It stayed open all night. His customers were mostly expatriates, Englishmen, and NATO servicemen from the States who recognized the picture over the bar and were glad for beer that was always served ice-cold. He lived in Majorca five years, until one morning when Franco's *Guardia Civil* busted in and ripped his license off the wall. Afterward, Flood returned to the mainland and settled for a while in Andorra.

In 1976 Flood went home to Oakland. His case by then had made it all the way to the Supreme Court. The majority opinion, delivered by Justice Harry A. Blackmun in the summer of 1972, acknowledged that baseball's special antitrust status was an "aberration" and an "anomoly" but refused to overturn previous rulings. The case was closed.

Nonetheless, by then the days when owners wielded unchecked power over their players were numbered. In 1975, baseball arbitrator Peter Seitz, exercising authority granted him through collective bargaining, upheld claims to free agency by two pitchers, Andy Messersmith and Dave McNally, effectively killing the reserve clause and opening the way to free agency. Flood's battle was lost, but now the war was won.

"Did Flood advance the ball despite being a losing case?" Miller wondered. "Very difficult to say. I think, though the term consciousness raising has been overdone, it surely did that among the players. It surely did that among the press. It surely did that among the fans."

Back home in Oakland, Flood drifted. "I kind of fooled around, did the same things that I always do when I have nothing to do. I started drinking too much, fooling around too much, chasing girls too much." A friend got him a job doing radio color commentary for the A's in 1978. Later he worked on special projects in the A's front office. For a time he was commissioner of the Young America Little League in Oakland. Last year, for his efforts, the city named a park in his honor.

Four years ago, *Sport* magazine published a special anniversary issue, profiling the forty most influential figures in the world of sports since World War II. The editors ranked Flood number thirty-two, between Avery Brundage and Bob Cousy. I went to Los Angeles to interview Flood. We met at his home in Baldwin Hills, where he lived with his second wife, actress Judy Pace, and her two children. The house was near the top of a steep, twisting canyon road. From the living room, through a glass wall, you looked out over the populated valley to the Hollywood Hills and the mountains beyond.

Flood sat cross-legged on the couch, occasionally sipping a soft drink (he said he had given up smoking and drinking). When he spoke—often pausing for a long time between words—he clasped his hands together prayerfully. A self-portrait—meticulous, detailed, almost a photographic likeness—hung on the wall. At the time, Flood was collecting his major-league pension and working on a sports cartoon series he hoped eventually to sell for syndication.

"I'm trying to get myself established in art again," he said. "I really don't like anything else as much as I like baseball. I really don't know anything else. I can't tap-dance or sing. But more than anything else I just wanted to find something that I could do from now on, instead of bouncing around so much. I have a lifetime job in Oakland if I ever wanted to go back. I really plan to make Judy happy, and the kids happy, and myself. I certainly know that we deserve it."

Inevitably, the conversation returned to the past, to what Flood referred to wearily as "not the central fact of my life," though clearly it was that.

" 'Til this very day, I guess someplace way back in the back of my mind, I'm really not sure that the decision itself was decided on the merits of the case that was presented to the Supreme Court." Flood spoke softly, twisting his hands. "I think that a lot of other things entered into it, be it, uh, any of the, uh . . ." And then he flared, giving vent to something deep inside. "Jealousy. Prejudice. What do you call that conglomeration of things, all of those things that are rolled into some Americans? I don't know. The good old boys got together and decided that this little black kid wasn't going to change the great American game."

"Was it worth it?" I asked him.

"I think now I can say, 'Yes, it was worth it.' During the time that it was happening, God, I had many, many second thoughts. It's not easy to turn your back on the only real thing that you know, that you do well. You find yourself in a really very complicated situation, and you wonder how you got there. I actually wonder what would have happened if I just said, 'Well, I'll go with the flow and let it be.'

"Sometimes, though, you find yourself saying, 'Goddamn, I wish somebody would do something about that,' whatever *that* is. And nobody ever does. You find out sometimes that that somebody who should be doing something is *you*, and nobody else could."

"Are you bitter?"

"Not bitter. What am I? It's been a long time since I even thought about it. What *was* I? I guess after the fact, and when I look back on it, there were times when I was just most unhappy. They talk of me as if I'm an entity, rather than a person who really feels. Hopefully, they, whoever *they* are, will remember how difficult it was for me to give it up, just cold turkey like that, how difficult it was for me to do what I did. Reading about myself in my own book hurts, sometimes. There were a lot of unpleasant events that I would rather forget, but no one will ever let me."

Among those who testified on behalf of the owners in the Flood case was a former player, Joe Garagiola. Several years later, according to Miller, Garagiola admitted having made a "terrible mistake," and apologized to Miller. It is not known whether Garagiola ever apologized to Flood personally, but in the spring of 1989, when Jim Morley was calling around, soliciting candidates for commissioner of his new league, he got through to Garagiola, who recommended Flood.

Flood became the third employee of the fledgling enterprise. He signed a three-year contract potentially worth more than one hundred thousand dollars a year in salary and bonuses. Flood gave the league instant credibility. Players liked him because he was one of them and could be counted on to look after their interests. Among liberal members of the generation of baseball fans who came of age in the sixties and seventies—precisely the senior league's target audience—Flood was widely admired as a symbol of resistance to authority. And to the media Flood was an intriguing story. If it weren't for Flood, a league official later admitted, Howard Cosell probably wouldn't have bothered to attend the first senior-league press conference in May 1989. Cosell, himself a virtual recluse in recent years, lent star quality to the occasion and helped make it a happening.

Since then, Flood had moved his family to Miami to be near the league office. Like any commissioner, Flood was expected, in theory, to mediate disputes between players and management, oversee the umpires, and issue rulings on protests. But the senior league also had a president and an executive director, who together managed the day-to-day affairs of the league. Flood's duties tended to fall more within the realm of public relations. He was the league's goodwill ambassador, and that, more than anything else, was what had brought him tonight to Fort Myers.

"I'm from Philadelphia," said the next man in line, and then he waited for Flood to respond.

"I love Philadelphia," Flood said flatly.

Laughing: "No, you don't."

"I love Philadelphia," Flood repeated, his tone of voice unchanged.

"You wouldn't go there, though, would you?"

No, he wouldn't. Did the fan think he was being witty? Did he think Flood hadn't heard the same jokes a hundred times before? For Flood, the act of signing autographs could never just be about memories of youth and fame. It always had to be about pain, too.

"W. C. Fields and Curt Flood!" said another.

"One to Dick, one to Joe, and one to Lew—L-E-W," said yet another, handing Flood three souvenir scorecards. Then, "You still shoulda gone to Philadelphia. I'm from there. Hah-hah-hah!"

RICK WAITS WAS PITCHING FOR THE SUN SOX TONIGHT AGAINST BRA-denton. With his pinched face, marble eyes, knobby chin, bushy mustache and ever-present chew, Waits looked like a ballplayer from another century, one of those inscrutable black-and-white visages you see in old team photos of the Brooklyn Excelsiors or the Rockford Forest City nine. The difference, of course, was that Waits sat before me in living color, pink-complexioned, milky-blue-eyed, red-haired, and all done up in a green-and-gold Sun Sox uniform.

Waits, a six-three left-hander, was never overpowering during his twelve-year major-league career. He was wild, he had arm problems, and he played for a lot of bad teams. Three straight years—1978–80—he won in double figures for the Indians; two of those years he finished with a losing record. In 1985, he was released by the Brewers. He went to camp with the Giants in '86 and was released for the last time but not before Roger Craig taught him how to throw a split-finger fastball.

That summer he took his family to Florence for a vacation, got sidetracked, and ended up pitching and managing in the Italian league. He'd had good success in Italy the last four years with the split-finger, and so far in the senior league he was un-stoppable. Waits entered tonight's game with a perfect record in his three starts and an earned run average of 0.39.

Waits's success was somewhat surprising considering the fact that with the splitter, he always threw a lot of ground balls. "You know," said Waits, "during the preseason games the word around here was that you better get 'em to hit it in the air 'cause every-body was thinking that the middle infielders—the speed and the range of the players—wouldn't be as good, and so therefore a ground-ball pitcher might not succeed as much. I don't know about the other clubs, but that's certainly not true for this ball club. Me and [Wayne] Garland and [Dennis] Leonard and even [Steve] McCatty the other day, we're all getting ground balls and our infielders are picking it."

That said, the Sun Sox went out and committed five errors, three on ground balls, two by hard-luck second baseman Pepe Frias. Incredibly, the Explorers also committed five errors (all on grounders) for a grand total of ten, making this by far the sloppiest game I'd ever seen. (Not, however, the sloppiest ever played. The major-league record for errors in a game is *forty*, twenty-four by Boston, sixteen by St. Louis, on June 14, 1876. Imagine *that*.)

Where the Sun Sox failed with leather, they more than compensated with wood, which spelled the difference in the contest. The Sun Sox collected fifteen hits, five each off three different Explorers pitchers, and scored nine runs. Waits, meanwhile, allowed just two runs in the second inning, neither of them earned, and coasted the rest of the way. Jim Slaton finished up with a perfect ninth.

Waits's record was now four and 0. His earned run average was 0.29 and falling fast. "If his ERA gets any lower," manager Pat Dobson said after the game, "they're going to have to start carrying it out another decimal point."

FORT MYERS • *November 22*

Sun Sox shortstop Tim Ireland was lying on his back on the floor in the trainer's room, his knees bent to his chest, trying to make the stiffness go away. Ireland was thirty-six years old. He had come to the senior league three years removed from pro ball and with only four days to prepare (he had to borrow a shortstop's glove) and he had been hurting ever since. "If I really told you how I felt that first week you wouldn't believe it," he said. "First day I felt all right, but after that I was so sore that I could barely walk. The next day I just gutted it out and good things happened."

Ireland's first game, he went four-for-five, knocked in two runs, scored two, and successfully executed the hidden-ball trick. Now, nearly a month into the season, he was batting .385 and ranked among the league leaders in hits and runs. His success had brought him more attention than he'd ever had before. People wondered who he was and where he came from.

Ireland played professional baseball for thirteen years. He was released—he had to guess about this, he wasn't sure—oh, about eight times. He played all over the United States, plus Venezuela, Puerto Rico, Japan, and Italy. Ireland was with Nettuno in the Italian League when he got released for the last time. "That was my farewell to baseball," he said. "That's the bottom rung, getting released by an Italian team."

"After how many years?"

"Six weeks. I wasn't into the Italian baseball scene."

After that, Ireland, like so many others, found that the only way he could escape the pull of the game was if he quit cold turkey.

"Didn't play at all," he said.

"Not even softball?"

"Nope. Once I hung 'em up, that was it. I didn't wanna be one of those softball players and play with those guys who wanted to play pro ball and couldn't and now they're playing softball with a vengeance and sometimes malintent. Those games don't do much for me."

Then, again, like so many others, he'd come back. Last year he was manager of the Giants Class A farm team at Salinas. This year he'd be coaching in Phoenix. He hoped one day to manage in the big leagues.

With his hat on, Ireland looked like he had a full head of hair. When he took his hat off, he showed a head that resembled an egg sitting upright in a nest of grass. If I'd had to choose his profession, I might have guessed accountant. His eyes were black and hard and small—maybe an especially repressed accountant. In the minors, he had been known all over for his hot temper. Water coolers cringed whenever he came near.

Ireland had brought that same attitude with him to the senior league, a sort of grim determination to succeed, to win whatever the cost. Fans loved him. He got hits with two outs, made big plays, never quit. His uniform was always dirty. Yet he was not nearly as popular with the other players. Anyone who made a specialty of the hidden-ball trick, as Ireland had throughout his career, was bound to make enemies. He was used to that. He knew the play was borderline bush-league.

But for some reason it seemed to make people even madder in the senior league. Ireland didn't know exactly why. "I'm just trying to win the game, man," he insisted. "You do what you can to win it."

Maybe it was the setting. In the senior league, a spirit of casual, collegial competitiveness prevailed. For the most part, these were men who had fought their wars on other fields, in other times. But Ireland, like the Sunday softballers he claimed to despise, was still fighting his own private war. His crime, if you could call it that, was that he tried too hard.

Ireland was listed in *The Baseball Encyclopedia*, he could say that much. It would have been much worse if he'd never made it. At least he'd had his cup of coffee.

"Eleven games," he said.

"Who with?"

"KC."

"Get to bat?"

"Seven times."

"Any hits?"

"One."

"Single?"

"Yup."

"Where'd you hit it?"

"Infield single, deep short."

"Did the shortstop go to his right or to his left?"

"Right." Ireland chuckled. Of course he remembered every detail. "A real blast. It was in a rain-delayed game, fourteen-two, and it had poured for about an hour. They got all the regulars out of there and threw me in."

Ireland got up off the floor and twisted his trunk, stretching. He looked around for his hat. "In fact, the guy that I got the hit off of is in this league now."

"Who's that?

"Easterly, Jamie Easterly, for Orlando."

"Did you ever mention it to him?"

"I haven't talked to him about it. He probably don't remember. Or give a shit."

IN THE TOP OF THE SECOND INNING, AT EXACTLY 7:29 P.M., a tiny rip appeared in the black sky beyond the wall in left-center field and a piece of white fire poked through. The rip climbed higher and higher in the sky, and soon the crowd began to cheer.

"Ladies and gentlemen," said the PA announcer, "that is the space shuttle."

One hundred forty miles northeast of Fort Myers, at the Kennedy Space Center, on the opposite side of the Florida peninsula, the space shuttle *Discovery* was lifting off. Rich Gale, who was on the mound, stopped and turned and stared like he was watching the flight of a long home run. For a moment, every player on the field turned his back to home plate. A few seconds later, the rip was gone.

Inspired, both teams did their best with bat and ball to imitate the rocket launch. Up 3–0, the Explos exploded with three more in the fifth, highlighted by a home run by Wayne Nordhagen. The Sun Sox answered with back-to-back leadoff homers in their half by Ron Jackson and Marty Castillo, followed five batters later with a grand slam by Ron Pruitt. That tied the score at six. The atmosphere in the press box grew tense as beat writers from two newspapers struggled to come up with some way to work the launch into their leads.

As the game entered the late innings, Ireland took control. In the seventh, he led off with a single and eventually came around to score the go-ahead run. Bradenton answered with two more of its own in the top of the eighth to regain the lead, 8–7. In the bottom of the eighth, Ireland drove in the tying run with a two-out triple, then scored on Pruitt's single to regain the lead for the Sun Sox. But when Bradenton tied the score with a run in the ninth, the game went into extra innings.

Pat Putnam led off the tenth for Fort Myers with a single. Pinch hitter Bobby Jones sacrificed Don Hood, pinch-running for Putnam, to second. Then Larry Harlow flied out to center. With two outs, it was back to the top of the order and you know who. Ireland stroked a clean line drive in the gap, scoring Hood and winning the game.

It was Ireland's third hit of the evening, all from the seventh inning on, all of which either tied the score or put his team ahead. The performance raised his season average to an even .400.

A FOOTNOTE FROM WINTER HAVEN. CECIL COOPER, STILL THE ONLY player I'd met so far who insisted he was *not* having fun, today announced he was quitting the senior league and going back to his family and his regular job as an agent. As of today, Cooper was first on the Super Sox with three homers and fifteen runs batted in and was batting .407.

"I'm a forty-year-old family man," Cooper explained. "I haven't lost too much at the plate, but I've lost the killer instinct I had as a player in the big leagues and you can't play the game without that."

BRADENTON • November 25

GRAIG NETTLES LOOKED SURPRISINGLY RELAXED FOR A MAN WHO had no money and had just been fired. He'd gotten off to a rough start as manager of the St. Lucie Legends, that was true—two wins and nine losses. But he hardly expected to be axed just like that. Hell, not even George Steinbrenner would have fired his manager after only eleven games. Joe Sprung, the New York accountant who owned the Legends, seemed to be on a mission to out-Steinbrenner Steinbrenner himself. Nettles referred to him as *Sprung*brenner, the nickname the players had given him. It was an insult, of course, but Sprung didn't see it that way. The comparison actually seemed to please him. Later, when I asked him about it, he blushed and offered to mail me a clipping all about it.

Anyway, things could have been a lot worse for Nettles. He was in Bradenton now, no longer managing but playing every day at first base. He'd signed a contract at the beginning of the season for the maximum amount—fifteen thousand a month—and it was still in effect. He collected two paychecks now: ten thousand from Bradenton and five thousand from Sprung, who had to agree to pick up part of Nettles's salary in order to make the deal. Nettles needed every penny. The fact was, like Rollie Fingers and Rick Wise, to name two other senior leaguers who came immediately to mind, Nettles was flat broke.

"It can happen, you know," he said while we sat on opposite sides of the picnic table in the center of the Bradenton clubhouse. "You're busy playing ball, you're not watching your money, you leave it to somebody else, and it gets lost." Nettles laughed softly. It wasn't so bad, he was only broke.

"It was a curious trade," Nettles said. "The owner never did talk to me, never told me why, but I found out the reason he was so upset was that I let the guys have a day off rather than make them work out. I felt we were so injured, everybody was so hurt, that the day would be better spent resting their legs. He didn't see it that way, so that's why he traded me."

Nettles shrugged and rolled his blue eyes. "He was just trying to dump some salaries over there. I think he realized he was in over his head and he wanted to cut his losses."

"Was it a trade you wanted?"

"Not at the time, but since it's happened I'm very happy to be out of there. It was just a bad situation. He's grown up reading about Steinbrenner and he wanted to come as close to being a Steinbrenner person as he could. I don't know, maybe he held me responsible because all of the guys were injured. I know when the season started, I mentioned injuries to him and he said, 'Don't worry, there won't be any injuries.'

"He's running it like he's running one of those Rotisserie leagues. He gets real excited about calling press conferences over there. He called one press conference the day before opening day just to announce our starting lineup, and he expected all the players to be there. A couple of guys didn't show up, and he wanted to release them right there on the spot. Over there, nobody knew what was going on. The owner was confused, the general manager was confused, and the players were confused. It was just mass confusion over there."

ACROSS THE DIAMOND, OVER BY THE OPPOSITE FOUL POLE, THE late bus filled with visiting Gold Coast Suns was just arriving at the other clubhouse. I saw Earl Weaver sitting outside on the concrete stoop, already in uniform (Weaver always took the early bus to the ballpark). Weaver seemed preoccupied so I stepped around him and made my way toward the raucous party sounds that were coming from the clubhouse. Once inside, I found myself face to face with a big, brown-skinned, bald-pated man who had startlingly bright eyes and a great, droopy mustache that fell heavily over the corners of his mouth—Luis Tiant.

Tiant was strictly a monochromatic dresser. The first time I saw him out of uniform, he had been wearing brown. Today he had chosen white. A white jacket over a white shirt (open at the collar, with white hairs peeking through), white pants, a white belt, white shoes, and white socks. The only part of his wardrobe that clashed was the long, brown Dominican cigar he wore between his lips. Tiant's chest was fully expanded. Even as he stripped off his clothes (down to his white underwear), he appeared to be strutting. It pleased him, obviously, to talk to a reporter again, to be in a roomful of men, to do things like pull down his fly, and shout "Ey!" to a teammate, "I got something for you right here!"

"I wanta try it one more time and see what happens," Tiant said by way of explaining his return to baseball. He hacked loudly, removed his cigar, cleared his throat, and spit in a cup. Then he put the cigar back in his mouth. Tiant's English was better than my Spanish, which is another way of saying I don't speak Spanish. In a quiet room, without the cigar, I might have been able to understand a good half of what he was saying. As it was, I did the best I could.

"It's something, doing all your life. That something never get away from you, after you play, especially as many year I play . . . You get a chance to come to the park, do something you like, get together with the guys you used to play, the guy you played against. I think it keep you younger, keep you . . . in shape . . . People ask me now, 'You coming for the money?' Well . . . I had to leave my job . . . I work for the State Treasury, Massachusetts [he does promo work for the lottery], I leave my job for three months, get permission to come down . . . Over there you don't have the chance to get killed, somebody hit a line drive back to you, get a heart attack, or do something, you know? We no get younger, especially me. I just turn forty-nine years old, yesterday before yesterday."

Tiant was giving me the party line on the age-old age question. The figure he gave was consistent with the date listed for his birthday in all the standard references—November 23, 1940—but almost nobody believed that. One thing was certain: he was old enough to play any position he wanted in the senior league.

"Congratulations," I said.

"Thank you . . . I think it's good to play baseball for a long life. The younger you feel, the longer you gonna live. Supposedly, we don't know." Tiant removed his cigar and grinned so widely that the ends of his mustache turned up and the whole became parallel with the horizon.

"To me it's a good thing," he went on. "Plus it puts your name back in the public. No like it used to be but still, you know, name in the paper, TV, and radio, and that's good for us, really. After you retire, no matter what kinda name you got or what you do in baseball, your name keep going down, down. . . . That's one of the reason I came down here, I think it's good.

"I guess I like pitching. That's what I learned all my life, that's the best thing I learned in my life, pitching. That's what I do for twenty-five years, now I come down here, I have an opportunity pitching again, have a good time, that's good. Unfortunately . . . I'm on the disabled list now until Wednesday. I supposed to pitch maybe Wednesday or Thursday next week, maybe Friday. Hopefully, can I get ready. Hopefully, can I pitch before the season over. Maybe they gonna ship my ass outta here!

"You have to come here and do good because if you get paid, you have to give a good show to the people. I know they don't wanna think we are twenty years old again, but they wanna see a good game. . . . We have to be proud and get in good shape and do what we supposed to do because we get paid for it. . . .

"When you lose, *pheeeww*, it's tough. You try to be funny, but it don't work. When you win, everything is fun."

After a while, I wandered back outside. Weaver was gone. When I looked to my right, toward the dugout, I thought I saw him again, a white-haired man playing a creaking game of pepper with another white-haired man; that would be Speedy Hecht. Closer by, Bert Campaneris was bouncing baseballs off the low brick wall in front of the grandstand and bending over to pick them up. Bend and throw, bend and throw. He looked surprisingly fluid for a man in his late forties.

I turned to my left, and that's when I noticed for the first time a sign that was painted on the outfield wall, just outside the foul pole. "Bradenton, the friendly city," it said. The phrase rang hollow. How many "friendly" cities were there, anyway? But beneath that it said, "A little bit of paradise." This last I was willing to accept; I took it to mean the ballpark.

Bright, blustery, the wind blowing out. Today's was the final game of a three-game series between the Explorers and the West Palm Beach Tropics. The Tropics won the first two, including yesterday's four-hit complete game by Tim Stoddard that lifted them out of a tie with the Fort Myers Sun Sox and gave them sole possession of first place in the southern division.

Dave Kingman was the Tropics' hero at the plate yesterday, going three-for-five with a homer and three runs batted in. Of course he hit the ball hard; you expected that of someone who hit four hundred forty-two homers in his career. What you didn't expect was the way he reacted to a lob pitch tossed by Bruce Kison in the fifth at a time when there were three infielders playing to the left of second base. In the old days, there was no middle ground for Kingman. Either he bludgeoned the ball off true or else he popped up or struck out; a pitch like Kison's lob he might have swung at three times and already been on his way back to the dugout by the time it reached catcher Stan Cliburn. But this time he waited, and waited—as patient as a statue— and when the time was right, laid out his bat and poked a ground ball through the gaping hole in the right side of the infield.

"Hitting it where nobody is is a lot easier than hitting it where three guys are," Kingman said the next day, as if he had always been so reasonable. Kingman spoke while he pedaled furiously on a stationary bicycle. Sweat dripped from his brow and ran in streams down the trunk of his kingly six-five frame. He smiled while he worked, that same blank, raised-eyebrow smile he wore like a mask throughout his career.

"Would you have reacted the same way five years ago?"

"No," Kingman said, and he laughed. "Probably not."

For Kingman, the discipline to wait on a change-up and go the other way was something that had come to him with age. In his case it was a lesson that, had he learned it earlier in his career, would not necessarily have made him a better player. "I wasn't paid to hit singles," he pointed out. "If I hit singles I'd have been gone a long time ago."

But Kingman wasn't the only old dog who was learning new tricks. The same thing was happening all around the league, in a thousand different ways. Old and washed up, some of them, they'd come here for no other reason than to relive the past, only to surprise themselves by making progress. For some it was as simple as discovering what they were capable of once they were free of the crippling pressure to perform that defined life in the big leagues. Others were blindsided by some simple realization that had eluded them all their lives. In baseball, it was almost never simply a matter of raw skill and athletic ability. It was *insight*, too, the tiny adjustment that solved the riddle and unleashed the talent that had been there all along. That insight, when it came, was thrilling.

If only it wasn't too late. "If only," as Al Holland said, "I knew then what I know now."

Tito Landrum's major-league career began in 1980 and ended in 1988. His *professional* career began long before that, in Orangeburg, South Carolina, in 1973, and was not over yet. Released by Baltimore in '88, Landrum signed with Texas and finished the season in Oklahoma City, the Rangers' AAA affiliate. Last spring he'd gone to camp with the Pirates, failed to make the team, quit, reconsidered, and later signed with Nashville in the Reds' organization. He'd missed the last part of the season when he was diagnosed with a herniated disc. As recently as two weeks before senior-league fall training began, he was home lying in bed in the fetal position, having refused surgery. Lately, though, he'd made dramatic progress with help from a physical therapist and had come to Florida "to help me stay on the minds of people in baseball, to let 'em realize that I left on the DL [Disabled List] but I am healthy, I can still play and I feel real good about myself."

The reason Landrum felt so good was simple. After seventeen years of spotty progress and limited results, he had finally learned how to hit.

"I was an up-front hitter all my life," Landrum explained. "I would never stay back. If you threw a breaking ball, you had me. That was the old adage, 'If you get two strikes on Landrum, throw him a breaking ball in the dirt, he swings at it,' because I was always so far out front."

Five years ago, when he was with the Cardinals, Landrum had come up with a weird batting stance that was supposed to cure the lunge. He'd start out leaning forward with the barrel of the bat pointing toward the mound, then rock back and settle into a hitting position as the pitcher completed his windup. It helped, but it wasn't the answer. Then Landrum went to spring training last year and met up with Hal McRae.

"There's a lot of ways to discuss and tell people about hitting," Landrum said. "Some of them click, and some of them don't. Hal McRae's clicked for me. It took me about a month after I received his tutoring to really get into what he was saying, but I think right now I'm being more consistent as a hitter than I have ever been in my career. I've been able to stay back, see the ball, and use my hands more than I ever did. There were times when you'd get into a good groove and you'd do that, but you're not really conscious of what you're doing. Now I'm conscious of what I'm doing, and I'm able to do it with more consistency. Over the long haul that's the difference between a .250 hitter [Landrum's career average was .249] and a .300 hitter, that consistency.

"I'm confident when I'm up at the plate now. Unfortunately, I'm thirty-five years of age, but, you know, I'm still very proud of that. There's a couple of things might happen. There's expansion, there's still Japan, people down here are talking about playing in Italy. I'd like to get the opportunity. I want to be able to take the uniform off, not have somebody *tell* me it's time to take the uniform off."

ALFIE RONDON NEVER PLAYED IN THE BIG LEAGUES. NO NEED TO look it up. You knew from the way he smiled at strangers and drew them into conversation instead of the other way around. Rondon came to the Tropics through an open tryout in the fall. He was from the Dominican Republic originally but lived in Pompano now, where he owned his own construction company. So far he had seen only limited action, but he made a point of greasing his cheeks before every game, going to the batting cage on his days off, and generally doing everything he could to make sure he was always ready. When I walked by him on the way to the press box, he was swinging a leaded bat, loosening up for batting practice. Before I knew it, I was hearing his life story. The words came so fast they sometimes tripped over one another on the way out.

"I signed with Houston 1969," he said by way of introduction. "I stayed in the farm team for about five years, then I got traded to the Yankees for about five years. I went to Europe, Bologna, and I played in Caracas, Venezuela. I play in Mexico for three years. After that I been around playing all over, Santo Domingo for five years. I love baseball. I been playing in over-the-thirty league, you know? Ron LeFlore played, too. He here now, yeah. Look at him, talking with Mickey Rivers over there. He had a problem with Bobby Tolan, you know that kind of situation? He got hurt a couple times and Bobby Tolan told him, 'You don' wanna play every day I cannot use you.' You play baseball before?"

"High school," I said. "Not professionally."

"Yeah? So I hit .300 for four years. I never got the chance to come up to the big leagues, you know what I mean?"

"Did you hit with power in the minor leagues?"

"Excuse me?" The way he said it, it sounded like "askew." "Oh, yeah!"

"I saw the guys were razzing you yesterday when you hit the long ball in practice, like you're not capable or something."

"Oh, no, no, no! Everyone kids me around. I got the power. In case—I be honest with you—in case I play every day. I no been playing every day. You have to play every day in this game to get your timing and feel strong when you come out. I got fourteen, twenty home runs when I play winter ball in Mexico, Santo Domingo. I used to make a combination with Tito Fuentes, remember Tito Fuentes? So I played with him two years."

Rondon spat assertively in the grass.

"I can hit it out anywhere, in practice, no practice, as long as it's the right time and the right timing for me, too. It work both way, you know? You be surprise. I can hit two, three home runs anytime. That's life. You have to have the timing and play every day. It tough but I don't mind. I play good."

The closest Rondon ever came to playing in the big leagues was when he went to spring training with the Astros in 1970 and '71. Though he gave away nothing, I wondered if he held any lingering disappointment at never having made it to the top.

"Well," he began, pausing for the first time to think before he spoke. "No. In life you have to take what God give you, you know what I mean? That's life. You love baseball, and you know you can play it, and you no make it, what can you do? Nothing about it. You know what I mean? So you can go play the best you can all over the world like I did."

"So it's been a good life?"

"Oh, yeah! Good memory, and I play good. You learn more and more as the baseball go by. I been playing for eighteen years the baseball. The more you see, the more you learn. You never know what can happen after this league. You're only thirty-seven, thirty-eight years old. In baseball, you never know. 'Til the last out you never win the game. I never want to stop play 'til one day, that's all. That's life."

"I'LL BE THE GUY WITH THE BEER WEARING AS FEW CLOTHES AS possible."

That's what Rick Horrow had said when we made plans to meet in the left-field bleachers for today's game. So I knew what to look for. I also had some idea of what to expect, thanks to Horrow's thoughtfulness in providing me with a twenty-two-page (plus covers) bound booklet of press clippings all about Rick Horrow, which arrived at my door yesterday morning via Federal Express. This was what I learned just by skimming through:

Horrow was "Founder and President" of Horrow Sports Ventures, a "multi-faceted sports development firm." Prior to striking out on his own, Horrow had held a number of impressive sports-related posts in south Florida, in both the private and the public sectors. As executive director of the Miami Sports and Exhibition Authority, he was "responsible for the creation, funding source, selection process, business plan and development scheme of the 16,000-seat Miami Arena" and was "credited as one of the driving forces behind the establishment of the Miami Heat professional basketball franchise." Horrow had written a book about the legal aspects of violence in sports and lectured on that subject at "more than 95" colleges and universities. In 1984, Horrow was among two hundred seventy-two up-and-comers identified by *Esquire* magazine as "The Best of the New Generation." He graduated "first in his class" at Northwestern and earned his law degree at Harvard. The most recent of "his many accomplishments" came last August, when he was named president of the senior league. "At 34," the booklet informed me, "he is the youngest person ever named to the presidency of a major sports league."

I found Horrow in the far corner of the bleachers, about six rows up. He wore long dark pants and a blue polo shirt. His shirt sleeves were rolled up to the armpits—he was otherwise completely dressed—and he was drinking a beer. On the bench beside him was a portable telephone the size of a pocket calculator which every so often made a chirping noise. He had the kind of haircut that hid the tops of his ears but not the bottoms and stood its ground in a stiff breeze. His chin was hidden behind a gray-spotted beard, lush and trim as a putting green, as sure a sign as any of unconcealed vanity.

"So you went to Northwestern," I said, just to get things rolling. "That's where my parents met."

"Yeah," Horrow said, "principally because I won the high school debate championship for three years in Miami and they offered me a debate scholarship. But it was also a ten-minute El ride from Wrigley Field. In inverse order of importance. I've always been a diehard Cubs fan."

"You and Don Sider," I said, referring to the co-owner of the Tropics, who grew up in Chicago.

"Don Sider never from six years old on got up at five every morning and cut out every box score of every football, baseball, basketball, hockey, indoor soccer, and outdoor soccer game ever played, and then before he went to school, starting in second grade, glued the box scores to a book."

Probably not, but Horrow had. In fact, the scrapbooks still existed. Just last week, on a visit to his mother's, Horrow had slipped out to the garage and taken the scrapbooks out of the boxes where they had been carefully put away, and leafed through them again. He marveled at the yellowed scraps of newspaper, loose in the pages now that the glue had dried, and at the wavering line drawn in a childish hand (his own!) down the middle of each page, dividing the National League from the American League. "For some kind of moral inspiration," he said, attempting to explain why he'd gone back to examine his roots. "To try to decide what motivated me to do all that I do. I'm neurotic today, but I guess that confirms I was even more neurotic then."

Horrow was an only child. His father died of cancer when he was eleven years old, leaving him to be raised by his mother. "I basically grew up on sports," he said. "I'd go to—even at Northwestern and in high school—you know, seventy games a year of some kind—football, baseball, basketball, hockey." Though he dabbled at golf and claimed he was a devotee of racquet sports, Horrow had always been more spectator than participant, a fact confirmed by the way he filled out the seat of his pants. At Harvard, he was a confessed "oddball," driven neither to do good for society, nor to do well for himself, but really just to have fun.

"I remember the first day of my contracts class, which was the second day of school. This very imposing professor, who was basically like Kingsfield in *The Paper Chase* and known for his tenacity by everybody, I struck a deal with him. I walked up to him and I said, 'Boy, I'd really like you to call on me for this case.' It was the case of Napoleon Lajoie, a classic law-school case that defined what specific performance is. There were five hundred people in the section and the guy, with a dour expression, called on me and said, 'State the facts of the case.' Normally what you do is you spin a thirty-second recitation of the facts. I had a baseball cap, I put it on, went up to the blackboard, wrote down his career stats, put a diamond down, and started describing everything in metaphorical baseball terms. I had rehearsed the speech that night. This was the first time the students were exposed to me and after I finished the facts of the case and what the legal holding was, they all gave me a standing ovation! It was"—here Horrow paused and laughed out loud, his eyes sparkling like Ronald Reagan's before a gathering of veterans—"it was wonderful!"

Horrow's book, *Sports Violence: The Interaction Between Private Lawmaking and the Criminal Law*, grew out of a law-school thesis project that focused on excessive violence in hockey. After graduation, Horrow clerked for a federal judge in Washington, which led to contacts with lawmakers and eventually the task of writing legislation intended to curb violence in sports. While none of the proposed legislation ever became law, Horrow had the opportunity to testify before members of Congress and was invited to appear on "Good Morning America" and the "Today" show. He was off and running.

"Then I decided at that point that it was more important to me, more *gratifying*, to come back home, to work on a sports authority, to build a stadium, to build an arena, to develop an NBA team, as opposed to staying in Washington and being involved with a big firm that happens to do NFL work. I made that choice, and five sports authorities, sixty-five elected officials, forty-eight appointed officials later, we got the arena open, we got the Heat, we got the stadium done. That's kinda how it happened."

Horrow kinda grinned—*aw, shucks.*

"You know, I don't believe it. To this day I don't believe it. You don't write that script."

Then along came the senior league. The concept was so *right* for Horrow, a perfect match in every way. Outrageous, high-profile, lots of fun; it wasn't Horrow's idea, but once he came on board he moved quickly and easily to make the league his own.

"Many of us are under forty," he said, referring to five of the eight principal owners plus the league's president, executive vice president, and executive director. "We're entrepreneurial, we're not risk-averse, and there is that feeling—it's not antiestablishment, because my contacts are essentially establishment contacts—but it's a case of feeling you can do anything, and you don't have to wait your turn in life, and you can take risks that other people might not be willing to take until they're much older. Not to suggest this is a maverick league in any way—the business plan is based on being as conservative as we can for as long as we can—but yet there *is* that thirtysomething feeling."

Horrow had woken up this morning in cold, wintry New Jersey. He'd been invited to Seton Hall the day before to deliver one of his many college lectures on the subject of sports violence. The talk had gone well and afterward he'd returned to his room at the Turtle Brook Inn. He had chosen that particular hotel because that was where the New Jersey Devils stayed. Then, because he was alone, he went out—to a sports bar, naturally—and there he had had a deeply moving experience.

"This is just so *permeating* to me," he began cryptically, "because I'm sitting there at a sports bar, I was drinking a lot, alone, and I was just watching the Knicks game against Golden State and the Rangers against Winnipeg and MSG [Madison Square Garden network] does this promotion and I see college baseball, college basketball, pro basketball, Rangers—and senior baseball! I said, 'Shit, I'm the president of this fucking league! Great! Can't believe it!' "

To PARAPHRASE, SOME PEOPLE ARE BORN WITH BURDENS, SOME PEO-ple seek burdens, and others, like Wayne Garland, have burdens thrust upon them.

Garland gave little indication his first three years in the big leagues of what lay in store for him. He came up with the Orioles, who used him mainly as a relief pitcher. All told he won seven games, lost eleven, saved five. He averaged fewer than sixty-five innings a year. But in 1976, two things happened to change Garland's life: first, the owners failed in their attempt to overturn arbiter Peter Seitz's ruling in the Andy Messersmith case, thus opening the way to free agency, and second, Garland won twenty games.

Garland had played out his option that year on a salary of twenty-three thousand dollars. After the season, he declared himself a free agent, entrusted his future to superagent Jerry Kapstein, and waited to see what might happen. As it turned out, his was not the richest contract signed that winter; that honor went to his teammate on the Orioles, Reggie Jackson, who agreed to join the Yankees for $2.93 million over five years. Jackson's deal was staggering at the time, but it made sense; he was an established superstar, a World Series hero, a proven drawing card. Garland was none of those things, and yet the Cleveland Indians decided it was in their best interest to offer Garland $2.5 million over ten years.

Garland's contract was a watershed. If a twenty-six-year-old pitcher could command millions on the strength of one good season, what was to become of baseball's pay scale? The other owners shuddered to think.

What followed was a nightmare, for Garland as well as for the Indians. From twenty and seven in 1976, Garland's record fell to thirteen and nineteen his first year in Cleveland. The following year he underwent major surgery on his shoulder to repair a torn rotator cuff, an operation from which he never recovered. Over the sad remainder of his big-league career, Garland won only fourteen games and lost twenty-nine. In 1986, when he cashed his last check, Garland had been out of baseball for five years.

Of course, by then, two hundred fifty thousand dollars a year hardly seemed like a lot of money. If he hadn't been hurt, if he'd been able to pitch at anywhere near the level that was expected of him, he would have been a terrific bargain for the Indians. But instead it was Garland's fate to be remembered as the classic worst-case example of what can go wrong when a player signs a long-term contract. It didn't matter that it was the Indians who made the offer; it was Garland who took the rap.

After he retired, Garland went home to Nashville, where he coached at a local junior college and operated an indoor batting cage on the side. In 1987 he got a job with the Reds' AAA affiliate, the Nashville Sounds, but that lasted only two years. In the last year before the senior league came along, he had been without a job in baseball.

I found Garland sitting by himself in the visiting dugout at Al Lang Stadium, wearing the green-and-yellow uniform of the Fort Myers Sun Sox. He was leaning back on the bench with his arms spread wide and his legs crossed, half watching while his teammates took batting practice. His skin was puffy and red, and he wore a bushy mustache in the style that was popular among ballplayers in the seventies. The expression on his face was as close as it could come to being expressionless, a flat, blank look that I read as wary.

Garland sighed when I asked him about the contract. "It was all guaranteed," he said. "No trade, no cut, or anything like that. At the time I signed it it was the longest contract in sports."

"The money doesn't seem like all that much anymore," I said. "Not by today's standards."

"Nothing. Just a salary comparable to the twenty-fourth guy on the roster right now. You look at Rickey Henderson and Kirby Puckett making three million a year, that kind of money is hard to fathom. I don't want to come out and say somebody's not worth it—if somebody's gonna pay it to you, you're worth it. But I think it's only best for baseball that it stop someplace. You would've thought that the owners would try to put a stop to it, maybe like they do in basketball, have a cap or something like that. What's next, the four-million-dollar ballplayer? I can't see it. I think it has to stop sometime, and in the very near future, too."

This was unexpected. Here was Garland, of all people, taking the owners' side on salaries. I asked him if he thought the big contract was bad for his career. "Did it take away your incentive?" I wondered. "Or put you under too much pressure to meet people's expectations?"

"I don't think there was a point when I went out there and said, 'Well, I got this amount of money, I'm gonna try to prove to the people that I'm worth it.' I don't think I really changed my style of pitching or anything like that. I would like for it to be known that when I went out there and I stepped across the white lines, I gave one hundred percent every time and I was a competitor. I think a majority of the people who played with me and knew me would say that. Maybe a lot of people in the front office and stuff didn't say that, because if you make that amount of money they expect you to go out there and win.

"When I was coming up and young, I always heard that if you ever became a twenty-game winner, they're gonna expect you to do that every year, and I guess that was the case. One person can't turn around a ball club. I had a lot of people tell me in '77—hitters and stuff—that I threw a lot better in '77 than I did in '76. But you know, I was going from a first-place club to a last-place club in Cleveland. If I had to do it all over again I think I would pick the same situation because at that time Cleveland had a good young ball club, and I had known [manager] Frank Robinson. This was a team that was maybe five years away, a team that was gonna build. But that never happened. Still hasn't happened.

"I don't know what would have happened if I hadn't injured my arm. I could *still* be up there pitching. You never know. I mean, the man upstairs knows why that happened."

"So are you glad you signed the contract?"

"I *am* glad I signed it, yeah," he said impatiently. "I stay to myself a lot, I'm a very quiet person. I knew when I signed the contract that the publicity and stuff was gonna come. It's part of baseball, you gotta take that in stride. But no, I have no regrets about it. Baseball was good to me. That contract gave me a lot of things that I wouldn't have, which I don't have anymore." Garland smiled and shrugged his shoulders. "It's called divorce, but that's a different story.

"There's no doubt, I wasn't worth the money. After I signed the contract I called my mother—well, before I signed the contract, when I found out what I was gonna get, I called my mother and I said, 'You know, I didn't get the million dollars I was look-ing for.'

"She said, 'Well, that's fine, whatever you got.'

"I said, 'I got two million.'

"She said, 'You're not worth it.' Basically, that was it. She said, 'Wayne, you're not worth it.'

"I said, 'I know, but somebody else thought I was.'

"I had no idea. I was looking for a five-year contract, maybe a million dollars or something like that, at the very most. That was my farthest dream. When it was ten years and two and a half million, holy cow! I couldn't believe it. I wasn't worth the money, no. I don't think anybody was. I had won twenty games and I happened to be in the right spot at the right time, made the right choice to go ahead and play out my option, and it paid off for me."

Garland was doing well so far in the senior league. He'd pitched five innings of shutout ball in his first start, then had three no-decisions. His ERA was 3.05, second among the starters on the team behind Rick Waits. He was feeling some stiffness in his right arm, but that was to be expected.

"Back when I was nineteen years old, we had six and a half weeks to get in shape. Now that I'm thirty-nine, I came down here, got two weeks and then, hey, here we go. Right now I feel like I'm just at the end of spring training. I know the last couple of starts that's the way my arm's felt. In spring training, you go through a period when you get the dead arm. That's the way it's felt the last couple of times. I'm real stiff and I'm gonna miss a turn. But it'll work itself out."

COMINGS . . .

The Sun Sox brought a new shortstop along on this road trip, Johnnie LeMaster. LeMaster spent most of his career with the Giants, your basic good-field, no-hit infielder. He achieved last-ing notoriety in 1985 when he was traded twice, first to Cleve-land and then to Pittsburgh, and thus became the only person ever to play for three last-place teams in one season. LeMaster lasted twelve years in the big leagues and retired with a career batting average of .222; obviously, the Sun Sox hadn't signed him for his bat. What they were looking for was that rarest of senior-league commodities—an infielder who could play consistent defense. If LeMaster worked out, the plan was to move shortstop Tim Ireland over to second base, his natural position.

You get used to seeing unlikely bodies in baseball uniforms, but LeMaster was the strangest bird yet. In fact, he looked like a bird—an egret, to be exact—with his long, skinny legs and impossibly frail upper body. He was standing by the batting cage, waiting to hit, when I asked him what had inspired him to play baseball again.

"It's in the blood," he said. He spoke with a Kentucky accent so heavy I wouldn't have guessed he had the strength to carry it, not on those slender shoulders. "*He-heh-heh!* It's in the blood!"

LeMaster owned a sporting goods store in his hometown of Paintsville, Kentucky. He had recently been elected to the Paintsville City Council and was due to be sworn in on January 10. Before he'd left for Florida, he'd made arrangements with the town fathers to postpone the swearing-in until February.

"I didn't even put my name in the draft," he said, talking through a smile that never left his face. "Different clubs sorta called and I just kept saying no. Finally they called enough to where they wore me down. I couldn't stand it any longer. The call of the *waaald* got me, *uh-hah-hah*. It was *taaam* to go! *He-heh-heh!*

"The most fun part of the game is being around the guys, I don't care what anybody has to say. Baseball people are the craziest human beings. You sit in the locker room or you'll be on the bus traveling, and you just got a big smile on your face all the time. They're *crazy*. I think when people get out of the game that's what they miss the most."

Earlier this afternoon, just six days after joining the team, LeMaster had gone on the disabled list with a sore shoulder. He wouldn't be playing, not for a while. At least he was having fun.

. . . And goings.

The Juice fired Gates Brown. I heard Fort Myers manager Pat Dobson talking about it with his players soon after I arrived at the ballpark. Dobson used to play with Brown in Detroit. He seemed shocked by the news and a little disgusted, judging by the way he shook his head.

Later I ran into Jim Morley and asked him what he knew. He said he had talked to Wynne Dillard, Orlando's general manager, on the phone today. Apparently, Dillard was unhappy with the way the Juice were playing—their record was nine and twelve—

and wasn't satisfied with Brown's explanations. "You ask Bobby [Tolan] about the game and he'll tell you, 'In the first inning such and such got hits, I pinch-hit for this guy,' whatever," said Morley. "But Gates would scratch his chin and say, 'Well, I don't know, we gave up a couple.' "

Maybe Brown was trying to keep it simple. Dillard, after all, was an investment banker, not a baseball man. Then I remembered what I'd heard Dillard tell Brown just the other day, that what he really wanted most of all was not to play baseball but to manage. "I want *your* job" was what he said. At least Dillard didn't name himself to replace Brown; he gave the job to Dyar Miller, the Juice's pitching coach.

But what a shame for Brown. Of all the old ballplayers I'd met so far, none was more obviously euphoric about being back in the game than Gates Brown. Oh, well, I thought, that's baseball. Today was Friday. I guessed by Monday Brown would be back at work at the metal-stamping company in Detroit. He had said he liked it; I hoped he wasn't lying.

WINTER HAVEN · *December 4*

THE HOME BULL PEN AT CHAIN O' LAKES PARK WAS OUT PAST FIRST base in a grassy quadrangle bordered (counterclockwise) by the grandstand wall, the clubhouse, a netted batting range, and a chain-link fence that ran along the foul line. On winter afternoons, the sun would linger there past the time when shadows had fallen over the rest of the park. On such an afternoon I found Bill Lee wearing catcher's gear, conducting a tryout.

As long as you were old enough, you could play in the senior league. Every team had three wild-card roster slots; you didn't have to be a big-league veteran to fill one, or even to have played pro ball, you only had to be good. Consequently, people came through asking for tryouts all the time. Larry Livingston, a cellular-phone salesman and left-handed pitcher from Atlanta who once was an extra in the movie *Slugger's Wife*, spent two weeks crisscrossing the state, looking for a job. Every time I saw him he was wearing a different hat. In the end no one wanted him, although he did go home with a very nice collection of hats.

The guys like Livingston, they all wanted to be the next Joe

Mincberg, a successful drug lawyer from West Palm Beach. Mincberg walked off the team at the University of Connecticut twenty years ago, killing his dreams of a pro career, but in 1989 was born again in baseball heaven—wearing a Tropics uniform, hanging out with Dave Kingman and Rollie Fingers, and playing a little first base. Or Hoot Gibson, a career minor leaguer who happened to catch a game on TV at home in Bryan, Texas, decided he was good enough to pitch in that damn senior league, left his wife (temporarily, with her blessing) and his job, and drove to St. Petersburg in pursuit of his dreams. Gibson called Jim Morley from a motel on Highway 19, got an audition, made the Pelicans, and wound up starting eight games.

Pitching to Lee this afternoon was a trim, small-framed right-hander, looking dour in a green T-shirt, black sweats drawn tightly at the waist, black hat pulled low over his ears, black socks, and an old pair of black spikes. His T-shirt was one size too small, Marlon Brando style, and showed off a V-shaped torso. He threw with a deliberate, compact windup that began creakingly and ended with a snap. There was stiffness in the motion, which gave away his age, but his fastball popped and his screwball had some bite. The stranger looked good—obviously, he was at home on the mound. It was also obvious that he was way too old, even for the senior league.

A lot of baseball people would have taken one look at this guy and walked the other way, exactly what happened when he went to see Clete Boyer in Bradenton; the manager of the Explorers just turned around without saying a word and went back into his office. End of tryout. Bill Lee was too much of a gentleman to pull something like that. Besides, he loved this kind of stuff. An old man showed up out of nowhere, wanted to show what he could do, Bill Lee was interested.

"Mike Marshall," Lee said, tossing the ball back after the stranger threw his scroogie. "He's coming in next week."

"Is he?"

"Yeah, we signed him for one month. Came right out like you did." Lee waved at the clubhouse with his mitt. "Walked out of that same door."

"Yeah, you know, he's got more of a title, but I got a lotta stuff."

Silence for several pitches, then Lee asked, "Yeah, you know how you were snapping like that?"

"Yeah, yeah."

"He did a few stretches, he came out, he went—," and Lee, standing up, yanked down violently with his left arm, twisting his forearm clockwise so that the palm faced out.

"Yeah, that's where it's at," said the stranger.

"Like *that*. Velocity? Whoosh! Nasty screwball, nasty screwball. You're like Mike Marshall but ten years older. You got more experience than him." Lee dropped back down in his crouch. "How old are you, fifty-five?" Lee was being polite.

"Thereabouts. You're close."

"See, he's forty-five."

"I ain't tawkin' about it," said the stranger, sounding as if he might be from Brooklyn. "It's so disgusting—"

"Don't think about it. Age is relative."

"But they hang you on it."

"Sure," said Lee, "you're gonna carry that your whole life. That's why you're you. But the thing is, you have a love of the game. You may not be able to play here, but you can play all summer."

"Yuh," said the stranger, cutting loose on a fastball, all business now, not looking to be consoled yet.

Afterward, Lee hung around while the stranger cooled down. "You think I can get on the taxi squad?" the stranger asked. It seemed like the wrong question to be asking. Did he want to play ball, or was he just looking for a job? The taxi squad paid two thousand dollars a month just to stay ready—good money if you needed work.

"We're gonna have a decision to make in a couple of days," said Lee. "[Mike] Cuellar's having an operation today."

"Oh, he is? What happened to him?"

"He had hemorrhoids. Guy's my idol. I got him here because I idolized him."

"Yeah, oh yeah, he had a good one," said the stranger, meaning Cuellar's screwball, of course. "That shouldn't deteriorate with age. The more rotation you get, that's all that matters. I mean, it's not velocity."

"Nope."

"It helps, I would imagine."

"Well," said Lee, "the things that go first on a guy isn't your eye and your ability to swing the bat, it's your ability to field and your ability to get velocity to home plate. A lot of guys are taking it out on blood and guts alone. You can go maybe a month that way and then all hell breaks loose. Me, I pitched eight innings yesterday and I jumped in the pool and swam for thirty minutes."

"Yeah, it all depends on your delivery. If you got a jerk in there—"

"Yeah, you're right," said Lee, looking over the stranger's shoulder now toward home plate, where his teammates were taking batting practice. "Well, I'm not gonna know anything until tomorrow."

"All right," said the stranger. "Thanks anyway."

"I gotta shag some fly balls."

"Should I call you?"

"Uh, where you gonna be?"

"I'm in Sarasota. So, uh—"

"Yeah, call in about two days."

"Two days. All right."

"We're gonna know more after the operation."

"All right, thanks a lot, buddy. Take care."

THE STRANGER'S NAME WAS TOM HAYES. HE WAS BUILT, ACCORD-ing to his own description, exactly like Carl Erskine, another great screwballer, who was five-ten, about one hundred sixty pounds when he pitched for the Dodgers in the fifties. Hayes did grow up in Brooklyn, which explained the accent. He lived in the city now but was vague about what part: "The, uh, the East Side, Upper East Side." And he wouldn't say exactly how old he was, either: "Very. Very. That's how old I am. I don't feel old."

His impressive upper body was due to an exercise he claimed he did "religiously." "I'll show you," he said. Hayes leaned over, propped himself with one hand on the edge of the bull-pen bench, clutched his bicep with his free hand, and stretched both legs out behind him. "Stay like this," he said. "Then you go right under"—he dropped down until his head was all the way under the bench—"then you come up. It's like a one-armed chin. I showed this to Reggie Jackson, and he fell on his face trying to do it. Couldn't do one."

Hayes took off the ancient black spikes, stowed them in (what else?) a black bag, and changed into a pair of no-name running shoes with Velcro straps. The sunlight was gone from the bull pen, and the nightly Winter Haven sound and light show was underway. Fluorescent bands of pink, yellow, and green shimmered in the sky over Lake Lulu. Someone in the press box had turned on the tape player and an old rock-and-roll keyboard classic—"A Whiter Shade of Pale"—was wailing through the empty park.

Hayes's thousand-mile journey to Winter Haven in a borrowed Toyota ("all beat up but I made it") turned out to be only the latest episode in a long life spent on the fringes of organized ball, a litany of lost opportunities and near misses, all the times he came *this close,* only to be disappointed again. He said he once signed a contract with the Yankees but was drafted into the army. Later he pitched briefly in the Pirates chain. But in fifteen years of playing pro ball, it was revealing that the best team he said he ever played for was a semipro club in Gibsonton, Florida, on the east shore of Tampa Bay. "We woulda beat anybody," said Hayes. "Not all the best ballplayers are playing professional ball. These were guys who just didn't want to go away from home. Big, strapping guys. Great catchers, great arms. And I was ten and o with them."

A chance encounter many years ago with Earl Weaver on the streets of New York was all the encouragement Hayes needed to pay his own way to Florida in hopes of catching on with the Orioles. Weaver finally told Hayes he couldn't help him. Another time, out of the blue, he called Oakland A's owner Charley Finley. Finley listened long enough for Hayes to think that if he showed up in Arizona, he might have a shot with the A's. When he got there, Finley told him he was a "kook." Consequently, Weaver and Finley had both earned spots on Hayes's personal shit list, along with Whitey Herzog, Willie Wilson, Clete Boyer, and the first baseman on a semipro team Hayes played for in San Angelo, Texas, who one day swiped Hayes's warm-up jacket. Hayes jumped the bastard in the hotel lobby, but all he got was kicked off the team. "I got released!" he said, still indignant. "See, I expected this guy who caused the trouble to confess, but it never happened."

Hayes was unclear on the subject of how he earned a living. "I'm an inventor," he said. "I have a toy on the market, and I get royalties and that's what I do." Among his inventions, he said, were an abdominal builder designed to be used standing up ("see, people don't want to get on the floor") a device that used steel tape to define the strike zone without interfering with a hitter's swing, useful in batting practice, and a supersonic helicopter, patent pending, which, he conceded, "is a little far out."

"I do mostly anything that comes into my mind," he said, talking rapidly, his eyes shifting from side to side. "I found I had a brain after baseball, you know? Hah! Baseball is actually arrested development in a lot of ways because all you think about is the ball. Guys neglect their thinking processes. That's why I like Bill Lee. He's a thinker. A lot of the time you're ostracized for thinking. You're a kook, they call you a kook. I been called that a lot."

Hayes reached into his black bag and pulled out one of his inventions. "It's called a wrist activator," he said. "I showed it to the White Sox and the pitching coach liked it." Hayes's wrist activator resembled a one-foot ladder with only three rungs, two at one end and one at the other. You gripped it like you would a fastball, two fingers wrapped around the inside rung. The short end of the activator braced against your wrist; the long end was weighted. To activate the activator, you gave it a yo-yo motion.

"Bring it up and pull it back fast," Hayes explained to Bernie Carbo, who happened by on the way to the clubhouse and stopped to see what was up. "The higher you go, the tougher it is. The more you get this popping, the better the hop on your ball." Carbo flicked it once or twice and smiled ambiguously. "Nice guy," Hayes said after Carbo moved on. He meant it. "Lotta jerks in baseball."

Of all Hayes's baseball-related inventions, the one with the best shot at revolutionizing the game was also the one that had brought him the most grief. "I have another thing," he said under his breath. "It's very radical. I didn't even tell it to these people because—," and he paused. "It's a new type of slide. I show it to people and they want to kill me. When you meet a guy that likes it it's surprising. I was actually signed with Kansas City with this slide. When I showed Whitey Herzog this slide, he lost his mind."

What was he talking about, a *new slide*? I was definitely interested, but Hayes was playing it safe. He refused to demonstrate. "It's the only way that hasn't been done," he offered. "That's the only thing I can tell you. You go head first and feet first—I don't want to divulge it right now, but it's the only way that hasn't been done. It requires a special shoe. It's very wild."

After some more prodding, Hayes reached back into his bag and pulled out the shoe. It was a left shoe, black, and looked like an ordinary baseball shoe except for an extra piece of leather padding on the outer ankle. But seeing the shoe only raised questions that Hayes wasn't willing to answer.

Hayes was understandably reluctant. He had had no luck at all convincing the baseball establishment to take him or his slide seriously. The closest he came was more than ten years ago now, when he rode the bus down from New York to meet Earl Weaver at a spring-training game in Fort Myers. (Weaver, when I asked him about it later, didn't remember anything at all about Hayes or his slide. "It could have happened," he said.) Hayes said that when he tried to explain his new slide to Weaver, the manager dismissed him with a curt "I can't help you."

"So I said, 'You're not helping *me*, I want to help *you*.' See, this is the general attitude in baseball. You can't help them, 'cause they're geniuses. So I was walking out, and Herzog was talking to reporters, and I took a chance. I went over after the reporters left and my opening line was, 'What the hell's the matter with Weaver?'

"He says, 'Whattaya mean?'

"I said, 'I spent five hundred dollars coming down here to show him a new slide.'

"So he says, 'What kind of slide?'

"I said, 'You can't tag me. Hah!'

"He says, 'What?' He says, 'Get your stuff.'

"I got my stuff. I went in the locker room. Everybody's looking at me like I was crazy. I'm putting on the shoe and this guy comes over to me, Willie Wilson. He's a wise guy. He did time [on drug charges]. He says to me, 'What's that shoe?'

"I said, 'You'll see.'

"And he says, 'Where you from?'

"I said, 'New York.'

"So he yells out—this is the kind of shit I don't need—'I know he's crazy, he's from New York!'

"Herzog says, 'C'mon, hurry up.' So I got the stuff on. When I came out on the field, he lined up the whole team. He puts a towel down in the outfield for a base. Immediately there's too much pressure on me. It's do or die. I give him the ball, I get back about forty feet, and I take off.

"I get up there, I do the thing, and he doesn't even try to tag me. He's flabbergasted. I went in so fast that I ended up wrong and I missed the base, but I was in there.

"He says, 'You got anything else?' Now he loves me. I go in the locker room with him and he makes a phone call and he comes out and he says, 'You're on the team!' I almost shit a brick! Now I want to hug the guy! He says, 'You're from New York. Meet me there on May first.' "

On May Day, as instructed, Hayes reported to the hotel where the Royals were staying. He tried to board the team bus. "I figured they knew me," he said. "They kicked me off." So Hayes took a cab to the Bronx, to Yankee Stadium. He told the guard he was a batting-practice pitcher, and got past the gate. But when he met up with Herzog in the clubhouse, the news was bad.

"[George] Brett had evidently tried to do the slide without me teaching him and he hurt his shoulder," Hayes said. "Herzog says, 'I don't want to do it.'

"I said, 'Oh, my God!'

"So that was my shot in the big leagues."

Hayes came to the end of his story and laughed, staccato-like: "*Hah-hah-hah!*" The laugh was baffling and offered no clues.

"I had very bad luck," he said, "Brett getting hurt like that. *Very bad luck.* I woulda been famous. I was on the club!"

THE BRILLIANT AFTERNOON FADED TO A COLD, LONELY WINTER HAven night. It really wasn't that bad, maybe forty degrees, but in Florida that sometimes felt like zero. Retirees weren't used to it, which is why most of them stayed home in their trailers, electric heaters turned up all the way, no doubt watching the Bills and the Seahawks on "Monday Night Football." Tourists would sooner risk hypothermia than admit the weather in Florida was lousy; I counted only a few, though, underdressed and miserable. I was just guessing, but a lot of what was in the stands tonight looked like it came by way of the Grove Lounge (the bar where the ballplayers all hung out) and probably couldn't wait to get back there.

Came the break between innings when the PA announcer said, "Now it's time to play guess the attendance!" No one guessed, they counted. Heads bobbed slowly, panning from foul line to foul line . . . one hundred thirty-seven, one hundred thirty-eight, one hundred thirty-nine, that was it, another record low for the senior league (I found out later there were thirty-four names on the players' pass list, all included in the total). Leon Roberts's double in the gap off Rich Gale in the sixth, which drove home two runs and put Winter Haven on top, generated not so much an ovation from the audience as so many tiny popping sounds, random and distinct.

I sat with Hayes during the game. We were in the grandstand behind home plate, ignoring an open invitation from the PA announcer to move down to field level and take a box seat. Hayes was shivering in only a T-shirt. Just when I was starting to worry about him, he disappeared for five minutes and came back wearing a sweatshirt. I offered to buy him a hot dog, but he turned me down and bought one for himself. I had read him wrong. Evidently, all he wanted from me was that I listen.

"I thought of starting a league like this years ago," he said. "We needed this. Most guys just take up daily drinking. Hah! I go to AA meetings now because of daily drinking. I got over twenty years of sobriety. A lot of players drink, mainly just to go to sleep. And then when you quit playing and you feel like you miss it, you drink to stay happy, you know?"

Hayes didn't last the whole game. He had to drive back to Sarasota. "I'm staying with a kid I met in AA, and he's a nut," he said. "He's drinking all the time, and I can't take it. I gotta get a job or something. I'd like to get on this taxi squad, just to get into it, you know? I'm fairly desperate. I got only a few more teams to try out with."

Before he left, Hayes wanted to give me something. "I'd like to show you my book," he said. "Yeah, I wrote a book!" He disappeared again, and when he returned he handed me a sheaf of papers, maybe half an inch thick: *The Crucifixion of a Fireballer*, by Tom Hayes. In a footnote at the bottom of the title page, Hayes had defined the word "crucify": "to mortify; subdue" and "to torment; torture."

Hayes wanted me to take the manuscript home and meet up with him three days later in Bradenton. That made me nervous; he said this was his only copy and he had no phone number, no address.

But Hayes wasn't worried. He said he got "good vibes" from me. Just to make me feel better, though, he scribbled a name and a phone number on a blank page in my notebook. "My toy agent in New York," he said.

"THIS IS THE STORY OF A LITTLE GUY; A GOOD LITTLE GUY, AND THE snares and entanglements of professional baseball life in the 50's. He pulls no punches. Why should he? No one ever pulled one thrown at him."

I read that much of *The Crucifixion of a Fireballer* later that night before I turned off the light and went to sleep. Hayes showed up a few days later in Bradenton, as promised, and I gave the manuscript back to him. I had made a copy, and I told him that I'd read it as soon as I had time. He called a few weeks later, collect, to ask what I thought, but I hadn't read any more. He never called again.

Hayes's book lay buried in my box of files, almost forgotten, for three months. It was not until after the season ended and I returned home from my three months in Florida that I came across the manuscript again. This time I read it through without stopping.

"My father I now realize was an alcoholic," Hayes wrote, "my mom was a manic depressive and my sister was a C.P.A., a Chronic Pain in the Ass." When he was sober, Hayes's dad was "great sometimes . . . I loved my dad," but there were always episodes. "He . . . disgusted all of us by his treatment of Pirate, our one-eyed dog. We all loved him even though he couldn't see well. He hugged the inside of the stairs on the way downstairs because of the limited vision from the one eye. Dad would beat the hell out of him if he came out of the kitchen and Pirate used to piddle uncontrollably when Dad came home . . . What chance did we have with a sadist like that?"

Hayes's best chance, he discovered early on, was his own right arm, "this serpent hung from my shoulder with a baseball in its fangs." One day Jackie Morrison, who lived across the street, challenged Hayes to a snowball-throwing contest. It was the day the serpent awoke: "The contest was to see if you could throw a snowball over the El. He was about ten years older and big, but neither he nor I knew about the hibernating serpent hanging drowsily from my right shoulder. He threw first and hit the El, about a sewer and a half. We measured everything in sewer cover lengths. We really were Brooklyn against the world.

"Now my turn. I had a well packed snowball which was an art in South Brooklyn. We made snowballs that you could fungo, or use for infield practice. It was an art, and I'll never tell. The sleeper suddenly dehibernated, its coils tense like a boa with a rabbit in its clutched fangs and with a reptilian whip lash which I have repeated tens of thousands of times since then the icy ball started its glorious launch—my first thought was damn, too high; this is new to me. But the frozen comet just kept going and going and going; completely over the El. Jackie Morrison never spoke to me again. . . ."

Hayes played a lot of stickball growing up. He remembered a tall, skinny left-hander who used to come by the "stadium" on Bay Parkway every now and then, name of Sandy Koufax. "Nobody wanted him on their side. He couldn't hit. He used to swing one foot under the ball in a groove all the time and against the Murray Sour Cream Bloop, you ain't got a chanst [sic] if you're an undercut guy. I think he threw a few innings but didn't impress any one either."

After high school, Hayes signed a professional contract with the Yankees, but his career was put on hold by the war in Korea. "I got drafted; so did Edward [Whitey] Ford. He went to Monmouth, New Jersey. I went to Camp Gordon, Georgia."

During the war, Hayes played ball for an army post team, the Camp Gordon Ramblers. Once he struck out five batters in a single inning (no one could handle his curveball, not even the catcher) and eleven more over the next four innings before the game was called because of rain. He challenged the local grenade-throwing champion to a contest and won with a throw of eighty-two yards. "I was very proud when I was standing in the ranks and called out by the captain and cheered by the whole company."

But it was in the army that Hayes first set out on the road traveled by his father. "About this time I started drinking because of the inactivity, then depressions came over me. I used to go up into the hills by myself and just sit."

After the war, Hayes lived the life of a baseball vagabond. He traveled all over the country, anyplace there was a team. He'd stay until he got homesick, or got in a fight, or got released. These were some of the stops he made along the way:

Radford, Virginia: "About as low on the B.B. ladder as you could go. We got $1.50 per day to eat on. The meat on a hot open sandwich looked like it was Xeroxed on the bread. Radford was the home of a girls college and the Radford Rockets never reached ignition. . . ."

St. Augustine, Florida: "Two things stand out in my memory. I had a girl in St. Augustine and I got knocked out in a fist fight for the first time. In between was weird . . . The fight was over the girl, naturally. Some dirty old man of 25 was messing around. A teammate; ugly creep. I knocked him down and let him up. Suddenly I was resting comfortably on the ground and didn't care if I ever got up. My eyes were crossed for a few hours which wouldn't have helped my control none, or maybe it would have. . . ."

Brunswick, Georgia: "They had a paper mill in Brunswick and the stink got into your bones. We stayed in the Oglethorpe Hotel which was of pre–Civil War vintage. They served rubber chicken and army style scrambled eggs. It was ridiculous and they had their experts."

Tri-Cities, Washington: "Kennewick, Pasco and some other wind-blown God-forsaken town; oh, yeah Hanford. The song now was 'Ebb Tide' and I was missing my Georgia girl in Brunswick; but I couldn't be further away unless I went to Alaska."

My copy of *The Crucifixion of a Fireballer* stopped abruptly in the middle of a sentence on page fifty-eight, with Hayes in Yuma, Arizona, "where the suffering serpent could get some pain-relieving heat while pitifully trying to strike." Hayes was all washed up. He read the bush-league standings in *The Sporting News* every week from the bottom up, looking for any team that needed help. Not a happy ending.

And what did Hayes have to show for all his years in baseball? One memory stood out overall, of a day he pitched batting practice in Newport News, Virginia, for the Norfolk Tars—The Day of the Serpent.

It was March 1951, the spring after he left the service. Hayes was twenty-three years old. Things hadn't worked out with the Yankees and so he'd made his way to Vero Beach, hoping to catch on with the Dodgers—"*my* ballclub . . . *my* hometown team." They kicked him out of camp. He stopped in Cocoa, where there was an independent club in the Florida State League, and when that didn't work out either, he tried Daytona Beach—"I don't remember much except that the mosquitos were trying to devour my calf muscles and ankles right through my . . . sanitary socks." When Daytona let him go, there was nothing left but to head for home.

"I hitchhiked up toward New York, passing through the Norfolk, Newport News area one night. I was thinking of talking to Mickey Owen of the Norfolk Tars and telling him what a mess I'd made of my life . . . But I was too depressed and broke. In Newport News, while walking to the outskirts to hitch a ride north, I saw the lights of the minor league ballpark. They attracted me like the moth to the flame. When I got closer, the crack of the bat meeting ball sent a miniature Ty Cobb running and sliding up and down my spine. I jogged to the Piedmont League club's ballpark. It was about the 7th inning and Newport News, a Dodger affiliate, was getting scwumped. A beefy pitcher with a nifty Dodger uniform was getting blasted, so I took a chance. I saw the manager, Stan Wasiak, and asked him if I could pitch batting practice the next day; he said okay.

"I slept part of the time in the bus station in Newport News and part of the time in the back of a parked bus in the rear of the station. I was a nervous wreck and didn't need the fags inviting me home with them in the station. Somehow I lasted until the next day and showed up at the ballpark.

"From the first warmup toss I knew the serpent had returned, angry and needing Ks to assuage his injured pride. The ball reached the mitt before I knew the serp released it. The Newport News catcher backed up and looked at me in awe. . . . This was the Day of the Serpent! The baseball felt like a golfball and looked like one to the batters. . . . No excuses for the prima donna, pampered, pouting, puffing peleteros. And no contact: I went through the entire lineup once, then again, and thundered the rising horsehide meteor past *all* of them. Bonus babies with crouching styles, Punch and Judies with their hands halfway up the bat. All fastballs; it was me and the serp against the world. All mundane activity stopped. Pepper games were abandoned. Coaches mouths became strange caves for wandering flies and gnats. Time stood still. The birds hovered without moving their wings. All you could hear was the pounding of the ball into the mitt of the entranced catcher . . . I believe that *no one* has ever had a better day than the serpent and I had that day. It is physically impossible for bone, muscle, sinew and blood to throw a baseball any better than I did that day in Newport News.

"I took a shower. I was a little sore, but the hot water reassured and comforted the serp. The ballplayers came in and started their ego-regaining bullshit. No class. One suggested that I get a job in the shipyards. I was going to tell him that he'd do better with a rivet gun than he did with his bat, but who needs snidisms at a time like this?

"Wasiak called me into his office. He had a class-A contract on his desk, green instead of class-D orange or brown. He said 'Sit down.' He asked me where I was from. I said Brooklyn. His eyebrows lifted. He said I was just going to sign you but [Anthony] Cincotta told me you were wild in the army and they kicked you out of Vero Beach. I can't sign you. . . .

"I walked towards New York. I don't know how I got home. There was a rain cloud a foot over my head all the way back to Brooklyn."

WINTER HAVEN • December 5

I KNEW THE CHANCES WERE SLIM, BUT I WENT STRAIGHT TO THE clubhouse anyway to find out if Tom Hayes had made the team. I found Bill Lee in the manager's room; he hadn't wanted to give up his privileged quarters so he shared the space now with his replacement, Ed Nottle. There was a new book in Lee's locker, *Summer of '49* by David Halberstam, about the Yankees–Red Sox pennant race of that year. It occurred to me that Lee was a rookie in 1969, only twenty years after the events described in the book, and that now it was 1989, only twenty years later. Nineteen sixty-nine I could grasp. Nineteen forty-nine was ancient history.

Lee looked puzzled when I asked about Hayes. "Oh," he said finally, "the old man. No." Hayes must have called Lee this afternoon. "I told him it wasn't his age or his desire that was lacking. It was the fact that he had a rotator cuff injury and he couldn't throw strikes. He was very erratic. I told him his love of the game was great and I appreciated him coming down."

So that was that. Sad, but surely Hayes saw it coming. "I'm assuming nothing's gonna happen," he'd said last night. "That's a good way not to get disappointed."

Today was also decision day for Mike Cuellar, Lee's idol, now fifty-two years old and hobbled by hemorrhoids. Before his operation, Cuellar had pitched only eight innings for the Super Sox and given up fourteen earned runs. He was feeling better now, but the Sox had decided to let him go. "He still thinks he can pitch," said Lee, "but he can't fucking walk. I gave him enough time, you know."

Despite Lee's reflexive use of the first person, the decision to release Cuellar had not been his. The ball club belonged to Nottle now. For whatever reason, the Super Sox were winning under Nottle. They were thirteen and seven since the change was made and had climbed into second place in the northern division, only three games behind St. Petersburg.

I'd met Nottle for the first time last week. He was leaning on the cage then, watching batting practice. Nottle was a Baseball Man—raspy-voiced, foul-mouthed, quick-witted, and tan like a farmer (face, neck, and forearms). He was fifty years old, one of those who had spent most of his career looking up from the bottoms rungs of the baseball ladder. When I told him I was writing a book, he said, "So's everybody, I think. See, I'm gonna write one about Bill called *Rooming with an Alien*."

"Do you really share a room?"

"No, just the locker room. That's as far as I'll go."

I asked him what he'd be doing if he wasn't managing the Super Sox this winter.

"I'd be doing shows. I sing in the off season."

"Did you say you sing?"

"Yup, that's what I said. It's the only other fucking thing I can do. If I could weld I'd weld for a fucking living. You spend thirty years in the minors you better do something to eat on."

Now, only half an hour before the game, Nottle invited me to ride with him over to the Holiday Inn. He wanted to give me a copy of his album. I said sure.

In a couple of months, Nottle would begin his fifth season as manager of the Red Sox AAA farm team in Pawtucket, a job he hoped would eventually lead to Fenway Park in Boston. "I had a shot last year and they gave it to Joe [Morgan], rightfully so. They didn't want him long-term and then he went nineteen and one, so that's the end of that."

Nottle figured that if the Red Sox didn't get off to a good start next year, he might still get his chance. "If not, then I told them

I'd take a coaching job. I turned it down the last two years but now I figure I'm fifty years old, I better get some fucking pension time. I'll be sixty and my wife and I'll be fucking saving up quarters to go to Coney Island."

Nottle drove a big car, but he was not a big man. He sat behind the wheel in full uniform, as unself-conscious in gaudy double knits and baseball stirrups as any other man his age would be in a suit and tie. What he chose to tell me about his life in Pawtucket had nothing to do with his work as a baseball manager; to him, I suppose, it was just a job. Instead, he told me all about where he lived. It was the more interesting story.

"Great situation. There's a guy there that's a clown, Ringling Brothers. He's got a little condo and he leaves April first, comes back September fifteenth. Leaves everything there. I pay him X a month and he leaves TVs, VCRs, the whole bit. Works out *unbelievably*. I bring somebody in, they clean the whole place up before he comes back. It's tremendous. Before that I lived three years in HoJo's. Fuck, this is my sixth month in the same room down here. Spring training, instructional league, and now this."

"This" was the senior league.

"*This* is very good for me and mine, I'll tell you *that*. Fuck, thirty years in the minors don't make you rich. I got a daughter in college, and this takes care of the last three years of college. *Tremendous*. And it's a great opportunity for me. It's the one area—well, I don't think anybody's worried about my handling the media or the community, but it's not that easy to be a minor leaguer in this league and handle a major-league club. Some of these guys aren't just major leaguers, they're *great* major leaguers. So I think, for myself, for my own self-doubts or whatever, this is great."

We turned in at the Holiday Inn and drove through the parking lot all the way to the back. Nottle's room was a corner unit on the ground floor. I waited in the car while he went inside. The door to the room was open, and a maid was standing there with her cart. Nottle said something to her on the way out that made her laugh.

"My compliments," he said, handing me the album after he got back in the car. *To Baseball With Love*. So he was sentimental, after all. The songs were mostly nightclub standards— "Always on My Mind," "On the Road Again," "New York, New

York." I asked him what it was like listening to your own voice
on a record.

"I fucking love it. Fucking A, I jerk off. Somebody says he
don't, gotta be an idiot."

On the cover was a photograph of the Oakland Coliseum with
an inset of Nottle in an A's uniform wearing a catcher's glove.
Nottle was bull-pen coach for the A's in 1983, the only year he'd
ever spent in the big leagues.

"Once I get to Boston, that cover comes off, Fenway goes on,
and the sound track is in the fucking vault," he said as we pulled
up outside the clubhouse at Chain O' Lakes Park. "If I couldn't
sell a hundred thousand of them in New England I'll kiss your ass.
That's six hundred thou' to me—no agents, no nothing. I could go
mute tomorrow, but that sonofabitch will never shut up."

JOAQUIN ANDUJAR WAS THE STARTING PITCHER TODAY FOR THE VIS-
iting Gold Coast Suns. Andujar had joined the Suns late. He
flew in from the Dominican Republic one day in early November, threw a little "beePEE," and immediately joined the rotation, despite not having thrown in almost a year. Now about to
turn thirty-seven, Andujar was yet another aging star who hoped
openly for a chance to return to the big leagues. "Yessir!" he
said. "You never know! I like to get back if they give me the
chance because my arm is there, nothing different."

Andujar's stormy career peaked in 1985, when he won twenty
or more games for the second straight season and helped the
Cardinals capture the National League pennant. St. Louis
jumped to a 3–1 lead over Kansas City in the World Series that
year, then crossed over into the Twilight Zone and lost everything. The Series ended for all practical purposes in the ninth
inning of game six, when umpire Don Denkinger blew a call at
first base that led to a game-winning rally by the Royals. After
that, game seven was a wash. The Cardinals used seven different
pitchers and were humiliated, 11–0.

One of the most memorable images of that final game is of
Andujar, who was livid after walking Jim Sundberg in the fifth
inning, being ejected from the game. In retrospect, it was then,
in the final moment of the season in which Andujar's career had
finally come together, that Andujar came apart. After that he
was never the same. Over the winter he was traded to the Oak-

land A's, where he was fifteen and twelve over two seasons. He finished his career in 1988 in the Astros' bull pen.

So far, Andujar was dominating opposing batters in the senior league. He had given up three earned runs in fourteen innings of work, and already there were rumors of an invitation to big-league camp. Watching him today, I thought he looked trim ("I don't wanna be fat"), that he threw probably as hard as ever ("I never have sore arm in my life"), and that he seemed to want to show whomever might be watching that his famous temper was no longer an issue. Once, after he threw a fastball in tight on a Winter Haven batter, Andujar walked three-quarters of the way from the mound to home plate just to say he was sorry.

My companion in the stands for most of the afternoon was Mitch Maxwell, just back from the latest round of owners' meetings. They'd talked about expansion, about what the league might do to increase its national exposure, and, of course, about attendance. Maxwell, you remember, was the one who refused to worry about attendance ("Quite frankly, I think it's a stupid question"). That was three weeks ago. Now he was worried. Through thirteen home dates, Winter Haven was still averaging fewer then six hundred fans per game. Orlando was doing even worse, with fewer than five hundred, but that was hardly a consolation. West Palm Beach, the franchise that had emerged as the envy of the rest of the league, was first overall with fifteen hundred fans per game, or about half what they needed to break even, and that was according to the most optimistic projections. Thanksgiving weekend—traditionally the beginning of the winter tourist season—had come and gone; if the snowbirds were in Florida, they certainly weren't coming to many ball games.

"I made a mistake," Maxwell said now. "I fell in love with the park. I saw Fort Myers, which is probably one of the best markets we have—it was available when I went down there—and I thought the ballpark was ugly. I fell in love with this ballpark, which is a mistake in my business. You never fall in love with the theater, and you never fall in love with the star." Maxwell chuckled. "Sometimes you screw the star, but . . ."

He couldn't help himself. His mind worked that way.

"All in all, I'm disappointed in the response of this town. I just think this town is too small or too poor or too apathetic. We've got about three hundred people that are terrific, but that's not enough. What the league needs is strong markets. St. Pete's a strong market, there's two million people there. Fort Myers's a strong market, there's half a million people there. And Miami, of course, and West Palm. I just don't think you can put a club with a six-hundred-thousand-dollar payroll in a town with twenty-five thousand people. We're not a minor-league team where all the expenses are paid for by the big-league club.

"If my club continues to play well and we stay two, three games behind St. Pete or even catch them, and I don't start drawing a thousand people on a regular basis, which is what I had hoped to draw, then I'll make a statement sometime around the end of December. You know, 'You've got two weeks to show me that you want a baseball team.' I've had calls from other cities. I'm willing to look into it."

"Go look," the citizens of Winter Haven might well have said, the way the Sox played today. Andujar and Ken Clay combined to shut them out on six hits. Mark Bomback, the Sox starter, was awful. Final score: Suns, 8, Sox, 0. Attendance on a warm, sunny Tuesday afternoon: five hundred two.

WINTER HAVEN · December 6

EARL WEAVER WAS NOT HAPPY. HE'D JUST HEARD THAT JOAQUIN Andujar was spending Christmas back home in the Dominican Republic and would likely miss two starts. It was in his contract. Weaver was sore but not at Andujar. He'd have put the same clause in *his* contract if he didn't live in Miami. No, Weaver was mad at the fool who wrote in a full slate of games for December 26. "Christmas and then the next day you're playing baseball," Weaver said disgustedly. "Seems kind of sacrilegious, doesn't it?"

The schedule, the stupid damn schedule. It galled Weaver to think of how much aggravation he'd put up with all winter long just because some idiot with the power to make decisions didn't know the first thing about putting together a baseball schedule. Like today. Today was a night game, the last of a three-game series. Yesterday was a day game. If only the night game had been yesterday and the day game today, then Weaver could have driven back to Miami this afternoon immediately after the game, had dinner with his wife, slept in his own bed, played golf tomorrow (an off day), and rejoined the team the following day in St. Petersburg. As it was, Weaver had had to check out of the hotel at noon and spend all afternoon hanging around the ballpark with nothing to do. By the time the game ended, it would be too late to go back to Miami. He'd have no choice then but to go on to St. Petersburg, which meant another night in a strange bed followed by another long, empty day away from home.

"Tomorrow's gonna be hell for me," Weaver said. "An off day on the road."

Weaver was killing time before the game, lounging in a corner of the third-base dugout, his face puffy and red, his legs dangling from the bench (barely scraping the concrete). As always, he wore long johns under his uniform pants; he was easily chilled. Bob Murphy, the veteran Mets radio announcer (he could "paint the word picture") was there, too, fresh from a week at a resort in St. Martin, looking more tan than healthy. This winter Murphy was doing a weekly senior-league game for the Florida Radio Network. He wanted four minutes of Weaver's time for the pregame show, but evidently that could wait. The microphone was off for now, and the two old friends were chatting.

"The worst part about the league," Weaver was saying, "is we're not gonna get the big names. Golf got all the big names, you know what I mean? Every one of them, the guys we grew up with. We're just not gonna get the nine-million-dollar ballplayer. Number one, they got families, and it's tough to be away from them. I don't know why I'm here, to tell you the truth. When you win and you're at home and you're taking your wife out for dinner, what could be better? But when you're on the road away from your wife again, what could be worse? 'Til the game starts, then you enjoy watching the games. A manager gets just as much enjoyment out of watching a game as the fans, but you're responsible for the wins and the losses. Losing is shit."

"How's your owner?" asked Murphy, trying out his singsong radio voice, "nice guy to be around?"

"Yeah, except that he's like me when I owned the thoroughbreds. I wanted to know everything the trainer was doing, you know? 'When are we gonna breeze 'em? When are we breaking 'em out of the gate? Get the condition book out.' We've only had one or two meetings since the season started, but when he's here, we go over the whole team, player by player. You can't blame the guy. The guy's just interested and wants to know. It's a toy for him."

Weaver's Suns were on a roll lately. Nine and four over the last two weeks, enough wins to lift them past St. Lucie and out of last place in the southern division. "What turned it around for your club?" Murphy asked now with his tape recorder running. "Just getting those guys healthy?"

Weaver agreed, but there was more to it than that. He'd started platooning at several positions and that, more than anything else, seemed to make a difference in how his players performed. "I hate to make 'em play over three or four games at a time," he said.

"They need more time to recover?" Murphy asked. He was thinking about muscles and bones. But that's not what Weaver meant.

"Well, it seems like it keeps up the interest level," Weaver said.

Murphy asked more questions, timing himself with a stopwatch, inserting breaks for commercials. When he had all he wanted, he gathered up his equipment, said, "Thanks, so much!" and went off in search of something to eat. Weaver watched him go.

"See, I missed talking baseball a little bit when I was away," Weaver said after Murphy had left. He crossed his legs and lit another cigarette. The sky above the wall in right field was a cold, bright red. " 'Cause the guys at the country club, they don't know that much about it. That's a fact."

"Will you come back next year?" I asked him.

"I don't like to be asked that question when I'm on the road. Ask me after we've won a game at home."

"Is that the whole thing? It's just no fun to be on the road?"

"It *is* for younger people," Weaver said. "If you want to cheat on your wife and run around and drink—I drink a lot, but I'm home by eight, nine—but if you want to do all that stuff, you love the road. There was a time when I loved the road. But that's over. If you don't mind catching herpes or AIDS or all of that shit, you might enjoy it. But not at this stage of life. You gotta look ahead. How many years do you have? Ten? Twelve?"

It was time for me to start thinking about dinner, too. I left Weaver sitting in the dugout, alone now except for a man in vacation clothes who had somehow gained access to the field.

He claimed to have met Weaver once before, years ago. "How's the season going?" the man asked, just as I was leaving.

"We're almost halfway," Weaver said innocuously. "Seems to have gone pretty good. By the time it's over you look back and you say, 'Aw, shit, that went fast.' "

S TAN B AHNSEN , THE A MERICAN L EAGUE R OOKIE OF THE Y EAR IN 1968, had lousy stuff tonight. Seven of the nine batters he faced reached base, and eventually all of them scored. All told, the Super Sox sent thirteen batters to the plate in the first inning and ran up an 8–0 lead. Bad, but it could have been worse, and soon enough it was. The damage was 9–2 after two, 13–2 after three, and 17–2 after four. Suns reliever Grant Jackson finally set down the Super Sox in order in the fifth. Refreshed, the home team came back to score five more in the sixth and one more in the eighth on Leon Roberts's second homer of the night (Roberts's roommate, Pete LaCock, also had two homers). By the time Weaver's Suns trudged down the left-field foul line to the sanctuary of the visitors' clubhouse, the score was 23–4. Losing is shit.

The spectacle was witnessed by a grand total of two hundred fifty-six fans, one in ten of whom was a visiting member of the Hobart College swim team. The shiny-haired swimmers, dressed in shorts and T-shirts despite the cold, kept up an intermittent chant of "Let's go, Sox!" as the touchdowns mounted. During the silences between, Bob Murphy's play-by-play could be plainly heard throughout the park, even without a radio. I thought of the highway traveler, scanning the stations away somewhere on a frosty winter night, surprised to come upon a baseball game, amazed to hear Murphy paint his word picture of Ferguson Jenkins pitching to Bert Campaneris.

At age forty-seven, Campaneris was the oldest everyday player in the league. But even Campy was still a child of thirteen in 1955 when his Cuban compatriot, Pedro Ramos, made his major-league debut.

"I started in baseball as a catcher," Ramos had explained the first time we met. "Then because I run and hit they put me in the outfield. I said, 'I wanna pitch!' So they put me at shortstop. I said, 'I wanna pitch!' So I get to pitch my first year in the States, 1953, and I don't do too good as a pitcher. I throw hard but I got bombed. They released me first year. So now I'm afraid. I don't even have money to come back to Cuba. I said, 'Oh, shit.' So they keep me there for a few days, then they sign me again, and then I come back and pitch. If I got hit, they put me in left field. I hit seven home run! The next year I come back to the league, I say, 'I wanna pitch!' So then I went sixteen and four and here we go!"

Ramos wound up pitching in the big leagues for fifteen years, accumulating enough at-bats along the way as a switch-hitting outfielder and pinch hitter to earn a dual listing in *Total Baseball*. Now fifty-four, Ramos threw batting practice for the Suns and served as Weaver's pitching coach.

"Some guys come back because they love it, like me," Ramos said. "And some guys, like me again, to make money."

And?

Ramos's eyes danced, and the edges of his mouth turned up. "And, perhaps, I believe I can still pitch. On a nine-one-one call."

Tonight, with his team down by eleven runs and six innings left to play, Weaver put out a call for emergency help. Ramos ran in from the left-field bull pen, white hair visible beneath his cap. He was making his first appearance in fifteen years.

Dalton Jones led off against Ramos with a home run (the only homer he would hit all year and one of only six hits total). Tommy McMillan walked. Gene Richards lined out to first base. Joe Pittman was hit by a pitch. Rodney Scott struck out looking. Two outs, two on. Ramos grinned at his catcher—*Hey, I'm not doing so bad!* But LaCock, next up, hit a three-run homer. That brought Weaver out of the dugout and sent Ramos to the showers. In two thirds of an inning, he had compiled an earned run average that exactly matched his age.

And yet when I found Ramos after the game, he was grinning like a rookie—shy, maybe, but too overwhelmed to hide his elation. "To be honest, I was a little exciting," he said, jumbling his verb endings. "I was. I never run to the mound coming in to pitch and I did tonight and I rushed myself too much. I don't usually throw that many balls, even now. *But I was so exciting!*"

"Were you ready to pitch tonight?"

"I was ready. I mean, there's no excuse, I was ready. I was just a little excited and I kept the ball too high, off the strike zone, which I not usually do that, even now. 'Cause I have good control. But you don't pitch for a long time, you don't have as good rotation on the ball."

"Did you try your fork ball?" Ramos had showed me the pitch once when he was fooling around playing catch. His version acted like a knuckleball, no spin at all.

"They didn't give me time! I was trying to see if I could get 'em out with this"—he made a fastball grip with his right hand— "and pretty soon, bang-bang and that's it. But I feel I threw pretty good. It was fun. When I got back to the bull pen, my pitchers over there, they were making little cracks. One of the guys said, 'See, it's not so easy!'

"I said, 'I been there, I know it's not that easy. They just got my cherry today, that's all!' "

BRADENTON • *December 7*

Drove down to McKechnie Field today to meet up with Tom Hayes and return the manuscript. Hayes was nowhere to be seen (I was early) so I wandered down the left-field foul line to a favorite hangout next to the visitors' clubhouse. Ron Pruitt, Eric Rasmussen, and Johnny LeMaster were all there in their Fort Myers Sun Sox road uniforms, leaning back against the wall in plastic chairs, enjoying the air and the sun. The subject of their pregame conversation was the economic aspect of baseball cards.

Most of the money paid out by the card companies went into a fund administered by the Players Association. At the end of the year, every uniformed employee in baseball shared equally in the proceeds. Pruitt's last check, cashed the year he retired in 1983, was for two thousand seven hundred dollars. By the time LeMaster retired four years later, it was up to twenty thousand dollars a man. LeMaster wasn't sure, but he'd heard that last year it was thirty thousand dollars. Hearing that, the others shook their heads in wonder. (By 1990, the per-player share of merchandising royalties would reach eighty-five thousand dollars.)

Players knew what their cards were worth to collectors. The fact that strangers made money off *their* likenesses and *their* signatures (never mind the royalty checks the players cashed at the end of each year) was infuriating to a lot of them. But it wasn't just the money. There was a generational factor as well for these men as they approached their forties, a feeling that "kids today" didn't have their priorities straight.

"New York's the worst," said Rasmussen, formerly with the Cardinals, Padres, and Royals. (Rasmussen was actually named Harold by his mother. He changed his name to Eric because, he said, "I never felt like a Harold.") "They get you when you're boarding the bus to go to the ballpark. The bus takes forty-five minutes or so. You get to Shea Stadium and there's the same fucking guys. They took the subway and there they are again. Same fucking guys. I read about one kid—Young Entrepreneur of the Year. Made a hundred thousand dollars trading various baseball stuff. You hear these kids talking in the stands, 'Yeah, I got Darryl Strawberry's autograph, it's worth sixty-five dollars.' I hate that. I got a son who's almost thirteen. He'll say, 'Yeah, I got this card, it's worth so much.' He doesn't even know anything about the guy, but the card's worth that much money."

"Did you collect cards when you were little?" I asked him.

"I had, not a million of 'em, but a couple of shoeboxes full or something. I just looked at 'em. I wanted to be like Eddie Mathews, that was my hero. I lived south of Milwaukee, Racine. The Braves were my team. I followed baseball, you know. I knew every game, every box score. When they moved out of Milwaukee I completely quit. I was so bitter, like the whole state of Wisconsin. Didn't even follow anything anymore except what Eddie Mathews did. I didn't give a shit what Atlanta did."

After a while, I left Rasmussen and his teammates and went inside the clubhouse. As my eyes adjusted to the dim light, I saw that the room was empty, save for a lone figure on a stool in front of a corner locker. His elbows were propped on his knees and he was smoking a cigarette.

"You throwing today?" I asked him.

Wayne Garland looked up. He nodded. His face was puffy and without expression. "I'm hurting," he said.

Of course, the dead arm, I remembered now. Last week when we met he'd said he was a little stiff. Nothing to worry about, right?

"I think I tore it," he said.

Tore it? I didn't say anything. There was only one "it" a pitcher worried about tearing, and that was his rotator cuff. It had happened to Garland once before, in 1978. If it had happened again, he was finished.

Garland volunteered nothing, and I didn't feel like pressing him. I left him sitting on the stool and went back outside where the sun was shining brightly.

GARLAND WAS AWFUL IN THE FIRST. HE TOOK THE MOUND WITH A four-run lead and promptly squandered it with two walks, one wild pitch, one single, and one home run. He was somewhat more effective in the second, stranding two Explorers and preventing any more runs. Over the next two innings he faced the minimum six. But in the fifth a wild pitch cost him another run and, with it, the lead. Hayes, who sat with me during the game behind home plate, observed that Garland was "short-arming" the ball—throwing with his forearm and favoring his shoulder. After he retired Al Oliver on a fly ball to center to end the fifth, Garland retrieved his jacket from the dugout and headed for the clubhouse. His day was done.

Fort Myers scored a run in the top of the sixth to go ahead, 6–5. The lead held, and so Garland got credit for the victory, upping his record to two wins and no losses. When I spoke to him after the game, he was holding a beer in his right hand.

"What happened today?"

"My arm died."

"You knew you were hurt before the game. Why'd you even go out there?"

"My turn was up."

He transferred the beer can to his left hand and raised it to his lips. "Thank God I wipe my ass left-handed," he said.

I smiled, but he didn't. It was no joke.

FORT MYERS • December 9

GARLAND LOOKED A LITTLE BETTER WHEN I RAN INTO HIM AGAIN two days later in the Sun Sox locker room. By now he could raise his right hand as high as his shoulder. "I'll see how it feels in a couple of days," he said, rubbing his right shoulder. He wore a yellow long-sleeved T-shirt over white, green-striped baseball pants. "I'm scheduled to pitch Wednesday, but I don't know whether I'll be able to make it or not. I'll just go day by day and see what happens."

"Do you know yet what the problem is?"

"A couple of weeks ago I had trouble sleeping because my arm would fall asleep all the time. Doc thinks it's some kind of pinched nerve in my neck or something that's causing that, maybe not getting enough blood to my arm and that's"— Garland paused, took a deep breath, and exhaled loudly—"that's what the trainer thinks it is, too. It's been going numb and stuff like that off and on all day. But I'm not gonna rule out a tear. Doc says I coulda tore it again, but I might just be sitting there with all the scar tissue and adhesions and mighta broke those loose and just be going through a period right now. He doesn't want me to pitch for ten days, but if it doesn't get any worse, I might as well run back out there."

I could understand why an athlete might feel that way if he were pitching in the big leagues. But this wasn't the big leagues. Why would anyone risk permanent injury in the senior league? I asked him, "Is it really worth it at this point in your life to put yourself through all this pain?"

Garland was quiet. Across the room, Pat Putnam's Labrador retriever, Curley, growled playfully at Marty Castillo, who had hold of him by the jowls. The Sun Sox were nine and one since Curley moved into the locker room. Curley had his own stall now and a fitted jersey with his master's number, twenty-three, which he wore to chase baseballs in the outfield during batting practice.

"That's hard to say," Garland said finally. "I think it's worth it, you know, 'cause we got a good ball club. I think anybody'd tell you they came down here to win. We got a good chance at that so in that sense I'd say it's worth it, yeah. I mean, I'm not gonna go out there and take a chance at really hurting myself. I think I know my limitations and if it gets to that point, then no, it won't be worth it. Then I'd have to have an operation, have a 'scope, something like that because, you know, I can't go through the rest of life like this. You still got other things you wanna do. Play golf, stuff like that. Brush your teeth, comb your hair."

This time he smiled faintly.

"I've pitched with pain before, I think everybody has. You gotta play with some pain. But like I said, if it gets to the point where it's unbearable, then no, I'm not gonna go out there. I don't think I can go out there too many times like the last time, that's for sure. It can't keep going on like this."

PAT DOBSON, THE SUN SOX MANAGER, WAS SIX-THREE, TANNED, AND handsome with a full head of wavy, brown hair. A dedicated smoker, he could have played a cowboy in a Marlboro commercial. The high point of his eleven-year major-league career came in 1971, when he entered the record book as one of four Orioles starting pitchers to win twenty games (Dave McNally won twenty-one; Jim Palmer, Mike Cuellar, and Dobson won exactly twenty). Dobson's current job was pitching coach for the San Diego Padres. His current preoccupation was the fate of free-agent Mark Davis, his bull-pen stopper last year in San Diego. Dobson was resigned to the fact that Davis was going elsewhere; now all he wanted to do was steer him away from signing with the Yankees. Dobson played two and a half years with the Yankees during the middle seventies and was of the opinion that no amount of money could compensate for the experience. (Two days later Davis signed with the Kansas City Royals.)

I found Dobson in the manager's office, a windowless cubicle that opened off the locker room. He didn't smile when I stuck my head in, but he didn't growl, either. There was a chair beside his metal desk, and he pointed at it. I sat down. I began by asking him about his old field boss, Earl Weaver. Dobson knew Weaver as well as anybody. Was he surprised to see him back managing in the senior league?

"I don't think he woulda done it anyplace else except Miami." Dobson spoke in a very low octave, a voice roughened by years of inhaling quantities of tar and nicotine. "Takes away too much of his free time. They're paying him top dollar to do it, and he can live at home."

"Do you think he enjoys it?"

"Oh, I think he'll always love baseball. I mean, it's his life, you know? I think he's like a lot of guys that went through the era of the one-year-at-a-time contract, where management really had control of the players, to the era of the two- and three-year contract, where the fucking players have control of the manager. It's a different breed of player, and their priorities are different. It's pretty hard for those guys to swallow that, that they don't have more control than they do. You have to remember that when he was managing in the early seventies when I was in Baltimore, he was probably making as much or more than any of the players. And then it got to the fucking point where it turned around, and he was making as much as the twenty-fourth guy and running the team. I think that stuff kinda eats at you."

"How about you? Are you having fun?"

"I enjoy being around these guys," he said. "They're kinda throwbacks to when I played, you know? You look in this club-house and you see ninety percent of the guys smoke cigarettes and drink beer. In the big leagues it's ninety percent *don't* smoke cigarettes and *don't* drink beer. I mean, it's like a fucking throw-back to when I used to go in the clubhouse when I was playing in the late sixties and early seventies. These are guys from my era."

The main reason I'd come looking for Dobson was because I wanted to ask him about Garland. There was something very wrong, I thought, about a man Garland's age risking permanent injury to pitch in the senior league. It seemed, too, that perhaps Dobson was partly to blame for sending him out there. I won-dered how much he knew about Garland's condition. If he was pressuring Garland to take his turn regardless, I wanted to hear him say it.

"What's wrong with Garland?" I asked him.

"I think he's got bursitis now is what he's got. That can prob-ably hurt as much as the rotator cuff thing. I've been through that. A lot of times I'd end up getting it, sleep funny, you know, and get one of those vertebras pinched in here"—Dobson reached back and touched the top of his spine—"and it cuts off the fluid into your bursa sac and your fucking bones just grind together. He's gonna see a chiropractor on Monday."

"Should he have started that game two days ago?"

"I know he was hurting before and he has been for quite a while. But he still wanted to pitch. When he does that for you and goes out there, you hope that you can let him pitch five innings and get him a win. I would've hated like hell to have him get out of there with a no-decision or a loss. I was gonna bunt for one run to try to get him a win. As it turned out, we ended up starting the inning with a double and got a two-out double to score the run and got the lead and won the game and he got the win. So it really worked out quite nicely, you know?"

I realized now that I'd read the situation all wrong. Dobson wasn't using Garland, he was looking out for him. The only part I still didn't understand was what was driving Garland, why pitching still mattered so much to him. "I know there was a lot at stake in the big leagues," I said. "But that's over. I'm puzzled why he still wants to put himself through all the pain and disappointment."

Dobson was sitting in a swivel chair. He leaned way back in it now and regarded me blankly through a blue veil of cigarette smoke. He sighed, and then he undertook to explain.

"Yeah, but not knowing what his financial condition is, how do you know that there's not as much at stake now as what there was then?" Dobson leaned forward again. "That's the point, see. He doesn't have a job in baseball right now. He doesn't have anything else to do besides what he's doing right now. He can pitch for me anytime he wants to. As long as he wants to go out there, I'm gonna let him pitch. He can use his own judgment on whether he thinks he can permanently hurt himself or whatever, but as long as he's capable of pitching he'll pitch for me. Anytime. I know what kind of financial condition he's in. I have a pretty good idea what financial condition most of these guys are in. See, a lot of times you may just go an extra mile with a guy and try to get him over the hump 'cause I know it's not easy. I've been there myself, when I got out and had to go into coaching and was making fifteen thousand a year. It's not easy."

It was as if I had been looking through a kaleidoscope all along at the senior league. Dobson's answer jiggled the kaleidoscope, and now I saw a new pattern and new shapes, not as cheerful as before. There was no future in the senior league, that was obvious all along. So why play? Maybe you were coaching or managing and this was a fun (and profitable) way to spend your winter vacation. Or maybe you already had enough money and you came down here to enjoy yourself, one last fling on your own field of dreams. Most likely, I saw now, you desperately needed work and this was a terrific job. Where else were you going to get paid excellent money to run around outdoors all winter in Florida (not working, even; *playing* a game), to hang out with old friends, to laugh, to tell stories, to hear strangers applaud your accomplishments, to revisit the most glorious episode of your life? For those who had stumbled when they left the game, the coming of the senior league was almost too good to be true. There was more than a hint of desperation, I realized now, in the way they lunged back into the embrace of the game they'd left behind.

"I hadn't realized there were that many here just because they needed the money," I said.

"There's a lot more than you think," Dobson said. "A very big percentage are here because they need the money. They're going through a divorce, or they need the money for child support, or whatever the hell it is. They're the guys that are gonna play [in the senior league]."

"So you think only a small minority are here only because they love the game?"

"Very small."

POMPANO BEACH • December 12

FROM MY DIARY: MADE A SNAP DECISION THIS MORNING TO DRIVE down to Miami and finally catch a game at Bobby Maduro Stadium before the season snuck away from me. Made excellent time down I-75, nice weather, good music on the radio. Exited on Florida 82 and pointed toward Everglades City, for variety's sake. Drove through a run-down settlement of migrant workers; houses and a school made of concrete block. Waited at a stoplight on Florida 29 near Immokalee while dozens of schoolchildren crossed the road. Stopped in Everglades City, the end of civilization. Mailed a postcard, bought a plastic alligator for my unborn child, then joined U.S. 41, east to Miami. Stopped after a few miles to eat leftovers for lunch out of a plastic tub. Sat at a picnic table in a grove of palms, between the highway (whizzing trucks) and the dark, still Tamiami Canal, surrounded by a low wall (that to keep out the gators?). Was joined at my table by a green, stock-still lizard. On the road again. Peaceful meditations, interrupted suddenly by the thought of gas. Yikes, empty! No towns, no settlements, no lonely quick stops for mile after mile after mile. Attention divided between exotic birds ruffling their plumage by the side of the road, thick tropical landscape (road was a tunnel through the jungle), and gas needle, dropping deeper and deeper into empty. Tried to stay calm (I never knew the needle went down that far!). *Certain* the car would start chugging any minute, I'd coast to a stop, have to thumb, and miss the game I'd driven so far to see. Then, gas! Picked up five bucks' worth at a roadside shack that also had for sale taxidermic alligator heads. Final approach to Miami on 41 was slow, slow, stop and go. Darkness fell. Where is it, where is it? There it is, Bobby Maduro Stadium. Aargh! No lights, no cars, no people. No game. Ticket window all shuttered up. Found a convenience store, bought a *Herald,* scanned the agate to find that the game was moved to *Pompano.* Crawled out of Miami on I-95, dodging construction, semitrailers, and mad commuters at the height of a midweek rush hour. Only to arrive . . . on time! In my seat now, deep breath, play ball!

CHUCK MALKUS, PR DIRECTOR FOR THE GOLD COAST SUNS, excused himself to answer the press-box telephone.

"Hi, Russ," he said, not waiting to find out who was calling. "We got a base runner on first, no outs, two strikes. Here's the pitch. It's a single, runners on first and second." Silence for three beats. "Here's the pitch. It's low inside for a low ball—okay, it's one-and-o."

Not exactly Red Barber but enough to satisfy Russ Berrie, toy magnate and owner of the Suns, calling from a pay phone in an airport somewhere in America, just to check up on his boys. Berrie used to stay on the line for entire games at a time but gave that up when one of his limited partners, also curious, nearly blew a gasket after three hours of busy signals. These days, Berrie politely hung up between innings. "You'll see," said Chuck. "He knows exactly when to call back."

Ringggg. "Hi, Russ . . ."

Berrie's interest, especially now, was understandable. As was often the case with teams managed by Earl Weaver, the Suns were coming on strong, picking up ground as the season progressed. After winning seven out of their last ten, the Suns' record was up to fourteen and sixteen, only three games behind second-place Fort Myers in the loss column, which was the only set of numbers Weaver looked at anyway. Tonight was the first of a two-game series against the Pelicans, themselves holding on to a slender lead over the surging Winter Haven Super Sox.

So it was a big game. I was interested, too, but I was also hungry. Tonight, alas, there was no food in the press box. One of Malkus's assistants came back from a hot-dog run with an I'm-sorry look on his face; the concessionaire, it developed, was awaiting payment from the Suns on an overdue bill. Until Berrie anted up, there would be no free eats for the working press. Grumbling (my stomach), I descended to the stands.

Two dogs and one soft drink later, I spied Jim Morley, sprawled familiarly across five seats in an empty region behind home plate. Morley was in a good mood, considering the fact that all we talked about was money. At this point in the season, all the owners had abandoned their dreams of first-year profits. The only question now was exactly how much everybody was going to lose. The latest best guess, according to Morley, was "right around a million," per team.

"I mean, we're talking a serious problem over in St. Pete," Morley said. "The team leading the league in the northern division in wins and attendance and everything else was the closest to being in default."

"Excuse me," I said, "did you say 'default'?"

"Aaah, I don't like to look at things that way," Morley said, clearly displeased by the way the word sounded on someone else's lips. "When I made payroll for December first, I didn't have enough money to cover it. The payroll service did the checks. I stood out about, you know, a hundred thousand."

Morley shrugged as if it was no big deal.

"We only had about eighty thousand in the account."

It wasn't supposed to be that way. If only Morley had been able to set things up the way he wanted, he wouldn't have spent the whole winter worrying about money. By late last summer, after laying out cash all spring, rounding up players, scouting locations, and putting on the big press conference, Morley was finally in a position to make some dough, he thought. Sometimes he had to remind himself, but certainly, that was the point of this deal: to make some dough. Nothing more, nothing less. Nostalgia was nice, but it wouldn't pay his mortgages back in Colorado Springs.

Morley had brought the potential owners together for the first time the last weekend in July. They met at the Marriott across from La Guardia Airport in New York. Morley made them a simple proposal: each of the seven other owners would pay Morley eight hundred fifty thousand dollars, or a total of almost six million dollars; half the money would go directly into a kitty from which all league expenses would be deducted for a period of three years, guaranteed by Morley; the other half would go into Morley's pocket, enough to recover his expenses, field a team, pay some bills, and, of course, reward him for coming up with the idea in the first place.

Morley thought it was fair. Everybody else thought it was outrageous.

"Being a real estate broker," said Morley, "I'm well aware. It was kinda like the real estate deal where you put the buyer and the seller together and they both look at the broker and say, 'What do we need you for?' It was a bloodbath the first couple of days, an absolute bloodbath."

Morley was "hung out," way, way out, and everybody else knew it. By the time he landed at La Guardia, his brilliant idea had already cost him three hundred fifty thousand dollars. To some of the others, that might not have meant so much. But to Morley it was everything. "I got basically no money left," Morley said. "If I don't cut a deal, get some of my money back, the league probably folds or waits until next year."

In the end, that was Morley's only real leverage. The senior league was his idea. He was like the little kid at the playground whose baseball it is; either the kid plays, or else he and the ball go home and *nobody* plays.

Eventually, a compromise was reached. While it was not exactly a windfall for Morley, it did allow him to play. Under the terms of the so-called Morley Agreement, he received one hundred seventy-five thousand dollars from each of the seven other owners: seventy thousand on signing, thirty thousand on opening day, and seventy-five thousand in staggered payments between the end of the season and opening day, 1991. If you took what the other owners had to pay and thought of it as a franchise fee, then Morley got his team for free.

Second, the other owners agreed to pay all league expenses for the first three years and leave Morley out of it. In the senior league, each team was responsible for its own player salaries (capped at five hundred fifty thousand dollars per team) and its own stadium lease (fourteen to twenty thousand dollars), but the league paid for almost everything else: not just legal and administrative costs but hotels, transportation, advertising, statistics, umpires, uniforms, even bats and balls. The preliminary budget for year one came to just over $1.5 million. Everybody else kicked in two hundred thousand dollars. Morley paid zip.

Finally, in the event the league were really to take off, Morley stood to make millions. That was his carrot. Morley was entitled to 100 percent of the proceeds from the first expansion franchise sold, 20 percent off the top of all future sales, and 25 percent of any profits the league might generate through the sale of television rights and corporate sponsorships. "Until I get $6.5 million," Morley said. "Once I've gotten $6.5 million, I'm vested like everybody else and then we all go down the road together."

Morley said that he began the season with about one hundred fifty thousand dollars in the bank, two-thirds of which went toward the first player payroll on November 15. Morley made some money in November: about sixty thousand in ticket sales, maybe another sixty thousand in outfield banners and program advertising. But there were also a lot of expenses—the stadium lease, staff and player salaries, workers comp, the Chicken (five thousand for a one-night gig), extra equipment—and by the time the first of December rolled around, a Friday, Morley's account was down to eighty thousand dollars. He needed one hundred six thousand dollars to meet payroll.

Morley knew he was taking a chance. But he also knew that not every player would cash his check before the weekend. That gave him a cushion of a couple of days, and he figured there were at least two ways he could make up the difference. Fort Myers was in town for a big weekend series. A terrific turnout, what with ticket sales, souvenirs, and programs, might bring in twenty thousand dollars. Maybe enough to avoid bouncing any checks, maybe not. Then there was Mike Mayes. For some time now, Morley had come to accept the fact that he was simply not a big enough player to go it alone in the senior league. Already he had sold minority interests to two small investors. At the moment he was working on a major deal with Mayes, a Dallas attorney, who was interested in buying a substantial share of the Pelicans. Interested, but not yet committed.

"So Monday rolled around," Morley said, enjoying the telling, "and I'm working with Mike Mayes on the deal to get the thing in order, and no call from the banker. Tuesday rolls around.

I'm sitting there, it's about ten in the morning, and the phone rings.

" 'Jim, it's J.C.'—J. C. Russell's the banker—'Jim, we've had a few checks come in. I'll clear these, but you're gonna be about eight thousand overdrawn.'

"Which told me some of the players still hadn't cashed their checks; I knew it was really about twenty thousand. I said, 'J.C., can you hold a sec?' I put him on hold, I let him stew there for a second so he thinks that I'm looking around in checkbooks because we got about four accounts. *While* I have him on hold, the Federal Express guy walks in with Mike Mayes's check. Two hundred thousand dollars.

" 'Yeah, J.C., yeah, I see what the problem is. Couple things just didn't get transferred. I'll be over in a little while, take care of it.'

" 'Okay. Thanks, Jim.'

" 'All right. Seeya, J.C.!' "

Morley laughed out loud. It was just like his friends always said: "Fucking Morley, man. He can step in shit and still come out smelling like a rose."

"Oh, I just had a *feeling*," he said, and he clenched his fist. "I mean, I was *feeling* it!"

St. Pete won, 12–7. I was long gone by the time the game ended. Too bad, as it turned out, because I missed seeing Steve Kemp walk *six* times in one game. I believed it was true, that when you went to a game, any game, you were bound to see *something* you'd never seen before. Thing is, you couldn't leave early. It was just that I was tired and I didn't know where I was going to spend the night and so I thought I better get going, get far away from this populated coast and back to Florida's backwoods interior, where I stood a better chance of finding a twenty-five-dollar motel.

Out to U.S. 27, north to South Bay, up the eastern shore of Lake Okeechobee, hoping for a glimpse of the big water beyond the dike, seeing nothing until Port Mayaca when I crossed the St. Lucie Canal and the road climbed up the bridge and there it was, black and still in the light of a full moon. On, then, to the town of Okeechobee itself, to a likely looking place with a bigmouth bass on the sign out front, where a room for the night (what was left of it) cost forty-eight dollars. I shrugged, I paid, I went to sleep. I figured four hundred forty miles was enough for one day.

ORLANDO, FORT MYERS • December 13

BEN KAUFMAN, THE HOPELESSLY GOOD-NATURED MARKETING MAN for the Orlando Juice, usually could think of something, anything, to make himself smile. Today he was having a hard time. He stood alone in the portal of the first-base grandstand, sipping hot chocolate just to stay warm, not worrying about blocking anybody's view because there was nobody behind him with a view to block. Attendance on this raw Wednesday afternoon in Orlando was one hundred fourteen, another record. It was also less than the total number of moms and dads of all those in uniform, a per-player attendance that was below what you might expect for a little-league game. What if one day the unthinkable happened and *no one showed up at all?* If a game was played, and no one saw it, would you say it had really been played?

Kaufman didn't know. His mind was far removed from foggy problems of philosophy. "You got the Mouse," he observed laconically, his face bent over his cup of chocolate, "and you got the Magic."

The Magic was the NBA expansion franchise. "The Mouse?"

"Mickey Mouse. Disney World. It's a tough nut to crack."

Kaufman, like his boss, Wynne Dillard, was from Arkansas. They were outsiders in a closed community; just *how* closed, they were only beginning to appreciate. They knew now that they had made mistakes. Probably the first was not saving the news of Gates Brown's hiring for Orlando *Sentinel* columnist Larry Guest, a local deity. Owner Phil Breen delivered the scoop (such as it was) to a TV reporter right before he met with Guest, who was furious at the unintended slight. In retrospect, a happy Guest probably would not have translated into measurably more ticket sales, but it might have saved the Juice from cracks like the one, reported by Guest in his column, that fugitive Manuel Noriega of Panama had avoided capture for so long by hiding out "in a place away from everyone—at an Orlando Juice game."

Really, though, the problems of the Juice in Orlando went far beyond the influence of one disgruntled newspaper columnist. There was not an owner in the senior league who wasn't guilty of having succumbed—even if just a little bit—to a romantic misconception inspired by a recent movie they'd all seen and loved, *Field of Dreams.* "If you build it, they will come," Kevin Costner heard a voice whisper one summer's night. And it happened, exactly as promised. Not only did the Black Sox return from the dead to play again but to this very day—and this isn't Hollywood, this is real life—tourists flock to the Iowa cornfield where the movie was shot, enough of them to support a thriving cottage industry for the lucky farmer who owns the land.

Well, it didn't happen that way in the senior league. The owners had thought the hard part would be finding players. Not so. The hard part was finding fans. They built the league. They sat back and waited. And no one came. Nowhere was this failure to promote and market the senior league more apparent than in Orlando. "This town is interesting," Pat Williams, general manager of the Magic, told *The National.* "There is such a high standard for promotion in this town. And the natives are used to it. And it's set by Disney, and if you don't market and compete at that level, you're in trouble by comparison."

As one who read Bill Veeck's autobiography—*Veeck—as in Wreck*—as a young man and admitted "it had the same effect on me that *Das Kapital* must have on a young Marxist," Williams was eager to do what had to be done in Orlando. His opening-night extravaganza, complete with manufactured mist, strobe lights, soul singers, and dancing girls, was described by Ed Hinton of *The National* as what you might expect "if a Las Vegas revue and a Disney Fourth of July celebration got married and had a baby." It was the Juice's bad luck to open with a whimper in Orlando the same month the Magic opened with a bang, knocking off the Knicks, the Lakers, and the Bulls at home and drawing more fans every single night (fifteen thousand seventy-seven, always a sellout) than the Juice would draw all season. You knew you'd come to the wrong place the moment you pulled into the gravel parking lot at Tinker Field and saw, away in the distance over downtown, giant columns of light crisscrossing the night sky above Orlando Arena, a sign that the Magic were in town.

All of this and more was in the back of Kaufman's mind as he gazed out over rows of empty seats and contemplated the latest humiliation visited on the Juice. Today at noon, an hour before the game, Williams himself had descended on Tinker Field with television cameras and a posse of civic leaders in tow to trumpet Magic owner William du Pont's (yes, of *the* du Ponts) recent purchase of the Orlando minor-league baseball team, the SunRays. Williams pled for support, maintaining that if Orlando ever hoped to attract a major-league team—which it very much did—the best way to impress the expansion committee was by buying lots of tickets for SunRays games.

It was a questionable theory, but so what? Within ten minutes Williams had pledges for seven hundred fifty-four season tickets. The *Sentinel* alone bought a block of one hundred. The following day it ran a column and a long story about the pseudoevent (together with a picture of Williams) on page one of the sports section. The other news from Tinker Field was that the Juice beat the first-place Tropics, 5–0, but that was buried on page two.

After Williams's press conference broke up, some of the local big shots were in no hurry to return to their offices. A few asked for free tickets to the game. The diplomatic thing to do would have been to say yes, of course, please be our guests. But Dillard and Kaufman weren't up to diplomacy, not at this late date. Today they made sure everybody paid, all one hundred fourteen.

TODAY ALSO MARKED THE RETURN TO AMERICAN BASEBALL OF RANDY Bass, once a hero to millions in Japan but virtually unknown in the United States. Bass, a left-handed clone of Greg Luzinski before Luzinski's weight ballooned, took batting practice for the first time before today's game. He used an aluminum bat because he hadn't played in so long he was afraid that if he used a wooden bat, he'd break it. Aluminum bat or not, the mysterious refugee from the Far East put on a stupendous display, sending ball after ball crashing against the concrete façade of the Citrus Bowl while teammates and opponents alike watched in awe. "I haven't picked up a bat or a baseball since May fifth of 1988," Bass explained after he was done, "so it'll take a few days before I'm ready to go."

Bass was a classic example of the minor-league phenom who, for one reason or another, never graduated to stardom in the big leagues. Playing in towns like Melbourne, Wisconsin Rapids,

Lynchburg, Tacoma, and Omaha, Bass hit two hundred twenty homers. In one incredible season in 1980, while in Denver, he batted .333 with thirty-seven homers and one hundred forty-seven RBIs in *one-hundred twenty-three* games and won the minor-league player of the year award. The Padres gave him a shot at first base the following year, but for the fourth time Bass failed to take advantage. All told, he hit only nine homers while playing parts of six seasons in the major leagues.

"When the [1982] season was over, Texas called me and said, 'There's a Japanese team interested in you, do you want to go?'" Bass, a native and still a resident of Lawton, Oklahoma, spoke plainly and without pretense. He stood casually behind the cage with his feet crossed and one toe planted in the dirt, leaning on a bat—the portrait of a slugger. "I said, 'Well, what's the deal?' They told me the money and I said, 'Sure, I'll go.' I mean, I'd been up and down in AAA and only had six or seven years in the big leagues so it didn't look like my career was going forward. It was backing up a little bit. Plus I was getting older. So I went to Japan."

In Japan, Bass was eventually paid more than a million dollars a year by the Hanshin Tigers to hit long homers and drive in lots of runs. In a country where foreigners are often shunned, *Ba-su* became a national hero. He led the Tigers to their first championship in twenty-one years and won two triple crowns, once with the highest batting average (.389) in Japanese baseball history. Bass might also have broken Sadaharu Oh's home-run record (fifty-five) if Oh's Giants hadn't walked him eight times during the last two games of the 1985 season. Bass's popularity was such that he was once paid one hundred eighty-five thousand dollars by Gillette to shave his beard on Japanese television.

In the spring of 1988, Bass's seven-year-old son, Zachary, was diagnosed with a brain tumor. Bass left Japan to join Zachary in San Francisco, where he underwent treatment. The Tigers didn't want Bass to go. They finally agreed to give him two weeks' leave, but when he didn't return on time, they released him. "My son was in a life-or-death situation," Bass said. "My son had a brain tumor. There was no way I was gonna be able to come back in two weeks and they knew that." Resigned, Bass went home to his eight-hundred-acre cattle ranch in Lawton (bought with Japanese yen) and resumed the life he'd left behind when he signed his first pro contract.

Then this winter, at age thirty-five, he got the itch to play baseball again. He went to the winter meetings hoping to find a Japanese team that would take him, but no one was interested. So when the Juice called and invited him to play in the senior league, Bass retrieved the carton of one dozen black Mizuno bats—each individually wrapped in plastic shrink-wrap—from his garage and headed for Orlando. He was anxious to prove he could still play. And if a major-league team saw fit to invite him to spring training, well, let's just say he'd be willing to listen.

"I made my money when I was in Japan," Bass said. "I guess the only reason I came down here for was to get in shape and have a chance to go back and play. I wasn't successful playing in the United States. I went to Japan, had a lot of success, now I'm back. Everybody's looking for a left-handed power hitter and they don't really know what I can do. They don't know how good the Japanese League was. It'll be interesting to see.

"If it happens, it happens. If it don't, it just doesn't and it won't make me one bit of difference. I have about five hundred head of cattle and I was happy doing what I was doing. I've built up my ranch pretty well. I won't feel bad. You know, I'll be thirty-six when the season starts so this is kind of a last shot, that's the way I look at it."

And Zachary? He was much better now, responding well to treatment. If nothing turned up by May, that would be two full years of remission. The doctors were saying now there was a 95 percent chance the cancer would never come back. Still, the tests were repeated every three months. Bass and his wife, Linda, lived with fear every day.

"It's hard when it's a little kid," Bass said. "If it was me it would have been no problem. I've lived my life. But to see your little kid sick, it really makes you sad."

OKEECHOBEE TO ORLANDO, THE ROUTE I DROVE THIS MORNING, WAS about one hundred miles north and west. Orlando to Fort Myers, which I set out to drive this afternoon, was one hundred sixty miles south and west. Another long drive, yes, but Wayne Garland was making his first start tonight for the Sun Sox since the day his "arm died" and I wanted to be there.

Besides, you could usually make good time on central Florida's lonely two-lane blacktops. This afternoon, it seemed like the only other vehicles on U.S. 17 and Florida 31 were semitrailers loaded to overflowing with oranges and grapefruits, driven by crazies who went faster than I would ever dare. I learned to roll down my window whenever they flew by in the opposite direction and inhale deeply.

It was after dark when I arrived in Fort Myers. The moon hung cold and bright between the light poles in right-center. The players huddled around the orange warmth of the electric space heaters in either dugout. Up in the press box, adorned for the holiday season with tacky Christmas decorations, we ate nuts and candies and watched the game through closed windows, grateful not to have to be outdoors. Mike Graham, the strawberry-blond owner of the Sun Sox who went to college in Malibu, stopped by during the middle innings to thaw out. He wore a fleece-collared leather bomber jacket, making no attempt to hide the fact that this was football weather. "Who's fooling who?" he said. "It's cold out there, and everybody knows it."

It was bad weather for hitters. Tim Ireland's twenty-four-game hitting streak ended when he grounded out three times and struck out once. But not so bad weather for pitchers. Mickey Mahler went all the way for the Explorers, holding the Sun Sox to two runs on seven hits. Garland, to my surprise, looked strong through five. He gave up an unearned run in the first inning, then settled down until the sixth, when he served up three hard singles and allowed the tying run to cross the plate on a wild pitch. The game was still tied at the end of nine, but the Explorers pushed across three runs in the tenth off reliever Dave LaRoche and held on to win, 5-2.

For Garland it was another no-decision, his fourth. I was cheered to find him in the clubhouse afterward drinking beer with his right hand, even if he did have to bend over to touch his lips to the can. He had this to say about his arm: "It's numb right now. The pain and the ache was there from the first pitch I threw in the bull pen. Obviously, it didn't hurt as bad as it did last week, but it was still there."

"What happened? Did you get a shot of cortisone or something?"

"No. I guess the main thing is this week I've been going to a chiropractor. He seems to think it's something in my neck. I found out I got a couple of pinched vertebras, and they're cutting off the feeling and the blood to my arm. He helped me out a little bit."

Garland was allowing himself to be hopeful. A pinched vertebra was bad, but not nearly as bad as a torn rotator cuff. Almost any pain was tolerable as long as you knew the chiropractor could make it go away.

"I felt good through five, but in the sixth inning it was just like I had never thrown a pitch, never warmed up or anything like that. That's why Pat [Dobson] got me out of there. He told me to go out there and go as long as I could. That's what I did. I couldn'ta gone back out for the seventh inning, no matter what."

It was nearly 11:00 by the time I left Fort Myers. I'd seen three ball games in the last thirty-six hours. In between I'd driven seven hundred miles. Home (and bed) was still a hundred miles away.

ORLANDO · *December 14*

Plastered all over the restricted regions of the ballpark this afternoon—on lockers, above urinals, in the dugout, by the clubhouse dryer, next to the "412" sign in center field, even on bats in the bat rack—were photocopies of a picture of a Tropics player wearing number twenty-five standing with his hands on his hips and his belly on his belt. Next to the picture, someone had printed, "Will the Real Joe Mincberg Please Suck IN."

Mincberg was number twenty-five on the Tropics, but the player in the photograph wasn't him. It was Jim Bonfiglio, who happened to be wearing Joe's shirt that day. The picture had appeared next to an article about the senior league in *Time* magazine. Not only did *Time* misidentify the player, it also spelled his name "Minceberg."

Now it so happened that the only thing inflated about Mincberg was perhaps his ego. His stomach was flatter than his batting average, .143 at the time. Mincberg was not thrilled at being introduced to the more than four million readers of *Time* as a fat man. His teammates, on the other hand, were delighted.

But there was an undercurrent of resentment in the collective mirth. The point was, Bonfiglio wasn't even a player, he was a lawyer moonlighting as the Tropics' bull-pen catcher. For that matter, Mincberg was a lawyer, too; he played some, but he'd spent most of the season on the taxi squad. Yet *Time* had chosen them to illustrate a story that poked fun at the senior league's "geriatric jocks," old men who, according to *Time*, had been hit with the "cunning humiliations" of age. Some of the ballplayers considered the article an affront to their professionalism. They were afraid people were laughing at them.

"Just a cheap shot," said one who was sitting in the dugout before the game.

"That's exactly what it was," said the one sitting next to him.

"Guys just sitting back in his office in New York . . ." another muttered under his breath.

The incident poisoned the atmosphere in the ballpark. Today, for the first time all season, I introduced myself to a ballplayer and was met with a look of unconcealed suspicion. Before he would allow me to turn on my tape recorder, Tim Stoddard wanted to know, "What are you trying to accomplish?"

Stoddard's jaw and chin were hidden behind a full salt-and-pepper beard. He stood six-seven, weighed maybe two hundred fifty pounds, and had a voice—deep and resonant, like the bass line in a Led Zeppelin song—that went well with his frame. A fastball pitcher, he appeared in four hundred eighty-five games in the major leagues with six different teams, all in relief, and averaged more than seven strikeouts per nine innings. As recently as last summer he had a 2.95 ERA in fourteen games in Cleveland, but the Indians let him go at the end of the season. At age thirty-six, he was coping with the realization that his career in all likelihood was over.

I wanted to answer his question, but before I could even try, he said, "Of course, all you read about this is that we don't want to grow up."

That that characterization was true in a lot of cases, by now I had no doubt. But it wasn't what I assumed the first time I met someone. "What's your motivation?" I asked him.

"It's fun," he said right away. Whoops, wrong answer. Okay, not wrong, incomplete. "I mean, you play this game your whole life, it becomes a part of you. It's just the fact that you've been an athlete since you were six or seven years old. You thrive on competition and trying to win. Maybe you could do the same thing joining a bowling league or a dart league or whatever but when you specialize in something, it's a lot more fun playing against the guys that have been your competition and your peers the whole time.

"You accept the fact that you're not what you were when you were twenty-two. I know that I'm not gonna be as good as I once was. I know I can't throw the ball ninety-five miles an hour anymore. But I know I sure know how to pitch, and I know these guys know how to hit. I'm not going out there thinking it's a joke. Every day I pitch, even now, I learn more about the game. The last time we were here I got knocked out. We ended up winning the game, but I think for me it was the only bad day down here. I was throwing the ball good, I was throwing hard, but it was the way I pitched and the way I let things happen to me out there. You get in ruts, sometimes. You go to one pitch that ten years ago was your main pitch, but now maybe you have to go to that breaking ball. So you try to learn by that, just like you did when you were twenty years old."

To me, Stoddard's attitude about playing in the senior league was the opposite of not wanting to grow up. The point, as I understood him, was not to relive the past. The point was to keep living, growing, learning, developing the craft that had been the object of his interest and devotion ever since he was a child. If the end of an athlete's career was like dying, then to quit while you felt you were still making progress was to commit suicide. Mike Schmidt, who probably retired before his skill was spent, was praised for exiting with dignity and grace. Steve Carlton, who let his talent burn down to the last red ember, was reviled. But which one had more courage?

DYAR MILLER GREW UP ON A FARM IN BATESVILLE, INDIANA, A LIT-tle bit north and west of where the Ohio River makes a left turn and heads toward its reunion with the Mississippi at Cairo, Illinois. There were fourteen seniors in Miller's graduating class and exactly nine boys on the baseball team, which played a seven-game schedule in the fall (spring was for track, and winter was for basketball; there was no football). Miller was a pitcher in high school—he once struck out nineteen batters in one game—but he never won a game. His scholarship at Utah State was for basketball. Unfortunately, he stopped growing when he got to six-one, too small to play forward, too gangly to play guard. So he switched to baseball to keep his scholarship and wound up being drafted.

By the time Miller made it to the big leagues with Baltimore in 1975, he was already twenty-nine years old. From the beginning, he was used mainly in long relief. Once, and only once, he complained.

"Earl," he told his skipper, "I need more work, I can't stay sharp."

"If you can't do it," Weaver replied, "we'll get somebody else who can."

"That was a good answer," Miller said years later when he told me the story.

After the Mets released him in 1981, Miller started over as a pitching coach. He made it back to the majors with the White Sox in 1987 and '88 and last year was a roving instructor in the Tigers' organization. For all his years in pro ball, Miller never made the kind of money that would have enabled him to take winters off. During the off season he was variously a substitute teacher, a gas station attendant, a plumber's assistant, an insurance salesman, and a carpenter. He also played a lot of winter ball. "I was always glad when spring training rolled around," he said.

This winter he caught on as a player-coach with the Juice, a job much more to his liking. Then when Gates Brown was let go two weeks ago, Miller was elevated to manager. I spoke with him before the game in the small private dressing room he shared with another player and part-time coach, Bill Stein.

"Yeah, I'm enjoying it," Miller drawled in a down-home, country-boy accent that made him sound a lot less smart than he was. He had thinning hair and sleepy eyes, and his cheek bulged with chew. While he spoke, he leaned way back in his chair with both hands behind his head. Now and then he reached forward and took a sip of coffee. "Shit, I guess! It's not like the pressure of the major-league thing. You try to let the guys have fun, rest 'em now and then, try to make it an easygoing atmosphere. Gates was trying to run this like a concentration camp. He had curfew. Hell, you don't have to have curfew in this league. I'm forty-three years old, I'm tired, I gotta get my sleep. I'm ready to go to bed at eleven. We *want* our sleep."

Miller chuckled, and Stein joined in.

"See, Gates wanted to get back in baseball. I think he was

trying so hard that he just put pressure on himself. I think the players felt pressure from him. He wanted to win so bad. You know, I don't think there's gonna be many guys go to the big leagues 'cause they managed in this league. Shit, you know, this is no stepping-stone. Bobby Tolan thinks it is. Probably ruined Gates, the way it turned out. Some of these players, they're in the game, they're gonna go back and tell their organizations how things were run down here. Gates is a nice guy. He's just not a real good baseball man."

I asked Miller what it was like to play night after night in an empty house.

"I played so many years in the minor leagues, it doesn't really bother me," he said. "You get used to it. You know, it's like when you go to Yankee Stadium, sixty thousand, you try not to notice the crowds. 'Cause if you notice the crowds at Yankee Stadium you get jittery. You try to block it out of your mind. Here you try to block out the silence. Yankee Stadium in reverse."

"It's hard to get the old adrenaline flowing," Stein put in.

It was time now to go back to work. The Tropics would be finishing batting practice soon, and then it would be the Juice's turn to take infield. Miller and Stein stood up, stretched, and headed for the field. I followed them out the door.

There were exactly nine people in the stands when we got outside—four in seats and five bunched together by a corner of the visiting dugout, hounding for autographs. Miller stood facing the press box, both hands jammed in his back pockets, and swung his head slowly from one end of the grandstand to the other. "Where are all the fans?" he said.

BRADENTON • December 16

A RAINY DAY IN FLORIDA, STEADY ALL MORNING, HARDER AS THE DAY wore on. But the man who answered the phone at McKechnie Field said not to worry, it was sunny in Bradenton. Of course I was skeptical, but I went anyway. The Skyway towers were invisible from the St. Pete side, so leaden and low was the sky, but by the time I topped the crest of the bridge and started down the other side the clouds were already busting up and the blue bay was white with reflected sunlight.

I poked my head in the visitors' clubhouse as soon as I arrived to see what was going on. The Legends were in there: Al Holland and Vida Blue, telling horror stories of Home Run Balls I Have Thrown; Walt Williams, sitting Indian style on the floor in front of a mini-screen color TV watching Saturday-morning cartoons; and Larry Livingston (the mobile-phone salesman from Atlanta, the one with all the hats), dressing excitedly in Legends road grays for yet another tryout.

I'd never seen Livingston throw so I followed him down to the bull pen. Luis Tiant—signed by the Legends as a pitching coach after the Suns released him—was waiting on the mound, throwing easily to Chuck Fick, the backup catcher. When Livingston arrived, Tiant flipped him the ball, then stepped back off the mound, crossed his arms, puffed out his chest, arranged his face in a big-league scowl, and prepared to pass judgment.

Livingston looked a tad distracted. When Fick stepped aside in favor of first-stringer Clint Hurdle, Livingston made the mistake of giggling. He was nervous, was all, but Hurdle got the wrong idea. "What's the matter," Hurdle said sneeringly. "You don't think I'm a real catcher?"

Poor Larry, of course he meant no insult. "I'm just happy to be here," he said, and again he giggled. Hurdle looked disgusted. He made a show of settling into his crouch.

It was as if a chasm had opened between the mound and the plate, the chasm that separated those who were once in the big leagues from those who weren't. Hurdle had no idea who this Livingston was. He only knew he hadn't "played," and to Hurdle that told him all he needed to know. When Hurdle's first throw came back wide and soft, and Livingston reached out and caught it with his bare left hand, Hurdle took it as another insult. From that point on, Livingston was doomed. When Livingston threw his fastball, Hurdle caught it in such a way that the pop was muffled. When Livingston threw his curve and it bounced in front of the plate, Hurdle took extra time to wipe the dirt off his glove.

Livingston was just getting warmed up when Hurdle shouted, "Hey, el Tiant! ¿Cuanto mas?"

Tiant looked at one more pitch, then asked for the ball. End of tryout.

GRAIG NETTLES, ONCE THE LEGENDS' MANAGER, HAD A FUN DAY
today against his old teammates. Nettles had three hits, including a three-run homer in the fourth off Vida Blue that broke
open a close game and sent the Explos on their way to a 14–5
romp.

"Those things happen," said Bobby Bonds, Nettles's succes-
sor, after the game. Bonds sat shirtless on a stool in the manager's dressing room, smoking a Players cigarette and eating from
a paper plate, which he held in his hand like a waiter's tray. The
sideburns I remembered were gone, but Bonds still wore his hair
in a longish Afro. "Vida didn't have his good stuff today," Bonds
said. "He'd be the first to tell you."

Ray Negron, general manager of the Legends, said the reason
he chose Bonds to replace Nettles was because Bonds com-
manded more automatic respect from his peers than any other
player on the team. Bonds played fourteen years in the major
leagues, the first seven with the Giants and the last seven split
among seven other teams. His unique gift was an unprecedented
combination of speed and power. Five times in his career he hit
thirty or more homers while stealing thirty or more bases. If he
had one glaring weakness it was that he struck out, on average,
once every four at-bats. Bonds set the major-league record for
strikeouts in a season with one hundred eighty-seven in 1969,
then broke his own record with one hundred eighty-nine in 1970.
Though he was a coach for four years with the Cleveland Indians, the Legends were the only club he had ever managed.

The first question I asked Bonds after we talked about the
game was "Do you want to manage in the big leagues?" Then I
listened.

"I don't think about that. They only got two black managers
in the big leagues, why would I think about that? They don't
hire black managers. Until that changes, I don't look at this as
nothing but doing it here. I'm not a dreamer. Reality is reality.
They don't hire black managers."

The clubhouse boy stuck his head in the room and asked
Bonds if he wanted something to drink. Bonds asked for a soft
drink.

"Reality is reality," he said again, "so why should I think this
is gonna get me someplace when that's something they don't
do?

"No [to the clubhouse boy], that's diet.

"If they were hiring black managers in the big leagues, it'd be different. It's hard enough for black people to get a coaching job in the big leagues, let alone be a manager. They keep saying it's getting better, but I don't see it. Until they honestly start making the decision to do it, I don't even worry about it."

The clubhouse boy returned for the second time and handed Bonds a Pepsi. Bonds thanked him, opened it, and took a long swallow.

"They didn't talk about two *men* battling for first place in the American League East [in 1989], they talked about two *black* men. It's almost the year 1990 and they're talking about two *black* men, that shows you how ridiculous it is. Tony LaRussa was just Tony LaRussa and Roger Craig was just Roger Craig. But yet if it's a black man, then they constantly use that. Until people come to the realization that a man is a man and a woman is a woman, that's the only time things are gonna open up. But as long as they want to pit color against color, it never will open up.

"Talk about Art Shell with Oakland [Raiders]. It's just a shame that you have to go so many years and they still bring that up. I don't care if he's black, white, yellow, green, purple, or any type of nationality. He's a man and that's the way you should look at it. When people understand that, are willing to accept that, then you'll see changes. Changes are made by a person's heart. When the heart changes, the person will change. As long as you have a hard heart, you will have a hard person. And the only ones that can soften the heart are the individuals themselves.

"Coming from when I signed in '64 to now, there have been changes in certain areas. Not rapid change, but there *has* been a very very very very very very slow process of change. But you know, that's just life. You just have to think about what you can do and not worry about it. If an opportunity's gonna come, it's gonna come. If it's not gonna come, it's not gonna come. I've learned through this game that nothing surprises me."

SAMMY STEWART'S PICTURE WAS IN THE SARASOTA PAPER TODAY, only it wasn't the sports page. His eyes were half closed, he was sort of smiling, and he was holding a sign under his chin that said "Manatee County Sheriff's Department." The headline read: "Pitcher Accused of Threat with Knife."

One week after the Pelicans sold Stewart to the Explorers,

general manager Rick Langford released him (thereby releasing himself from the obligation to pay Jim Morley two thousand dollars). Since then Stewart had been living in Bradenton with his wife, apparently hoping to catch on with another team.

According to the story in the paper, Stewart was arrested after a woman ran into the lobby of the Bradenton Police Department screaming that Stewart was beating his wife and threatening to kill her and two friends. "I will kill you all, nobody will leave this room alive," Stewart said, according to police reports.

When police arrived at Stewart's home, they found him seated in the living room with a sheathed hunting knife in his pocket. At the officers' request, Stewart placed the knife on a television stand. Then he tried to escape through the back door. Police arrested him a block away.

Two days later, Stewart remained in custody at Manatee County Jail. Bail was set at twenty-four thousand seven hundred ninety-five dollars. End of comeback.

BRADENTON · December 17

TODAY WAS CIVIC CLUB DAY AT THE BALLPARK, ANOTHER HALF-desperate, somewhat successful promotion. Lions, Kiwanians, Rotarians, and the like, together with their families, were admitted free. Santa Claus landed on the infield in a helicopter before the game and passed out candy canes. One thousand five hundred thirty-three fans passed through the gates, twice the average number for McKechnie. It was not known how many actually paid for their tickets.

The guy I was looking for today was Walt Williams. The last time I'd seen Williams before this winter was nearly twenty years ago. Three of us had driven down to Florida with our junior-high baseball coach for spring training. Most of the trip's details I'd forgotten (I was only fourteen), but Williams I remembered. One afternoon outside old Payne Field in Sarasota he had passed right by me on his way to the team bus, a muscular black man in red-and-white pinstripes who was about my height, maybe twice my weight, and, as far as I could tell, had no neck.

I found Williams in the clubhouse, both arms draped over the windowsill, watching the pregame action in the outfield. Williams had played for a couple of years in Mexico and Japan after his major-league career ended in 1975. Afterward, back home in Texas, he'd opened a body shop that specialized in custom paint jobs. Later he ran a rec center in Brownwood, his hometown. "I enjoyed that," Williams said in a surprisingly high voice, "because I played basketball and dominoes and those are two of my favorite pastimes."

Williams was happy on the outside. He wasn't looking to get back into baseball. But in 1988 he was offered a job as a big-league coach with Jim Fregosi's White Sox. It turned out to be a miserable experience. "It was right after the black thing," Williams said, referring to Al Campanis's "Nightline" fiasco, which forced baseball to examine its hiring practices. "I felt like they wanted me on the field for basically that purpose. I didn't really feel comfortable. I felt like an outcast."

Williams was fired after one year by the White Sox because, he was told, he lacked experience ("How can they hire you with no experience and fire you with one year's experience?"). Then last summer he joined the Rangers as a coach with their AA affiliate in Tulsa. It was a step backward professionally, but Williams didn't care. "It was the happiest year I've had in a long time," he said. "I felt like I was a part of the organization and that's a big thing with me. The front office was just super. It was like a dream, them being so nice. It was like it was scary. I felt like I wasn't just a token."

As long as it had been since Williams last played, people still remembered his nickname. PA announcers all around the league always made a point of introducing him as "No-Neck." I wondered if that bothered him, too. "Who gave you that nickname?" I asked him.

"I was seventeen years old," he said. "I'd signed with the Astros out in California, a place called Modesto. I was on a ten-day trial and then I was leading the league in hitting so they sent for me to come to Houston. You know, they didn't think they'd signed a guy that was capable of winning a batting title so they wanted to look me over, I guess.

"So Paul Richards and Eddie Robinson both came to my room, and, I can't remember which one said to the other one, 'Look, this guy doesn't have a neck.' And then the next day it was like blown up in the papers that Houston has a no-neck outfielder.

People was thinking I had literally no neck. And that kind of grew and grew, then everybody started in. When a baseball player gets some kind of joke on you, its kinda run into the ground.

"But I had a manager, named the late Grover Resinger, with the Cardinals organization. And he told me, he says, 'Look, Walt'—'cause I resented the name, at first—but he told me, 'Look, when you're gone out of baseball, people will remember your nickname a lot better than they will your real name.' And I always respected Grover. After that I didn't resent it anymore."

TONY BARTIROME, THE EXPLOS' TRAVELING SECRETARY, WAS OVERheard in the press box telling somebody on the phone that the Explos were going with Davy Crockett today. Of course he was kidding. In fact, today's starting pitcher was Daniel Boone—a former reliever with the Padres and Astros who really was a direct descendant (seventh generation) of *the* Daniel Boone. *The* Daniel Boone was a man (remember?), yes, a *biiiiig* man. But this Daniel Boone was only five-eight ("I can stretch to five-nine if I want"), weighed one hundred forty-five pounds, and wore a size seven shoe.

Boone was not the smallest man ever to pitch in the big leagues. Bobby Shantz, who won twenty-four games for the A's in 1952, was only five-six and weighed one hundred thirty-nine pounds. Boone thought he might have had the slightest build overall, height and weight, but that honor probably went to a fellow named Nick Carter, who won two games for the 1908 Philadelphia A's, then disappeared. Carter, they say, was five-eight, one hundred twenty-six pounds.

In any case, Boone was definitely the smallest pitcher Floyd Rayford of the Legends had ever had the pleasure of facing. Rayford sat on his hands in the dugout before the game, watching Boone warm up, salivating at the thought of the feast that awaited him. "I'm gonna kill that midget," he said over and over, "I'm gonna kill that midget."

Well, Rayford certainly tried. He swung hard every time. But Boone gave him nothing but junk and the result, predictably, was three soft grounders to third. Boone not only survived; he went seven and two thirds innings in his first start for the Explos and was the winning pitcher as Bradenton swept the three-game series with St. Lucie.

Afterward, I had to wait while Gary Carter interviewed Boone
for television. Boone, who last pitched professionally in 1982,
was until a few weeks ago working in construction for a developer
in Carlsbad, California. For several years now he'd been pitching
in an over-thirty league in San Diego. He would have liked to have
gone to camp with a senior-league team in the fall, but no one
invited him, and he couldn't afford to make the trip on his own.
Then the week before Thanksgiving, Bradenton manager Clete
Boyer called. The Explos were looking for help and John D'Acquisto had mentioned his name. Was he interested?

"So I told my boss," Boone explained as we walked back to
the clubhouse after his interview, " 'There's a chance I might
go to the senior league, what do we need to do?'

"He said, 'Oh, we'll try to get you a leave of absence.'

"Well, it happened to where I had to take off so quick. The
Wednesday before Thanksgiving, it still wasn't finalized. I didn't
talk to Rick Langford until Friday and I left without getting a
leave of absence. Gosh, they're pretty good people. I think I
might be able to talk them into taking me back."

Boone wore a mustache that was enormous, especially for a
man his size. It looked like a bow tie the way it sat on his lip.
His eyes were blue marbles, very serious. I asked him how many
different kinds of pitches he threw today.

"Gosh, fastball, curveball, slider, screwball, fork ball, and
knuckleball. Six."

"Does that mean you need a catcher with six fingers?"

"Well, the curveball and the slider is the same, it's two. Then
the fork ball is three and the screwball is four and the knuckleball is five." Boone wiggled all five fingers, the way his catcher
did when he called for the knuckler.

"Have you always thrown so many pitches?"

"From Little League on up. I watched big leaguers on TV and
listened to the different pitches they threw and just went out
and played catch and worked on them. I knew—you know, from
my size and everything—that I didn't have a whole lot of speed
on the ball so I had to develop these other pitches. That's what
I mainly worked at. It's always been easy to throw a fastball for
a strike, but then if you can throw all the other ones for strikes,
that's the big key. When I'm behind, and the hitters are looking
for a fastball, I got three, four, five pitches that I can use besides
my fastball."

The other day, Boone said, his boss back in Carlsbad had written him a letter, just to let him know that he was fired. Boone meant to write back. He felt he could explain. But so far he hadn't gotten around to it.

"Actually, I got something even deeper in mind." Boone half smiled and looked at the ground. "I'd like to go to spring training with the San Diego Padres," he said. "That's my big hope."

ST. PETERSBURG · *December 18*

Dock (not a nickname) Ellis was hanging out in the coaches' locker room before the game, waiting for the fog to break. Outside, the field was in pretty good shape except that a cloud was sitting on it. When you stood at home plate, you couldn't see the outfield wall. The men of St. Petersburg's Department of Leisure Services (that's Parks and Recreation everywhere else) were out there spreading sand in the infield and hoping for the cloud to go away, but so far it didn't look very promising.

Ellis hadn't even bothered to get dressed yet. He wore shower slippers and a pair of gray, knee-length cutoffs. The only visible hair on his body, apart from his eyebrows, was a scruffy goatee in black and gray, the official facial-hair colors of the senior league. The dome of his head was as shiny and round as a bowling ball. Burned into his left shoulder, I noticed, was a blue tattoo: "Manhattan Dock."

"Manhattan Dock?"

"They had Broadway Joe," said Ellis. "When I got to New York they had Manhattan Dock. They didn't play off my Manhattan Dock the way they played off of Broadway Joe."

Probably because he wasn't there long enough. More often than not during his twelve-year career—which began in Pittsburgh the summer Martin Luther King, Jr., was assassinated and took him to New York, Oakland, Texas, back to New York, and finally back to Pittsburgh in 1979—Ellis had no trouble at all getting other people to pay attention to him. He wore curlers in his hair, routinely spoke out against authority, exploded periodically in fits of rage, and generally did whatever he could, whenever he could, to force his black, defiant self down the throats of the timid white world of baseball fandom.

"It's the white man's game and they just allowed me to play in it, that's all. That's why I was a motherfucker when I played. I told them motherfuckers when I could not throw a ball, they were gonna kiss my ass out of the game and I would never look back and they would never want me back in that motherfucking game again. I told them, 'While you use me, I'm gonna use your ass.' Only thing I could not control was their money. I tried to get as much out of them as I could, and they got out of me as much as I wanted to give them and that was it."

But there was more to Ellis's story than one black man's rebellion against racism in the American Pastime. Ellis was also a drug addict, a fact he freely admitted now that he was in recovery and working with other addicts as a substance-abuse counselor.

"I'm a dope-fiend alcoholic," Ellis would say. Or else, "I'm a sick motherfucker." Then he'd look hard right at you with his eyes bugged wide open and a scowl on his face that was designed to elicit the maximum reaction. And then he'd laugh, an insane man's head-ringing cackle that turned out to be his way of putting you at ease.

Ellis was speeding on greenies when he made his major-league debut in 1968. He was high on LSD, he boasted, the June day in 1970 that he pitched a no-hitter against the Padres. In fact, Ellis claimed that until this winter when he joined the Pelicans—at the invitation of Bobby Tolan, a childhood friend—he had never once ventured between the foul lines when he wasn't high on *something*.

"An alcoholic always feels that they're in control," Ellis said, explaining. "They're the last one to know. There was no way that you coulda told me I had a problem. I knew that I could drink a lot and do a lot of drugs so how could I have a problem? I could stop when I wanted to, it's just that I didn't want to stop. *Heeh-heeh-heeeh!*"

"So what made you change?"

"What happened to me was, I started drinking Scotch. I drank Chivas Regal for ten months before I admitted to myself that that was Scotch. I called it high-class brandy. I went to sell a Cadillac one time and I found ten bottles under the seat."

"Full or empty?" The question came from Ozzie Virgil, Sr. He was the only other person in the room. Until now, he'd shown no sign that he was paying attention.

"They were empty," Ellis said.

"Aw, shit."

"It's just that I had started drinking Scotch," Ellis continued, "and I'd swore I'd never drink Scotch as long as I lived. It was like, if I drink Scotch, I'm a real alcoholic. *Heeh-heeh!* Yeah, a kid used to throw me drugs in the big leagues. I used to get the best drugs from the kids in the stands. They throw good marijuana, cocaine, amphetamines, black beauties, heroin, anything you want, they throw it to you."

"Why do they do that?"

"They know you cool. They know you get high. You cannot fool kids. It's your manner, your behavior. And management swear they can't see it! But they got a twelve-year-old in the stands that *knows* this motherfucker gets *loaded.* They got managers and coaches sit right there looking at the motherfucker and swear they can't see shit. Some of them really don't know!"

"All the years that I coached, I never could tell," said Virgil. "The only thing that I could go by was what I heard."

"Yeah," said Dock.

"I mean, I could see guys acting the way they act—'What the fuck's this guy acting this fucking crazy?' "

"Yeah."

"But I never thought—well, all that group we had in Montreal." Virgil was the Expos' third-base coach from 1976 through 1981. "I *heard* they were doing it, but I never saw 'em. I never saw 'em."

"It's gonna get worse now," said Ellis. "They got some new shit coming. They got a new drug out now called ice. Ice is like an amphetamine. It's a quick high and cheap. It's better than rock cocaine.

"They got a problem in the motherfucking game, and they don't want to admit it. That's all it is. Half the top executives in baseball are drunks. What are they gonna do?"

ST. PETERSBURG · *December 19*

THE FOG NEVER BROKE. IF ANYTHING TODAY IT WAS THICKER. OZZIE Virgil went outside early and hit fungoes in the outfield to Jim Morley and a couple of players, but they couldn't catch what they couldn't see and eventually gave up. I took a walk in the outfield and almost got lost. When I got back to the dugout, my shoes were covered with wet clippings from the freshly mowed grass. About four o'clock they turned on the stadium lights, or so I gathered from the blurry balls of colored lights that suddenly appeared overhead.

Bill Lee spent most of the afternoon in the visiting clubhouse playing cards with his teammates, though he did stick his head outside long enough to sniff the wind and go on record with a weather prediction: "It's raining to the north of us, it's hot to the south of us—record heat in Miami. So we're in a war zone, right in between. What'll happen is, the storm comes in when the fog is still here. Then it rains, cold front comes through— wind comes out of the northwest—clears up, drops to thirty."

Well, we'd see. Super Sox owner Mitch Maxwell was here from Winter Haven for the series with St. Pete, staying with the team at the Hilton across the street. He'd been sorry to see yesterday's game canceled. Under Ed Nottle, the Sox were climbing steadily in the standings—sixteen and thirteen since Lee was fired and only a game now behind second-place Orlando. It was a good time to be playing the first-place club.

But all he could do right now was wait and hope that the fog would lift. And as he sat in the dugout in the gathering gloom, his thoughts turned to money matters. Maxwell had just completed a round of visits with the other league owners, as many as would talk to him. According to Maxwell, the last couple of weeks had been a hard time for all of them. They'd been looking forward to Thanksgiving and the arrival of the first snowbirds. But when Thanksgiving came and went without any noticeable effect on attendance, their spirits plunged.

The fact was, their only real source of revenue was attendance and that was lousy. The TV contract with Prime cable network had brought in a grand total of one hundred fifty thousand dollars, or less than twenty thousand dollars per team. The deal with Merchandising Corporation of America for the league's licensing rights (including baseball cards) was worth another twenty-five thousand per team, one-third of the *per-player* revenue last year in the big leagues. Apart from the MCA deal, the only other corporate sponsorship the league had sold was an arrangement with AT&T for sixty thousand dollars, which, once it was divided eight ways, amounted to pocket change.

No, attendance was basically it, that and whatever local sponsorships the teams had managed to sell on their own. What that meant, Maxwell predicted, was first-season operating losses of between seven hundred thousand dollars and one million dollars per team, and that beyond the one hundred fifty thousand owed Morley under the original franchise agreement. Realizing that, Maxwell had felt the need to poll the other owners.

"Everybody was sort of down," Maxwell said. "I wanted to make sure we were all committed to next year because, quite frankly, if we weren't committed to next year, with the kinds of losses that we've suffered, we should all just close now. We're all gonna lose another three, four hundred thousand in the month of January. That's fine to lose if you're prepared to make it back next year. But if five of the guys said, 'This sucks, I want out,' then it would have been better to pull the plug on January first."

According to Maxwell, all the owners were still in. They'd agreed to stick it out until the end of the year on the assumption that they'd all be back for at least a year two of the senior league. Come next fall, though, there would have to be changes. For one, Maxwell saw a lot of fat in the league budget, originally projected at $1.5 million but so far running at $1.8 million.

"The league has not been run well in the first year," Maxwell said. "We've pissed away a lot of money. We've spent money on salaries for people that didn't perform. We've spent a lot of money that didn't put people in the seats. No disparagement to Rick Horrow, he's a terrific guy, but Rick should be in his office every day selling this league. And Curt [Flood] has got to do more for what he's being paid than be a figurehead. That's just wrong."

Secondly, there would undoubtedly be a shuffling of franchises, beginning with Maxwell's own. "I'll tell you today for the record," Maxwell said. "I'm not staying in Winter Haven." Maxwell had made up his mind in mid-December, on Chamber of Commerce Night at the ballpark. Maxwell and his staff spent weeks planning the event and were hoping for a strong show of support from the local business community. But that night only two members of the Chamber of Commerce actually showed up. "I was very, very angry," Maxwell said, and then he launched into an exploration of his favorite metaphor.

"Sometimes you go out with a woman and she goes to bed

with you because you say hello. And sometimes you go out with a woman and you woo her and you do whatever you think you have to do and she's just not interested in going to bed with you. Winter Haven is not interested in getting laid, they're just not interested."

Maxwell knew why. There were lots of reasons: Winter Haven was too small; it had no TV station of its own; no newspaper that everybody read; there were too many old people; the list went on. "People move to Winter Haven because they don't want this kind of thing," Maxwell said. "They move to Winter Haven because they don't want traffic. They move to Winter Haven to die. We need to be in a market where people want to live."

But Maxwell recognized that there was more to it than that. Winter Haven was not like the coastal cities of Florida. There were fewer nonwhites in Winter Haven, fewer eccentrics, fewer outsiders, and generally less tolerance. Maxwell had done his best to cater to the local establishment. He paid two hundred dollars to join the Chamber of Commerce, went to all the meetings, tried to fit in with the boys. But he had never felt accepted, and now he felt like he finally understood.

"I'm glad this won't be printed until after I'm out of there," Maxwell said, speaking confidentially. "They don't like the fact that I'm from New York. They don't like the background I have. And they don't like the fact that I'm Jewish. That's just a fact. It's wrong, it's unfair, but it's a fact."

LAST FRIDAY AT 9:30 A.M., Mike Marshall finished teaching his last class of the semester at Henderson State University in Arkadelphia, Arkansas, then got in his car and drove straight through, fifteen hours, to his home in Zephyrhills, Florida. On Saturday, after a few hours' sleep, he got back in his car and drove to Fort Myers, where he put on a Super Sox uniform, threw some BP, threw in the bull pen, and pitched one inning late in the game. It was his first appearance on the mound since he gave up playing semipro ball in 1985. "We were ahead, twelve-four, so it wasn't a big deal," Marshall explained, "and I was everywhere."

Marshall, a fourteen-year major-league veteran, earned a doctor's degree in physical education in 1978, after "delaying my entrance into the education field." His specialty was kinesiology, which combined principles of mechanics and anatomy in the study of human movement. At Henderson State, Marshall taught kinesiology and exercise physiology and was also coach of the baseball team, which gave him a laboratory for the practical application of his theories.

Marshall planned to spend this Christmas vacation pitching for the Super Sox. He would have started yesterday's game, but it was fogged out. If the fog ever lifted, he'd get his chance tonight.

"Are you excited about starting a game?" I asked him. We were standing behind home plate in the nearly empty stadium.

Marshall looked at me quizzically, as if I were a freshman who'd just made a queer observation in class. He puffed himself up like a professor at a podium and cocked his head a finger's width off-center. He had a sculpted, gray-stubble mustache and a microscopic goatee that was contained in the cleft of his chin. "I don't know about excited," he said. "I've been in baseball too long to think about excited."

All I meant was that he was starting rather than relieving. Of the seven hundred twenty-three games in which he'd appeared in the big leagues, all but twenty-four were in relief.

That was true, Marshall said. But after he was released by the Mets in 1981, he'd pitched for years in a college-kids summer league, where he was used exclusively as a starter. "I once pitched three complete games in one day up in Jacksonville," he said. "I pitched at nine, at noon, and then another game started at ten-thirty that night, finished at one, and I pitched a complete game there. Then I came back at noon the next day and pitched a perfect game. I finished all the games I started."

Marshall gave up competing four years ago, but he still threw every day during baseball season at Henderson State. "Just 'cause I love to throw," Marshall said. "I've learned more probably in the last five years teaching kids how to pitch than I ever knew before that, so now I can incorporate some of the things that I've taught. I've figured out a couple of things that would have helped me if I'd known 'em. That's what I tell my kids: 'If I could have thrown that pitch then that I can throw now . . .' "

There it was again, the senior-league refrain, a variation of the age-old lament that sooner or later occurred to everyone—not just ballplayers—who had a chance to grow old. Marshall was simply adding his voice to the chorus.

"They all look at me like I'm crazy, but that's the truth," he said ingenuously. "I never knew how to throw a curveball. I finally figured it out last year. There are secrets to all these pitches. I understand the secret to the screwball, there's no question about that. I *know* that. Nobody knows that one like I do. I figured out the secret to the fastball. That doesn't mean I'm ever gonna throw a hundred miles an hour, but I understand and I've taught some kids. Proper technique. Training and technique. I understand that now. But I never understood the curveball until last year. I finally figured it out. Down at Fort Myers I threw some great curveballs, some *unhittable* curveballs. Unfortunately, they fooled the umpire as well and he didn't call 'em.

"But in any case, I wanted to come down here, throw against some people that knew how to swing a bat, put this new stuff into play, see what happens. I'm gonna get a chance to step out there and let 'er go. It's gonna be fun."

If it ever happened. As we were talking, the cloud opened up and it began to rain. Not heavily, but enough to force the official postponement of tonight's game. Marshall's debut would have to wait until after Christmas.

SARASOTA • *January 3, 1990*

AL HOLLAND WAS LATE ARRIVING AT THE BALLPARK TONIGHT. THE game between the Legends and the Explorers was originally scheduled for Bradenton, but because of continued poor attendance the Explorers had booked Payne Park in neighboring Sarasota for two nights to test the market. Anyway, by the time Holland showed up, something didn't feel right in the clubhouse.

"Hey," Holland said in a low voice to teammate Roy Thomas. "Who's our manager?"

"Bobby [Bonds]," said Thomas, then added doubtfully, "I think."

"We had a team meeting?"

"Oh, that," said Thomas. "New owner."

Though the deal was not yet finalized, and no formal announcement was expected until later in the week, the players were told today that Joe Sprung and Burt Abrams had sold their controlling interest in the Legends to one Lenny Woolf of Detroit. The sale brought with it a fresh infusion of cash for a franchise that had long been operating on the brink of insolvency. Traveling secretary Doug Kemp was up in the press box before the game, stuffing envelopes with more than two thousand dollars' worth of meal money for the Legends' six-day road trip, money that in the past had been arbitrarily withheld by Sprung. According to Kemp, the funds had been drawn from a new account controlled by Woolf.

The Legends had a special fan in the stands tonight, none other than Don Cooper, the pitcher who was banished from the senior league in November because he wasn't old enough. Since then, another Legends pitcher, Randy Niemann, had also been expelled when it turned out he was only thirty-four. Cooper was originally from New York City but lived now in Sarasota. He had glass-blue eyes like a malamute and short blond hair he wore greased and spiked.

First question: "How old are you, Don?"

"Uhhh," he said. It looked like he was adding in his head. "I'm thirty-five."

"But, Don, *The Baseball Encyclopedia* says you're thirty-two."

"The records were burned in a fire. In an orphanage fire."

Jim Nettles, sitting next to Cooper, laughed out loud when he heard that. Nettles was a teammate of Cooper's on the Legends before he was released and signed by the Explorers. He was out of uniform tonight because he was injured. "You been around [Legends general manager Ray] Negron a long time," he said. "You can lie with the best of them."

Cooper tried again. "Legitimately, I do not have a birth certificate. Every year I played, I made myself as young as I could. If I went to another team, I'd try to shave a year off. If I had kept playing I would have retired at twenty-five."

That sounded plausible. It was an old trick, one ballplayers had been pulling for years. You made yourself younger so nobody would think you were too old to play. Usually, you did it when you signed your first contract. Of course you never dreamed at the time that there would come a day when you'd be too *young* to play.

"How old were you when you signed with the Yankees?" I asked him.

"Excuse me? I was twenty. Legitimately, between you and I, I'm gonna be thirty-four in January. But I know a lot of other guys in the league who are not eligible to play. What am I gonna do, blow the whistle on those guys?" Cooper lowered his voice. "Look, if I was in relief getting my tits lit up, nobody woulda cared. But I'm starting, doing well, overexposed a little bit, and now the jig was up. I don't see the big deal being thirty-four or thirty-five. Which I am, I'm thirty-four."

First he said he was thirty-five, then he said he was thirty-three, now he said he was thirty-four. The book still said he was thirty-two.

Again he lowered his voice. "Legitimately, I'm a little young. I did it because I wanted to have fun and play, you know? And to take it away, the fun"—Cooper pursed his lips and looked disgusted—"it's not like I was tearing up the league and blowing people away. I was just another player."

"How did you—"

"Think I'd get away with it? I looked at it like, 'Who would care?' Who am I? I'm not a big name. To me, you know what that's like? At the end of the day the bell rings and the teacher's forgotten to give you the homework. And some little nerd in the back says, 'Teacher, you forgot to give the homework!' Why would somebody want to be mean and take my fun away? Why would somebody care that much?"

Out on the field, Felix Millan climbed up out of the dugout on his way to the third-base coaching box. "Hey, Felix!" Cooper called out. "What's up? Why don't you play tonight? Gotta get your legs in there." Millan smiled, and Cooper watched him walk away.

"You take everything bad that happened," he said finally, "it still was a lot of fun, a real lot of fun. The best time was in the clubhouse, just being around a lot of guys who played a long time. Nice people. Nice people. I heard they put 'Youngster' on my locker when I left. It was fun—fun and a lot of laughs. That's what I miss most. They took away my fun."

A CLOUDY MIDDLE-OF-THE-WEEK AFTERNOON IN WINTER HAVEN, THE crowd better than average by Super Sox standards: six hundred seventy-seven humans and one cocker spaniel. The dog lay napping on the roof of the visiting dugout, nose on paws. When a foul ball rattled the screen behind home plate, he stood up, turned around in a tight circle, fretted for as long as it took Rick Wise to make two more pitches, then lay down, sighed pointedly, and went back to sleep. Zachary Maxwell, the owner's eight-year-old son, roamed the stands in a cowboy hat and new leather boots, waving his silver six-shooter in the faces of innocent fans, shouting "Bang-bang-bang!" Zachary paid no more attention to the game than did the cocker spaniel, until he had to go to the bathroom. Zachary preferred the private bathroom in the press box. He was there for some time. When he called out for updates, I called out the score.

Thanks to a couple of mid-December fog-outs, nearly two months had passed since the last series between the Super Sox and the Pelicans. The passage of time and two managerial changes in Winter Haven—Ed Nottle was out, Leon Roberts was in—had failed to improve relations between the two teams. The Super Sox were still fuming over the cumulative 47–16 drubbing they had suffered at the hands of the Pelicans in the first week of the season. The consensus in Winter Haven and elsewhere was that St. Petersburg had violated at least the spirit of the law in the senior league by packing its roster with scads of unknown journeymen who barely qualified under the age limit. Half the guys on the team no one had ever heard of, guys like catcher Butch Benton, a former first-round draft choice of the Mets who hit .162 over the course of a forgettable fifty-one-game major-league career before resurfacing this winter in the senior league. Benton had turned thirty-two—the minimum for catchers—on August 24, just six weeks before training camp opened. He was currently the Pelicans' leading hitter with a .355 batting average and a .524 slugging percentage. Benton had even inspired a new term, "the Butch

Bentons of the league," describing all players whose talent far exceeded their drawing power.

There was a historical precedent for this kind of development. Organized baseball began as a way for rich kids to amuse themselves. Early clubs like the New York Knickerbockers and the Brooklyn Excelsiors played the game for fun, not money. Membership was based on class first and talent second. The clubs banded together in 1858 to form the National Association of Base Ball Players, specifically to protect baseball's amateur status, and keep the working stiffs off the diamond.

"Almost from the outset, however," wrote Peter Levine in his book A. G. *Spalding and the Rise of Baseball,* "this amateur 'gentlemen's game' was transformed. . . . Those clubs that openly claimed high membership standards . . . found the desire to win so overwhelming that they increasingly admitted as members anyone whose qualifications consisted of baseball talent rather than of requisite social status. Indeed, by 1865 . . . such clubs were not above charging admission, paying ballplayers, or providing them with full-time jobs off the diamond because of their performance on it."

Now, a century and a half later, the undesirables weren't professionals, they were no-names. In all other respects, the issue was identical. The only way to keep the Butch Bentons out of the senior league was by changing the rules to require a minimum amount of major-league experience. Otherwise, not just the Pelicans but every other team would eventually give in to competitive pressures and go after the best players they could find, to hell with the spirit of the league. The Super Sox could cry foul all they wanted, but there was nothing they could do about it.

Thanks to a 2–1 win last night—the Super Sox's first ever against the Pelicans—the mood throughout the organization was somewhat brighter, although plenty of bitterness remained. Rick Maxwell, the Super Sox general manager, stopped by briefly during the game and whispered two anecdotal tidbits in my ear, neither of which appeared in the Pelicans' media notes. According to Maxwell, Sox reliever Pedro Borbon had known Pelicans manager Bobby Tolan when they were teammates in Cincinnati, "and Tolan was a jerk then, too," and the clubhouse boys hated to see the Pelicans come to town "because they're the worst tippers in the senior league."

Another win today would have meant a sweep of the two-game series, and no doubt made the Sox feel even better. They had their chances, but Bill Lee couldn't hold a two-run lead, and in the end the powerful Pelicans won again, 9–6. The loss buried the Sox deeper in last place in the northern division with a record of twenty and twenty-six.

Tomorrow the Sox would leave on an important road trip— three games in West Palm Beach against the team with the best overall record in the league, then across the state for a two-game series in Fort Myers, then up to Orlando for a make-up double-header, the first in senior-league history. Thanks to a format that generously awarded play-off berths to two teams in each four-team division, the Sox were still in the hunt, only four games behind second-place Orlando. But time was running out. With seven games to play in the next six days, the time for the Super Sox to make their move was now or never.

The Super Sox team bus was scheduled to depart from behind the clubhouse tomorrow morning at 11:00. I had already made plans to be on it.

WEST PALM BEACH · *January 5*

Bussie PULLED HIS LUMBERING RIG OUT OF THE CHAIN O' LAKES complex, turned right past the Citrus Showcase (a civic arena with a dome that's supposed to look like an orange peel), drove out of town on Cyprus Gardens Boulevard, and eventually made his way to old Florida 60, which crossed the peninsula at its midsection from Clearwater on the Gulf of Mexico to Vero Beach on the Atlantic. The day was young, and the journey was just beginning.

This was no luxury coach like the ones I'd been hearing about. There was no VCR, no deep-plush upholstery. The seats were narrow and vinyl-covered and reclined just far enough to tempt you into thinking that sleep was possible when it was not. According to the ancient custom of the road, the rowdies—led by Bernie Carbo and Scipio Spinks—commandeered the back of the bus. Being ballplayers, they played cards. A plastic cooler in the aisle, weighted down with beer and soda and covered with a clean white towel, served as a table. The rowdies played a game called pluck, an esoteric variation on bridge known to every ball-player from the time he first learned to chew tobacco. Pluck was strictly for fun. Boo-ray (another bridge mutant), on the other hand, was for money. The boo-ray players—Ferguson Jenkins, Gene Richards, Joe Pittman, and Ron Dunn—claimed the middle of the bus. Theirs was a quieter, more sober undertaking. Each came to the table with at least ninety-six dollars in small bills, meal money for the six-day trip (they knew that if worse came to worst, there was always the postgame spread). The front of the bus was for management types (Leon Roberts in the seat of honor, opposite Bussie; Rick Maxwell right behind him), nonuniformed personnel (trainer John Young, known to all as Doc; equipment manager Wayne Murphy, who answered to Clubbie or Murph), and the book readers. John LaRose, a taxi-squad relief pitcher and a one-time blackjack dealer in Atlantic City, was lost in *The Secret Lives of Marilyn Monroe*. Jim Willoughby had brought along a spy novel—"I like almost anything with an American flag and a hammer and sickle on the cover."

Every ballplayer, as soon as he is drafted and signs his first contract, buys a new car. It's tradition. But then all he does for years afterward, until he makes it to the big leagues, is ride the buses. To a ballplayer, the simple phrase "riding the buses" sums up every hardship and indignity he suffered while toiling in the bush leagues. The ones who survived talked about the endless hours on the road like it was time spent on a medieval torture rack, and, of course, the word gets out. Back when Bo Jackson was deciding which profession to pursue after college, what discouraged him most about baseball was the prospect of all those bus rides in his future. (Jackson must have made his peace with buses; after he signed with the Royals, he spent half a season in the Southern League with the Memphis Chicks, a team whose overnight caravans from Memphis to Orlando are the stuff of legend.)

For some in the senior league, the idea of piling back on a bus was abhorrent. Buses were a symbol of sacrifices already made. To go back now, in middle age, was to be reminded of all they had achieved, and all they had lost. Bill Madlock, who could afford to be choosy, said he would sooner rent a car and drive hundreds of miles by himself than get on a bus with his teammates. "Nooo," he said when the subject of buses came up. "Not me." And yet I had the feeling as our trip began that most of the passengers on this bus were comfortable enough and content not to drive. Here a man was temporarily liberated from family and responsibility, playing cards at 11:00 A.M. on a week-day, laughing at jokes he was too old to laugh at. Hell, it was only a three-hour ride.

Bill Lee was dressed for the road in shorts, a long-sleeved T-shirt, and a chartreuse fishing cap with a six-inch bill. He sat up front with the book readers and was working on two volumes simultaneously: *The Winds of War* by Herman Wouk and *The Denial of Death* by Ernest Becker—"one for pleasure and one for business." Lee had been thinking a lot about death lately, ever since his ninety-year-old grandmother called to say she'd seen him on TV and wanted him to shave off his beard because it had so many gray hairs in it that it made *her* feel old.

There was no way Lee was going to get any reading done, though, not as long as he was still stewing in the bitter recollections of yesterday's defeat. Lee was furious with Sergio Ferrer, the Pelicans' light-hitting shortstop, first, for making it all the way to third base while he was pitching, and then for trying to distract him by dancing up and down the line. "I hate that dancing-off shit," Lee said darkly. "I told him next time he tries that I'm gonna cut his throat."

Lee was mad at Lenny Randle, too, although no one knew exactly why. "I'm gonna hit Lenny Randle," Lee said for anyone who might be listening.

"You always say that," came a voice from the back of the bus, "and you never do."

"And I couldn't hurt anybody anyway!"

East of Winter Haven on Route 60, Bussie drove for miles past citrus groves laid to waste by the December cold snap; gnarly trees with brown leaves, their fruit freeze-burned and rotting at the bases of their trunks. Near Yeehaw Junction—a highway crossing with one stoplight and two truck stops—the land flattened and the sky grew large. Cattle grazed on marshy, copper-colored meadows. The bus became the high point on the landscape.

Yeehaw Junction would have been a good place to pick up Florida's turnpike, a new toll road built for the tourist trade and connecting Orlando with Miami by way of West Palm Beach.

Everybody thought so, except Bussie, who was probably under orders. Ignoring insults from the back of the bus, he barreled straight ahead on 60, another twenty-three miles to Interstate 95: less direct, more traffic, but free.

THE PALM HOTEL IN WEST PALM BEACH WAS CLEAN AND COMFORT-able, even luxurious. The players hated it. What the players looked for in a hotel—besides cable TV—was a nearby mall. At the Palm, without a car, you were stranded. So at 2:45, one half hour after we arrived, almost everybody climbed back on the bus and Bussie drove us to the mall. There, the players went their separate ways. Some had come to eat lunch, others mainly to cruise the aisles, looking at women. Ferguson Jenkins—today's big winner in boo-ray—spent part of his winnings on a present for his college-age daughter. Tommy Cruz—the middle Cruz brother between José and Hector—bought a pair of two-hundred-seventy-five-dollar sunglasses, which he proudly modeled on the short walk from the mall to the ballpark. "I need them 'cause I'm always losing my sunglasses," he explained.

There wasn't much happening in the clubhouse when I got there. The last bus from the hotel wouldn't arrive until after 5:00, one half hour from now, and the game didn't start until 7:30. I walked the length of the uncluttered room, past the neat row of stalls (each with a spotless, road-gray uniform hanging on a metal hanger), through the tunnel to the dugout. There I found Dalton Jones, already dressed. He was sitting on the top step, his back to a concrete wall, gazing reflectively at the playing field. By his posture and attitude, the grass might have been a lake and the wall he was leaning against a shade tree on the shore.

"This from *The Big Chill?*" Jones wondered out loud. "A Whiter Shade of Pale" by Procol Harum was playing on the stadium sound system (I hadn't heard that song in years, but lately it seemed like I was hearing it every day). "I didn't like that movie," Jones said.

In 1964, when he was twenty years old, Dalton Jones went to spring training with the Red Sox and won the starting job at second base. A tall, lanky, left-handed swinger, it was only natural that he be compared to Ted Williams. That would be a terrible burden for any young player to bear, but it couldn't compare with what Jones actually had to deal with. For when he arrived in Boston, he was already well known as the phenom who possessed a swing that Ted Williams himself had described as *the best natural swing he ever saw.*

Jones lasted nine years in the big leagues without ever coming close to fulfilling the expectations others had for him. After his rookie year he was used mainly as a fill-in around the infield or to pinch-hit. The high point of Jones's career was 1967—the year the Red Sox won the American League pennant and "A Whiter Shade of Pale" reached number five on the charts. During the World Series, which the Red Sox lost in seven games to the Cardinals, Jones split duties at third base with Joe Foy and batted .389. In 1970 he was traded to the Tigers. Three years later he was out of baseball.

Jones had left his job at a bank in Baton Rouge in order to play in the senior league. At this stage in his life the only expectations he had to live up to were his own, and so far he was coming up way short. To date he had appeared in just fourteen of Winter Haven's forty-seven games, and he was batting .176. Last night at Chain O' Lakes Park, he had picked up a ground ball behind second base and attempted a casual backhand flip to the shortstop covering. As a younger man he might have made the play look easy, but Jones was forty-six years old; he'd been out of baseball for seventeen years. His throw sailed wide of the mark and dribbled into center field.

"When I left baseball I wasn't even thirty years old," Jones said in a soft, wide-voweled accent that was straight out of Mc-Comb, Mississippi, his hometown. "I think most of the guys— waaall, I don't know ..." He paused. "... I think it wasn't very satisfactory, the leaving, because you didn't go out on a plus, you know? Coming back, just being around it again, has been real good, especially around guys like this that played some. I was impressed with how many guys came down here. I woulda thought that jobs or something would have interfered with that."

Jones asked me where I was from. When I told him I lived near Boston he said, "You musta been around in '67. Good year. Guy over there managed us"—he pointed to the Tropics dugout along the third-base line—"Dick Williams."

"*Dalton Jones,*" came a voice from down the bench. It was Doug Simunic, the backup catcher, a pup, comparatively speaking, at thirty-three. Apparently he'd been sitting there quietly for some time, listening. But as soon as Jones showed signs of falling into a reverie on the '67 Red Sox, Simunic spoke up. "Dalton Jones. I remember growing up in Detroit. He was up to bat with the bases loaded—"

"Hey, this is going in the book. You just leave that out."

"—he was up to bat with the bases loaded, and he hit a grand slam. The guy on first base tagged up. He passed him. He only got a three-run single. Dalton, that play didn't figure in the game, did it?"

"It *won* the game."

"Yeah, that's right," Simunic said. "I was working on a golf course, listening to the game on the radio. Dalton Jones."

While Simunic and Jones were remembering that day—Simunic fondly and Jones not—a young woman appeared at the top of the dugout steps. She wore a tag identifying her as a member of the television crew. Very politely, very professionally, she asked the men in uniform if she might borrow a helmet.

Simunic, eager to please, said, "Yeah, I'll get one, hold on," and headed for the tunnel.

"Preferably one with two, um, muffs on it," she called after him.

Simunic stopped dead in his tracks. "I don't know if we got one with two *muffs!*"

"Whatever they're called," the woman said. Now she was embarrassed.

"I'll ask somebody in there if they got two *muffs*, though," Simunic said, his eyes sparkling. A minute later, he came out and handed the woman a Super Sox batting helmet, one with two earflaps.

"Oh, you got one!"

Simunic looked up at her and smiled lecherously. "Yeah, but most of the guys only like 'em with *one* muff," he said. Simunic watched her walk quickly away, then he turned to Jones. "Be tough to nibble on two muffs at the same time!"

TONIGHT WAS PALM BEACH *POST* Night at the ballpark—if you clipped the coupon in the newspaper, you were admitted free. Before the game, Tropics owner Don Sider was saying he expected a crowd of about two thousand. As it happened, he got three thousand six hundred ninety-six, just short of a new league record. Overall the Tropics were averaging about fifteen hundred fans a game at Municipal Stadium. They were drawing better than anybody else in the league—about 30 percent better than Fort Myers and St. Petersburg, the only other teams that were even close—and still they were losing money, lots of it.

The reality of small crowds and inattentive media had dampened Sider's outlook since the last time we talked, about six weeks ago. He said now he expected to lose more than one million dollars, about the same as what I was hearing from the other owners. The remedy Sider favored was expansion into Arizona and southern California. Not only would the sale of new franchises generate short-term revenue for all the owners; more important, it would broaden the scope of the league. "So that it's easier to sell national advertising, get national TV," Sider explained. "Those are the two items that will make this league survive. I don't care how many fans we have in the stands; they're not gonna pay the salaries that these players are gonna need. It's gonna take TV money and sponsorship money."

Sider was having problems, too, with the Expos and the Braves, Municipal Stadium's major-league spring-training tenants. Neither was pleased that West Palm Beach had chosen to rent "their" ballpark during the winter. "The problem is the Expos in particular," said Sider. "I talked to Bill Stoneman, president of the Expos, and he said to me in no uncertain terms, 'Good luck to you guys, but we could care less about you and we're not gonna do anything to help you because we perceive you as competition in West Palm Beach for baseball.'

"They should welcome us with open arms. This league could be the best things to come along for the players in many, many years. If this league is successful, when they can't play in the bigs anymore, they can come here and still make fifty, sixty, seventy thousand a year instead of sitting behind a desk and making forty thousand a year. It doesn't mean anything to Bill Stoneman today, but it should mean something to the players. The players should be on the owners' case because the owners have to make the players happy, too; they have to negotiate with them."

The Tropics' starting pitcher was hard-throwing six-foot-seven Tim Stoddard, the most intimidating member of the best pitching staff in the league. Stoddard began the game by walking the first two batters on nine pitches. After Al Bumbry flied to center, Tony Scott singled and the bases were loaded. It was unlike Stoddard to be so generous; now it was up to the Super Sox to take advantage. Pete LaCock, batting fifth, hit a grounder to the right side of the infield; a run scored but now there were two outs. Next up was Butch Hobson, who drove a one-ball, one-strike fastball deep to left—and into the glove of Tito Landrum.

You knew it would happen; after the first inning, Stoddard settled down and coasted the rest of the way. He gave up just six more hits, didn't walk another batter until the ninth, and wound up with his league-leading third complete game. Meanwhile, the Tropics' hitters reached Sox starter Jim Bibby for one run in the first, three in the third, and one in the fourth. Final score: West Palm Beach, 6, Winter Haven, 1.

Underneath the stands in the Sox locker room, what had been order at 5:00 was chaos at 10:00. Uniform parts lay in piles on the muddy floor. Steam swirled like smoke in the rafters. Naked men waited for an open shower (there were only six). I turned on my tape recorder and went looking for some expert analysis. "Weird game," I said to Leon Roberts. He stood in front of the manager's locker, first one on the left, just inside the door.

"Whattaya mean?"

"Well, I counted ten times Stoddard fell behind in the count, two-and-o. Yet he only walked four—the first two he faced and two in the ninth inning, after it didn't matter anymore. He fell behind two-and-o to Gene Richards *four* times, but then it seemed like he was always able to find the plate again."

Roberts looked at me like I was out of my mind. It was late, he was tired, his team had lost. *What the hell difference did it make?* "He threw the ball pretty good," Roberts said. "Gotta give him credit."

I tried Bill Lee at the next locker. Tonight Lee had worn a T-shirt under his uniform that advertised the "1989 Zipper Open." It had a picture of a man holding a baseball bat in front of an open zipper, at the appropriate angle, of course. I asked him what he thought of Stoddard.

"I thought he was awesome," Lee said. "Thought he was wild, but when he had to make the pitches, he did. They don't make mistakes. Hell, they could beat the Atlanta Braves three out of four."

I passed on to Lee what Tropics pitcher Juan Eichelberger had told me before the game. Eichelberger—who spent his entire major-league career with the Padres, the Indians, and the Braves—said he actually believed that the Tropics were the best team he had ever played for. "They could probably beat two or three big-league teams right now," he said.

"I guarantee it," Lee said. "As long as he don't start. Hah! Tell him that, that'll piss him off!"

WEST PALM BEACH · *January 6*

CLUBHOUSE SCENES.

Besides Murph and Doc, the only passengers on the early bus to the ballpark were the wounded (Gary Allenson, Joe Pittman, Butch Hobson) and the lonely (Rick Wise, John LaRose). Upon entering the clubhouse, each was handed a fresh tin of Copenhagen by the local clubhouse boys, who stood at the door like butlers. The first thing Murph did was place two brand-new balls on the shelf in the locker of tonight's starting pitcher, Bill Lee. Doc unpacked his machine—an ominous black box with dials and gauges and a frightening cluster of electrodes—and plugged it into the wall. A few minutes later, Bernie Carbo showed up, tanned and happy after a day at the beach. "I bet I gave you guys a heart attack showing up so early," he said. Carbo was hungry so he sent one of the clubhouse boys out for fried chicken. "Breasts," he specified. "No thighs."

First up for "treatment" was Joe Pittman. He lay facedown on an examining table and read *People* magazine while Doc delivered an electrical current to his sore right hamstring. Pittman was called Shoes, a nickname derived from his taste in footwear at a time when white cleats were still a fashion statement. "Sir," Pittman reportedly told his first manager in the minor leagues, "those are the only shoes I got and I ain't gonna dye 'em black." The next day, so the story goes, Pittman found a new pair of black spikes in the bottom of his locker.

Hobson was kneeling chest-deep in the portable whirlpool. He looked like a gray-haired centaur. "Shoes," he said, needling, "I can't understand a word you say." Shoes had a tendency to slur his words.

Pittman didn't even look up from his magazine. "Mother-fucker—I'll—beat—your—ass," he replied. Very clearly, thank you.

Reliever Mark Bomback, otherwise known as Bomber, staggered into the clubhouse from the field. He was dressed in a plastic sweat suit drawn tightly at the ankles and the wrists. Sweat dripped from the exposed flesh on his brow. When he sat down in front of his locker, the bald spot on the top of his skull shone red.

Carbo regarded his teammate distrustfully, with the peculiar expression the slovenly reserve for the fit. "Keep working," he said.

"Pennant race," said Bomback, between gasps.

"Problem is, you can't run the ball across the plate. Hah!"

Glenn Brummer, the third-string catcher, arrived on the last bus. Brummer had toiled for long years in the minor leagues before being called up by the Cardinals at the ripe age of twenty-seven. Throughout his five-year stay in the big leagues, Brummer was always a backup. His busiest season was his last, with the Rangers in 1985, when he appeared in forty-nine games. He had never known the feeling of job security. The first thing Brummer did when he came to the park each day was check the lineup card. Not the starting lineup, he never expected that; Brummer's eyes went automatically to the list of available subs. As long as his name was on that list, he knew he still had a job. Today, thankfully, it was.

"I'm still there," Brummer said happily, his finger on his name. "Still on there. I made it again."

"Where'd that guy go to get the chicken?" Carbo moaned. "Fucking Kentucky?"

WHILE HIS TEAMMATES STRETCHED, MIKE MARSHALL STOOD STIFFLY in the corner of the dugout. His arms were folded across his chest defiantly, like Mussolini or Mr. Clean. He wore blue sneakers with Velcro straps, and he had pulled his uniform pants halfway up to his armpits. He looked more professorial than big-league, like a man in desperate need of a woman to teach him the elements of style. "Everybody believes in stretching," he replied when I asked him if he planned on joining his teammates, who were lolling in the grass in right field. "I for the life of me cannot figure out why they think stretching's good for you."

Last week in Winter Haven, while warming up before a game, Marshall had caught a spike on the rubber and twisted his knee. "Just a freak thing," he said. "Never happened before in my life." He paused for a moment, then remarked pedantically, "Now I can't say that." Marshall was not one to let a leg injury hold him back, however. He pitched four innings in relief that night, the last two "standing out there on one leg." This business about pitching with your legs—supposedly the secret to the longevity of pitchers like Tom Seaver and Nolan Ryan—was one of Marshall's pet peeves.

"I don't think the legs and the body add anything to the pitch. I'm always amused when Tom Seaver tries to talk about pitching, inasmuch as he doesn't have a clue about how the body works. For him to talk about how to throw a baseball is kind of silly. He talks about how you throw the baseball with your rear end. My challenge to him is, let me cut off your right arm and let's see how hard you can throw it."

Marshall was silent for a beat so that I might have space in which to laugh. I obliged.

"That's silliness," he continued. "You don't throw the ball with your legs. You don't throw the ball with your body. You throw the ball with your arm."

Now that I thought about it, I didn't remember seeing Marshall on the bus yesterday. Nor had he shown up for the game. Marshall's comings and goings were mysterious. Apart from the days he was scheduled to pitch, you never knew when he might show up. His teammates didn't seem to mind. Marshall moved about in his own world—he even washed his own underwear rather than let the equipment manager take care of it for him— and basically everyone else did their best to ignore him. Only Bill Lee, who was fascinated by anyone or anything that was out of the ordinary, seemed not to be threatened by Marshall and to take him seriously. As the eccentrics, they wound up being lumped together by their teammates, who spoke of Lee and Marshall as "two guys with one hundred seventy IQs" who used "those fourteen-letter words." Last week, to the horror of general manager Rick Maxwell, Lee had been spotted experimenting with Marshall's warm-up routine.

Basically, Marshall believed in throwing hard from the first pitch. "It doesn't take long to get the capillarization, the oxygen and all that stuff, going," he said. "Only takes a couple of minutes. I know how to throw my pitches so I don't need to rehearse those too much."

Never before had I heard an athlete say "rehearse" when he meant "practice."

"I remember when I was pitching every day in the major leagues, frequently I'd go into a ball game without having warmed up at all. I'd be sitting down in the bull pen and [Walter] Alston would call down and say, 'Tell Marshall he has the eighth and ninth.' I'd say, 'Thank you,' and I'd walk under the stands and into the dugout and sit down, and then go out and pitch. Of course the excitement of pitching in the major leagues pretty much gets you warmed up all by itself. You don't need much more than that."

What elevated Marshall's theories above mere quackery was the fact that he lasted fourteen years in the major leagues. Four times during the 1970s he led his league in appearances, including 1974, when he pitched in one hundred six games for the Dodgers, eclipsing his own major-league record, set the previous year, by fourteen. So why was Mike Marshall a journeyman throughout his career? To him the reason was obvious, and it had nothing to do with baseball.

"There's no question that my career suffered primarily because of my player-rep activities. I played for nine different major-league teams, and the reason I did that is that they kept trying to get me off the negotiating team. But as soon as they traded me to another team, they'd elect me immediately. It was certainly nothing that I ever wanted to do, but it was a job that had to be done and unfortunately I was the person in a position to be able to do it. I know Marvin [Miller, former head of the Players Association] takes all the credit, but I was the one who came up with the idea for the free agency thing. Andy Messersmith and I are the ones who put that thing together."

This time Marshall gave me no time to react. In a flash he was off again.

"Here's a little-known fact. I only played five full years in the major leagues where I stayed with the same team from the beginning of the year to the end, excluding the year I was injured, when I broke my rib with the Dodgers. Five: '74, of course, which is the best year any reliever's ever had; '73 [with the Expos], which is the second-best year any reliever's ever had, when I pitched in ninety-two games; then in '79 [Twins] I pitched in ninety games, the third-best year a reliever ever had; and then in '72 [Expos], when I had a 1.78 earned run average. The other full year was 1971 [Expos], the first year when I was trying to figure out how to pitch.

"But my point being, had I not been a member of the Players Association, and had we not had those battles to fight, and had I been allowed to just play and pitch, and had people evaluated me on my pitching instead of my ability to negotiate, I could have had a far larger career, and certainly a longer career."

RON WASHINGTON, THE TROPICS' SHORTSTOP, HAD THIS TO SAY about Bill Lee before the game:

"He's a competitor. I enjoy facing him because he's the kind of guy who might throw his junk, but he's gonna challenge you one time and say, 'Hit this, Mother Hubbard, if you can!' You enjoy going out there against guys like that. I know he's an older guy and always carrying on but he got a set, he really do. He got some *rocks.*"

This was what happened to Bill Lee in the first inning, pitching to the best-hitting team in the league: Mickey Rivers, the league's leading hitter with a .397 average, slapped the first pitch straight back up the middle for a single. Toby Harrah, batting .306, followed with a double to left, scoring Rivers. Tito Landrum (.324) singled to left, scoring Harrah. Washington, second in the league in hitting at .393 and the league leader in RBIs with sixty-one, reached on an error. Dave Kingman (five homers) doubled to left, scoring Landrum and Washington. And Lee Lacy (.333) singled to center. Lee finally retired Jerry White on a fly ball to center and Luis Pujols on an infield pop-up, but Rodney Scott singled to left and Kingman scored. Rivers, batting for the second time in the inning, grounded to first for the final out. Six hits, five runs, two men left on base. The score at the end of one inning: Tropics, 5, Super Sox, 1.

Lee left the game after five innings, having faced a total of twenty-eight batters, twenty-five of whom got a strike to hit on the first pitch. Lee challenged those Mother Hubbards, all right; lucky for him he escaped with his rocks.

Tonight the Tropics showed the Super Sox why they were the best team in the league. They hit the ball hard—Kingman's homer off Darrell "Bucky" Brandon in the sixth cleared two fences, the one in left and the one at the outer edge of an adjacent practice infield—and often. All told, the Tropics hammered out eighteen hits, including five by Tito Landrum, and scored twelve runs. The Sox rallied for four in the ninth, but it was too little, too late.

Lee was nowhere to be seen by the time I got to the clubhouse, having long since departed for watering holes unknown. Outside in the darkness by the idling bus, I found Darrell Brandon waiting for his teammates, drinking one beer while holding an extra in reserve. Brandon was forty-nine years old. He'd started out in the minors in the late fifties, played major-league ball in the sixties and seventies, and joined the senior league in the eighties. Now it was 1990, which meant that Brandon had played professional baseball in each of five decades. Tonight he had the look of someone who'd stayed too long at the party. He'd entered the game with a 12.46 ERA and managed to make it worse. Now he was trying bravely to pretend it didn't matter.

"I'll tell you," he said to teammate John LaRose, "there's a lot worse things in life than losing a Senior Professional Baseball Association game."

If only he hadn't brought it up. Now I felt sorry for him.

WEST PALM BEACH • *January 7*

Sunday morning. Day game this afternoon, then on to Fort Myers. The clubhouse coffee, on the burner all night, was thick as pudding; no matter, the yawning players gulped it down. Today's chosen target of abuse was first baseman Pete LaCock, a blue-eyed Californian who played during the seventies for the Cubs and the Royals. LaCock was the son of game-show host Peter Marshall, who changed his name.

"He just didn't think he could make it in show business with a name like LaCock?" I asked.

"Would you?" LaCock asked rhetorically. "Not unless you were really funny."

LaCock had good reason to be embarrassed today. In the seventh inning of last night's game, with a runner on first, he had fielded a hard-hit ground ball, then thrown to the shortstop covering second for what should have been the start of a double play. But no one was covering first. LaCock thought the play was the pitcher Brandon's, who thought it was LaCock's, the result being that both stood staring at each other accusingly while the runner crossed the bag.

"Shit," Gary Allenson said, "you were only two steps from the bag."

"Three," LaCock shot back, as if that made a difference. A pause, a grin, then, "Fuck you all!"

Glenn Brummer was lobbying for some recognition. He'd pinch-run in the ninth inning for Allenson and lolled home from second on a double. It was the first run he'd scored in the senior league and he wanted a game ball to commemorate the achievement.

"Pinch-run don't count!" someone said.

"Fuck it don't," said Brummer.

Bill Lee finally showed up, pale and saggy-eyed on the morning after, still angry at Roberts for giving him the hook in the fifth inning. It was obvious but I asked him anyway:

"How you doin'?"

"Lousy. I got a headache."

"What happened?"

"I got blottoed last night."

(Lee was in no mood for company or conversation. He spent the rest of the morning chasing a football around the outfield— kick it, go get it, kick it again.)

Doc sat on a stool while Bernie Carbo clipped his hair. Scipio Spinks pranced around the clubhouse doing his best imitation of LaCock's pigeon-toed walk. Pedro Borbon told a story in tortured English I had trouble understanding, something about swallowing too many greenies, getting in a fight with the Mets, and trying to eat Tommie Agee's hat. That brought the clubhouse conversation around to the subject of brawls.

"I remember my first day in the big leagues," LaCock began. "Rick Monday was the first hitter and Pat Corrales was the catcher. Not even a pitch had been thrown. And Rick got up there and said something to Corrales and Corrales just stood up and went *wham.* Just hit him! I went, *'Fuck.'* I didn't know *what* was going on. This was my first day."

Which reminded him: "Hey, I'll tell you one of the funniest things I ever saw. Amos Otis was hitting and Cookie Rojas was on third and Ken Brett was pitching for the Angels. I was on deck. Amos, you know, he has to get his gloves just right and his pants right and his helmet. Then he walks up to the plate and Brett gets ready to throw and Amos backs off again. He kicks his cleats, you know, and so Ken yells, 'Get in the fucking box!' " Amos looks at him and just smiles and kind of turns around and starts working on his gloves again. So Brett winds up and goes *whoosh,* throws one right over the top of his head! Now the catcher turns around and starts hauling ass after the ball and Ken runs right at Amos—but Ken doesn't know that Cookie broke from third! Amos is watching the catcher, he doesn't see Ken coming at him. Cookie and Ken collide in front of home plate and bounce in between Amos. They're both hurt and Amos is standing there going, 'Yeah, this is great!' "

"One thing you don't want to do in a fight," offered Ron Dunn, "is end up on the bottom. You throw guys out of the way and push guys out of the way and drag them out of the way, but if you get taken down, you gotta assume the fetal position."

"Turf burns and stuff," said LaCock. "Turf burns will kill you."

At LaCock's urging, I went over to the Tropics' clubhouse to look for Al Hrabosky, the bearded, hard-throwing reliever who earned the nickname "The Mad Hungarian" while pitching for the Cardinals in the early seventies. Hrabosky used to like to turn his back on the hitter in key situations, leave the mound, compose himself silently for several long seconds, then pound his fist in his glove, stalk purposefully to the top of the mound, and deliver his pitch. The shtick angered some hitters and intimidated others; in either case, Hrabosky had the advantage.

I found Hrabosky in the players' bathroom. He was standing over the washbasin trimming his famous black beard, heavily salted these days with gray.

"LaCock says I need to ask you about the big fight with the Cubs," I said after I introduced myself.

Hrabosky's eyes brightened. Speaking to my reflection in the mirror, he told the story. "It was a game in September of '74," he began, "in St. Louis, like on a Sunday afternoon. The

Cardinals and the Cubs got that great rivalry; it's about fifty-fifty Cardinals-Cubs fans, even at Busch Stadium. I came in in the eighth inning—the score was tied—and I got 'em out.

"In the ninth inning Bill Madlock was the first hitter. Bill was the first guy ever to step out and go back to the on-deck circle when I went behind the mound. All along in my mind I kept playing out the scenario, knowing that eventually someone was gonna do that. So I waited on the mound. When he got back in the batter's box, I could see he was laughing, like, 'I made you wait!' So as soon as he got ready, I went back behind the mound again. When I came back to the mound, he went back to the on-deck circle.

"Now the fans are starting to react. Shag Crawford was behind home plate. He went to Madlock in the on-deck circle and told him to get back in the batter's box. Well, whatever Madlock said, he made Shag mad, and Shag ran back to home plate and pointed to me. I knew exactly what that meant. So I wound up and threw a pitch. Ted Simmons jumped up and caught it"— Hrabosky jumps in the telling, to show how far he was out of the strike zone—"and Shag said, 'Strike one!'

"Now Teddy—see, I'd just come into the game, but Teddy'd been back there behind the plate all game, one hundred forty degrees in the turf—he's a little tired. He's taking his time getting the ball back to me. I wanted the ball as quickly as possible. I thought I could conquer *that* hitter."

Meanwhile, things were getting a little crowded around home plate. Cubs manager Jim Marshall stormed out of the dugout to argue the call; on-deck batter José Cardenal decided that if Madlock wasn't going to hit, then he might as well take his place; and finally Madlock changed his mind and returned to the batter's box.

"My pitch separated all three of them," Hrabosky continued. "There's a picture that shows Shag in perfect position calling balls and strikes, Simmons with his head turned reaching up for the ball, Cardenal and Madlock both trying to swing, and Marshall standing there with his hands up in the air, trying to get out of the way of the ball."

"Strike two?" I asked.

"Well, we had to wait for the fight. Somebody said something and Simmons got out of his crouch and just popped Madlock and both benches emptied and everything else. After considerable discussion they decided the first pitch stood and the second pitch was no-pitch, so the count was o-and-one. I got 'em out, got him one-two-three, and we got a run in the bottom of the ninth and won the ball game.

"So that was just one of my claims to fame—to throw one pitch with no batters in the box and then to throw another one with two batters and a manager."

Not only were the Tropics the winningest team in the senior league with a record of thirty-seven wins and thirteen losses, which made their clubhouse a fruitful setting for insults and practical jokes; also they had no fewer than three lawyers on the roster. Both factors helped make for the league's most active and interventionist kangaroo court.

On the docket this morning was a case involving a high-stakes wager between teammates. Reliever Felix "Ike" Pettaway, the defendant, had allegedly bet center fielder Mickey Rivers, the plaintiff, that Rivers would be unable to throw a baseball so hard that it would pass through a tarp. The tarp in question, it turned out, already had some holes in it, wind flaps, actually. Rivers hit a wind flap and the ball went through. Rivers claimed victory, Pettaway cried foul.

Attorney for the defendant was today's starting pitcher, Pete Broberg. Representing Rivers was the bull-pen catcher, Jim Bonfiglio. Joe Mincberg, like Broberg and Bonfiglio a real-life lawyer, was the presiding judge. We join the proceedings with reliever Will McEnaney on the witness stand.

Bonfiglio:	"Tell the judge and the jury what you saw and heard last night before the game concerning the bet between Mickey Rivers and Ike Pettaway."
McEnaney:	"What I heard down on the left-field line was that Ike Pettaway told Mickey Rivers that there was no way he could throw that ball through the tarp. I believe he said, 'I'll bet anything in the world you can't do it. *Anything in the world.*'" [hooting and hollering from the gallery]
Judge Mincberg:	"What prompted this discussion? Just general boredom?"

McENANEY:	"Just casual conversation. Mickey is proud of his arm. He thinks of himself as a hard-throwing pitcher. He said, 'I can throw the ball through the tarp,' and Ike Pettaway took the bet."
JUDGE MINCBERG:	"Can you identify the man you call Mickey Rivers?"
McENANEY:	"Yes, I can."
JUDGE MINCBERG:	"Where is he?"
McENANEY:	[Pointing] "He's right over there."
JUDGE MINCBERG:	"What's he wearing?"
McENANEY:	"Just a smile." [more laughter] "Now there were several attempts to make the ball go through the tarp—I believe it was within a half dozen—and on the last throw it went through. He said, 'All right, motherfucker, it's done.' "
JUDGE MINCBERG:	"On any occasion did Mr. Pettaway ever say, 'By the way, if it goes through a preexisting hole in the tarp, it doesn't count?' "
McENANEY:	"No."
BROBERG:	"We want a mistrial! The court is taking such an active part in this!"
JUDGE MINCBERG:	"No, this is federal court, it's all right."

Done with McEnaney, Bonfiglio called his client, Mickey Rivers, to the stand.

JUDGE MINCBERG:	"Take the stand, Mr. Rivers. Raise your left hand. Are you gonna tell the truth?" [Rivers nods affirmatively]
BONFIGLIO:	"Tell 'em what your story is." [general encouragement from the gallery]
JUDGE MINCBERG:	"Order in the court so we can understand Mickey!"

It should be noted here that Mickey Rivers characteristically expressed himself in a halting, creaky, painfully inefficient manner, not unlike the tortured way he pitter-pattered into the batter's box before stroking a base hit.

RIVERS:	"Big Ike—check his name back down to Little Ike now, he's not doing a good job—

	questioned my ability of throwing. He said, uh, a great arm like mine could throw eighty-five miles an hour. So, continued to talk about the great arm. So, looked around and say, 'Well, I bet you *anything* you couldn't throw the ball through the tarp.' "
JUDGE MINCBERG:	"Anything you wanted?"
RIVERS:	"Anything I wanted. A very knowledgeable man like me, a worldly man like me, known all over the world as a money-taker—"
JUDGE MINCBERG:	"Did you at any time say to Mr. Pettaway, 'By the way, Ike, there are preexisting holes in this tarp. What happens if I throw one through there?' "
RIVERS:	"No, he didn't want to. He just wanted me to throw the ball through! Through the tarp! He said that I would not throw the ball through the tarp in any condition!"
JUDGE MINCBERG:	"And what happened? Did you?"
RIVERS:	"Yes, Your Honor. A great man of my caliber do not need over one or two throws to throw a ball through a tarp."
JUDGE MINCBERG:	"Well, how many throws was it, one or two?"
RIVERS:	"Your Honor, I didn't need but one throw."
JUDGE MINCBERG:	"We've heard testimony from Mr. McEnaney that you threw the ball six times. Is that a lie?" [buzzing in the gallery]
RIVERS:	"Your Honor, I just explained. A great and just man of my knowledge do not need but a throw."
JUDGE MINCBERG:	"Now, the ball that you claim went through the tarp—did it go through an existing hole or did it break new ground?"
RIVERS:	"Your Honor, I will say it one more time. The bet was made to throw the ball through the tarp and the ball went through. To my knowledge, the ball went through."
JUDGE MINCBERG:	"Did it break cloth or did it go through air?"
RIVERS:	"It was on the other side of the tarp."

At this time, Rivers, apparently confident of the strength of his case, motioned to Judge Mincberg.

JUDGE MINCBERG: "Mickey, you have one more question?"

RIVERS: "I like to know, would he like it doggy style or standing?"

A full three minutes elapsed before the bedlam died down and Judge Mincberg was able to restore order in the court.

JUDGE MINCBERG: "All right, Mr. Broberg, go ahead and present your client's case."

BROBERG: "I call my client to the stand right away. Mr. Pettaway, when you were standing out there talking to Mr. Rivers about throwing the ball through the tarp, how many throws did he take at the tarp?"

PETTAWAY: "Mickey Rivers took two throws at the tarp. He was saying, 'I can throw the ball eighty-five miles an hour.' I said, 'Bullshit, you cannot throw no eighty-five miles an hour. If you can, throw the ball through the tarp.'"

BROBERG: "So what did Mickey do?"

PETTAWAY: "He grabbed the ball and tried to throw it through the tarp. The ball fell right on the tarp. It did not penetrate through the tarp. So he picks up another one. Then he throws it through a hole that's already been made. Then he hollered, 'I done throwed it through the tarp!'"

BROBERG: "Okay, when you made the deal with Mickey, did you think the deal was for him to throw the ball through a preexisting hole or just throw it through and make a new hole?"

PETTAWAY: "Throw it through to make a new hole."

BROBERG: "And that was your recollection of the deal?"

PETTAWAY: "Yeah, he recollect that and I recollect that."

BROBERG: "I don't have any further questions of this client."

Now it was Bonfiglio's turn to cross-examine the defendant.

BONFIGLIO:	"You never told Mr. Rivers not to throw it through the hole, did you?"
PETTAWAY:	"No."
BONFIGLIO:	"Now, you had an opportunity to look at the tarp, didn't you?"
PETTAWAY:	"Yeah."
BONFIGLIO:	"You've seen it there a long time, right? We've played three months, right?"
PETTAWAY:	"Yeah."
BONFIGLIO:	"You knew the holes were there, didn't you?"
PETTAWAY:	[unwillingly] "Yeah."
BONFIGLIO:	"But you didn't tell him he couldn't throw it through the holes, did you?"
PETTAWAY:	"No, uh, yeah." [hooting, hollering]
BONFIGLIO:	"No more questions."
JUDGE MINCBERG:	"Any other witnesses? I'm prepared to rule." [all eyes fix on Judge Mincberg] "It seems to me that in all fairness there was a misunderstanding of the terms of the wager. There was not a clear understanding of what the bet was to be. There was—no bet! No bet! And no one owes any money to anybody else!" [Pandemonium in the clubhouse.]

ANOTHER LOSS FOR THE SUPER SOX, NOTABLE BECAUSE OF TWO MOments.

The first occurred in the bottom of the second inning with two outs, runners on first and second, and Ron Washington due up. Under orders from manager Leon Roberts, Ferguson Jenkins issued an intentional pass to Washington, loading the bases for, gulp, Dave Kingman. This was not one of those proverbial "percentage moves"; Washington and Kingman both bat righty. No, this was a simple tribute to the kind of year Washington was having in the senior league; that the Sox would rather pitch to Kingman—he of the four hundred forty-two career homers—*and with the bases loaded,* than to Washington, a notorious free swinger throughout his major-league career who struck out a total of two hundred sixty-six times with only sixty-five walks and, unlike Kingman, lacked the power that would have compensated. But Washington entered the game batting .390, one hundred fifty points higher than Kingman. And already, with a double in the first, he had driven in his sixty-third run of the season—a pace that over a full major-league schedule of one hundred sixty-two games would produce an astounding total of two hundred thirteen runs batted in.

Lucky for Roberts, the gambit succeeded. Kingman ran the count to three-and-one, then popped up meekly to third base.

One inning later, in the bottom of the third, again the bases were loaded, this time with only one out. The batter was leadoff hitter Toby Harrah. Jenkins was struggling. It had taken him fifty pitches to get seven outs, and apparently fifty pitches was all he had in him tonight. Belatedly, Jim Willoughby began warming up in the bull pen.

First, Jenkins took a long walk around the perimeter of the mound. Then Doug Simunic unfolded himself from his crouch and ambled moundward. After Simunic, it was Roberts's turn. Then Jenkins indulged in a little housecleaning around the rubber. Then he knelt down and retied his shoelaces, first the right one and then the left one. The umpire tried to prod him, but Fergie would not be moved. "I told him, 'Throw me out of the game if you want to,'" Jenkins said later.

But no one stops time. Not even in baseball, which has no clock. Eventually, you have to make your pitch. And so, after what seemed like half an hour, Jenkins resignedly took his position on the rubber, eased into his stretch, glanced at the runners, and served up a big, fat lollipop.

I missed Harrah after the game so I couldn't confirm what I suspected. But this much I knew: that Harrah was a gentleman, that he was once a teammate of Jenkins on the Rangers, and that while he drooled over that lollipop all the way to the plate, when he finally got around to taking his lick he delivered a ground ball straight to the shortstop for an inning-ending double play.

Jenkins walked slowly off the mound and into the clubhouse, his dignity intact.

The postgame spread was hot dogs and canned corn, food fit for losers. It was hard not to feel bad for the Super Sox, swept as they were in the three-game series. To have come all this way, stayed two nights, played three games (twenty-five and one-half innings of baseball), and left without accomplishing anything! A road trip seemed like a lot of trouble to go through if you weren't even going to win one game.

Driving west out of West Palm Beach, Bussie managed to get himself tangled temporarily in the narrow roads of a country subdivision—"We've been horseshit all year," Bernie Carbo observed, "but the bus driving's been fucking worse"—before finding his way to Florida 80, which skirts the southern shore of vast Lake Okeechobee, then follows the Caloosahatchee River one hundred miles further west to Fort Myers.

We were in a part of Palm Beach County where tourists never go, an expanse that within living memory was still the Everglades but which had since been diked and drained and wholly given over to agribusiness. Still, it was beautiful. Gravel roads crisscrossed the landscape at sharp angles to the highway, carrying semitrailers traveling at high speeds, dust spiraling in their wakes. The sky was a pale, luminous blue, a sky I recognized from books as being the color of robins' eggs. The clouds in it were like the shells some mornings on Pass-A-Grille Beach—ivory, mainly, but tinged with peach and rose and amethyst.

Here and there on the horizon rose thick pillars of black smoke, so solid and arching that from a distance I almost believed that they were holding up the sky. It was winter harvest time in the Florida sugarcane fields. The cane was being burned before it was cut, a process that consumed the leaves but not the sweet, sappy stalks. As we approached the fires, it was like a vision of Armageddon. Whole fields were up in flames. Buckling waves of hot air crashed against the windows on the side of the bus, distorting our view. I caught a terrifying glimpse of the setting sun wiggling behind an orange curtain of fire.

"Shit!" yelled out Scipio Spinks, breaking the awed silence on the bus. "That's marijuana. Pull over!"

FORT MYERS • *January 8*

LAST NIGHT WE CHECKED INTO THE KIND OF HOTEL ONLY A BALL-player could love. So what if we were miles from the center of town and even farther from Fort Myers's famous beaches? Who cared if our rooms overlooked a parking lot? Why, out here there were not one but two multiscreened movie theaters, each with a full schedule of matinee performances; a couple of full-service shopping centers; several popular drinking establishments (hanging plants or flashing lights, your choice); and an international array of fast-food joints, all within easy walking distance.

The visitors' locker room at Terry Park was twice as big as the one in West Palm Beach. It opened onto its own practice diamond, which was like having a private playing field right outside your front door. There was also a separate office for the manager. That's where Mike Marshall, tonight's starting pitcher, finally located his uniform this afternoon. If this was somebody's idea of a joke, Leon Roberts was not amused, not after his team had lost four straight, and knowing the fate of his two predecessors. Marshall didn't laugh, either. Blank-faced, he gathered up his gear and transferred it to an empty locker. Marshall even peeled off the piece of tape with his name written on it, then carefully centered it above his new stall, taking care to smooth out the wrinkles with both hands.

It must have been a ballplayer's sixth sense that caused Gary Allenson to look up from his stool a short while later and see Roberts scanning the faces in the locker room. "Hey, headhunter," he called out. "Who you looking for?" He had to know that *he* was safe, otherwise he'd have kept his mouth shut.

Roberts tried to smile, but the set of his jaw said, "I'm only doing my duty." Bravely into the manager's office marched Dalton Jones, he of the best natural swing Ted Williams ever saw. Jones and his .162 batting average, I later learned, were removed from the active roster. Bernie Carbo, previously on the disabled list, was activated in his place.

Jones was my roommate on the Fort Myers portion of the trip. Later, when I asked him what his plans were, he said he'd be staying on until the end of the season as first-base coach.

"So they made you a coach," I said as optimistically as I could.

"I was always a coach," he said with an edge in his voice, and then I remembered that he had been hired to do both jobs. In other words, I should understand, no one was doing him any favors. Maybe they needed him more as a coach than they did as a player.

THERE WAS A FOUL ODOR IN THE PRESS BOX, AND IT WASN'T THE HOT dogs. It was a dead rat, exhumed this afternoon from the narrow space between the roof and the ceiling tiles and transferred—obviously by someone who didn't have to work here—to a resting place just outside the door. The problem with leaving the dead rat by the door was that the door was always open. The door stayed open because whenever a foul ball cleared the press box, every newsman in attendance, together with the PA announcer, the publicity man, the official scorer, and all the other hardened regulars leaped from their chairs and rushed through the door out onto the (unfenced) roof of the grandstand in a suicidal frenzy to get to the ball before it clattered over the side and fell to the pavement, forty feet below, where children waited hopefully.

To amuse themselves between foul balls, they told jokes and riddles and played parlor games, anything rather than watch the game. It seemed to be a point of honor among those who covered the senior league—especially here in Fort Myers—to affect a lack of interest bordering on disdain for whatever happened to be taking place on the field. Tim Ireland, the impish shortstop of the Sun Sox, successfully executed the hidden-ball trick three times during the course of the season and to my knowledge not one reporter (myself included) ever had the slightest idea what happened, any more than the poor runner who got tagged out.

Which explained the general confusion in the top of the first inning when Mike Marshall suddenly got tossed out of the game. Apparently he had committed a balk—no one ever saw those, either—and after he exasperatedly flipped the ball over his shoulder, which got him the old heave-ho, everybody looked at everybody else on the off chance that one among us had been paying attention. No such luck.

Thankfully, this was the senior league, where normal rules of access did not apply. I left the press box, walked downstairs, and wandered over toward the visitors' locker room. In the darkness of the empty practice field I intercepted Marshall on his way to an early shower. To say that he was fuming would be misleading. He was angry, definitely, but he tried not to show it. Marshall was one who usually took pains to encapsulate his anger rather than spread it around.

"What happened?" I asked him.

"I put my foot on the rubber," Marshall began in a reasonable tone of voice, "and I didn't have the grip I wanted on the ball. I just threw a screwball and I wanted to come with a curveball. So I stepped back off to find the seam. When I stepped back on he called a balk. There's no balk until you're ready to take your sign! When I walked back to him I said, 'A balk is deceiving the runner. I didn't deceive the runner! I hadn't started to check my sign yet!'

"He said, 'Get back on the mound and pitch. That's a balk. You gotta step off with the other foot.'

"I said, 'Hold it a second. There's no balk unless you deceive the runner.'

"He gave me another smart remark and I said, 'Between your stupidity—not knowing what the hell the rules are—and that asshole back there not knowing what the strike zone is, you can't pitch in this league.' So I turned around and said, 'You pitch,' and I heard him say, 'You're gone.'

"He said I threw the ball at him! I tossed it up in the air! Is that throwing a ball at somebody? I said, 'You're the dumbest sonofabitch I've ever seen. What you need is to get your ass kicked by someone.' I didn't mean literally. Figuratively."

Marshall paused for a moment, and then the anger spilled out of him.

"Well, I'd like to take him out behind the stands and talk to him straight about his attitude. Who the fuck does he think he's talking to? Who the hell we talking to here? It's the attitude more than anything else, for Chrissakes. It's not like you're dealing with a bunch of high school kids who are being smartass. This is the senior *professional* league, there ought to be a little bit of respect somewhere.

"It'll kill the league," Marshall said before he ducked into the locker room. "That's what's gonna kill the league. The game gets out of control. You have all the blowouts because the umpiring is so terrible. What the heck's he talking about, a balk? I'm not even looking at my catcher, I'm trying to get a grip on the ball! Silly, just silly."

"Are you going to pitch again tomorrow?" I called after him.

"No," he said. "I'm gone. I've had it. I got other things to do, better things to do. It's a joke right now. This is a ringer league with silly umpires. I got other things to do."

"You're leaving the team?"

"Yeah, I'm gone. I'll come back when they make it into a real league."

A few innings later, back in the press box, I talked to general manager Rick Maxwell. By then, Marshall was already on his way home to Zephyrhills, although he'd changed his mind about quitting. Before he left, Marshall promised Maxwell he'd rejoin the team the day after tomorrow in Orlando, and be available to pitch the first game of the doubleheader.

On a night when Roberts was praying for a complete game, Marshall's early exit forced him to rummage around in his scanty, overworked bull pen. Mark Bomback lasted into the fifth, allowing five runs, three of which were earned; Pedro Borbon pitched a scoreless inning and one-third; and in the seventh, with Winter Haven now losing 7–1, Darrell Brandon got the call for mop-up duty. Brandon allowed five hits, including a double and a home run by Dan Driessen, and gave up five more runs. Rather than waste another arm, Roberts let catcher Glenn Brummer pitch the eighth.

"Fuck," said Bernie Carbo, ripping through the curtain of quiet that descended on the Super Sox locker room after the game. "Turn the radio on or something."

The Sox were hurting. Bill Lee, who had stepped in a hole while doing his running before the game, had an ice pack wrapped around his left ankle. Shortstop Ron Dunn was wearing *two* ice packs on his throwing arm—one on his shoulder, the other on his wrist. Mark Bomback was coping with the news that he'd be out for at least a week with yet another pulled hamstring. And Gary Allenson was rubbing the sore spot on his foot where he had been hit by a foul ball.

"You know you're doing horseshit when Allenson's in the on-deck circle and he's gotta come out of the game," said Lee. "Way to go!"

Doug Simunic tried to look at the brighter side: "It really wasn't a bad game up until we didn't have a coach in the third-base coaching box for the last two innings."

"Then we ran out Bernie," said Lee, "and we still didn't have one."

"Shit," said Carbo, "this is boring. Reminds me of the year I was in the minor leagues and we got written up in *Harper's* magazine as the worst team in baseball. Knoxville, Tennessee. The Southern League. Lost one hundred one games out of a one-hundred-forty-two-game schedule. Got rained out twice. We had Johnny Bench, Stan Swanson, Hal McRae—had eleven guys who made it to the big leagues off that team. Don Zimmer was the manager."

"I know what we're gonna do," Lee said. "We're gonna get

the movie *Patton* and we're all gonna see it before the next game. Listen to George C. Scott's opening speech."

"You think that would help?" I asked him.

"Yeah, remember where he comes out behind the American flag? 'You don't win wars by dying for your country. You make the other sonofabitch die for his country! You stick your bayonet in *his* belly! You spill *his* guts on the ground!' "

I skipped the bus ride back to the hotel and rode instead with Lee in Maxwell's rented van. Poor Bill. He'd sat and watched the whole game. For him, the only thing worse than losing was not getting a chance to play. If it were still his decision, he'd have been in the lineup every day, playing left field whenever he wasn't pitching.

"You know who has the best batting average on this team against Jim Slaton [tonight's starting pitcher for Fort Myers]?" he asked me in the parking lot at the hotel.

I didn't, but I did. "Bill Lee?"

FORT MYERS • *January* 9

Today, everybody had his theories about what was wrong with the Super Sox.

"The age factor caught up with them," said Doc. Doc had been around. He was once trainer, clubhouse manager, and traveling secretary for the Nashville South Stars of the Atlantic Coast Hockey League, but even that was less demanding than his present job. "We peaked and started going pretty good, but now the age factor's caught up with us."

The way Bussie saw the problem, it was more an attitude thing. "Before in Pompano and down in Miami they were kicking butt," he observed from his throne behind the wheel. "You couldn't do no better than that, *nobody*. But this time they ain't won a one. I don't know what the heck the scoop is, but I heard some of the guys saying that some of them were not really putting everything in it.

"If you gonna play, you gonna play. If you gonna bullshit, you gonna bullshit—and you ain't gonna win."

Scipio Spinks—forever linked in my mind with Diego Segui

on the all-time all-name team—allowed that there was an ele-
ment of fact in both opinions. "First of all, we didn't believe it
was going to be as competitive as it is," he said. "We thought
we could all get together for a couple of months and get in shape
and come on out and play decent baseball. Then all of a sudden
you run up against kids—I say 'kids,' they're thirty-five, thirty-
six years old—and you gotta extend a little bit more. Some of us
have been out of baseball for ten years. Myself, I been out fourteen years. We still got time to make a run at second place—*if*
we stay loose and have fun. We got a ball club that can definitely
do that."

Spinks offered this hopeful prognosis while lounging on a
bench outside the locker room. The sun and the unreal warmth
of a seventy-degree January afternoon had drawn Spinks out of
doors, even though he was in the middle of dressing for the
game. So far he'd managed to put on a pair of white spandex
undershorts, a red T-shirt, and baseball socks—the all-in-one kind
with the painted-on stirrup that was preferred by almost everybody in the senior league.

The shorts stopped just above a shiny six-inch scar that wiggled grotesquely on the skin of his right knee—"Johnny Bench's
signature," Spinks said when he caught me looking at it. Spinks,
a former St. Louis Cardinal, had collided with Bench in a game
in 1972 while trying to score from second base on a single. Spinks
owned a fastball at the time to compare with Bob Gibson's, but
he tried to come back too soon and wound up blowing out his
arm. He was only twenty-six, but his career in baseball was over.

Spinks and I had started a conversation the night before in
the hotel bar. Most of what he'd told me I hadn't been able to
hear above the thumping and wailing of a band called Crystal
Reflections (something like that), and what I *had* heard, well, let's
just say it was a little foggy. I switched on my tape recorder and
asked him if he'd mind repeating himself. The subject was black
baseball fans. The question: why were there so few at the ballpark?

"The reason black fans don't go out to the ballpark," Spinks
began, "is because a lot of black athletes aren't coming back to
the community. We aren't giving back to the community what
we took from it. Of course, we don't owe anybody anything. But
still, when we were younger, the black athletes were the only
people that we knew. Our idols were people like Ernie Banks,

Willie Mays, Hank Aaron. We saw those guys all the time because they had to stay in the black community. I grew up in
Chicago. All the black athletes when they were on the road
stayed in one hotel and that was on the same side of the city
that I lived on, four or five blocks from me. You got to see the
Al Smiths, the Minnie Minosos, the Larry Dobys. You got to
say, 'Wow, if I ever play baseball I can be just like them.'

"My uncle had a place in Chicago, it was a restaurant and a
bar, and I used to bus tables for him. That's where a lot of
athletes would come and socialize. You could be around them,
you could actually touch them. Guys like Ernie Banks, Billy Williams, Tony Taylor, they'd sit and talk to you. Nowadays, to go
talk to Dave Winfield you'd have to spend five hundred dollars
on dinner.

"I'm not blaming Winfield. Some guys *do* go back to the community, but they don't stay. With a million-dollar contract, you
don't want to live on Sixty-first and Champlain in Chicago. You
want to live out in the richest part of town or wherever you can
go. And you can't fault them because they're making millions of
dollars and their habits have changed. But we don't take enough
time to go back and say, 'Hey, here I am, I came from here.' We
forget where we came from."

Like so many other ex-ballplayers, Spinks had gravitated into
sales after he left baseball. "I sold cars and I did real well at it,"
he said, "but it got to a certain point where I was burned out. I
don't get burned out on baseball. I was so bitter when I had to
retire. I didn't even want to go to ball games for five years. I
didn't even want to talk to anybody about baseball because
somebody would say something that would rekindle that willingness to want to play again in me. At that time I knew I couldn't
play, and why should I keep fighting myself, knowing I can't
play? Then this league came along and Mother Nature took care
of all my injuries and there was an opportunity to come back
and play.

"If there was an old car salesman's league, I'd just bypass it.
Hah! I really would."

Pedro Borbon returned to the clubhouse after batting practice
with an armload of coconuts, harvested with the help of his
young son, also Pedro, from the palm trees that leaned over the
outfield fence. Borbon dumped the coconuts on a picnic table
next to where some of his teammates were playing cards. While

the card players looked on sideways, Borbon picked two he liked, shook them one at a time, banged them together to soften the husk, chose one, whacked at it repeatedly with a bat while turning it slowly in his hand, ripped off the husk, cracked the nut on the edge of the table, poured off the milk, produced a machete (where did he get that?), chopped at the nut with the huge blade, and spread out the slices like pieces of melon for anyone who wanted to taste. The coconut was sweet, but the best part was watching Borbon work.

Tonight's game was a benefit for cancer patients. The organizers were having a picnic in a nearby tent. Bernie Carbo, in uniform, crashed the party and came away with a Styrofoam cup filled to overflowing with shrimp, another of cocktail sauce, and an unopened bottle of zinfandel. Carbo was proud of his heist— he wanted to open the bottle then and there, before the game— and Spinks was admiring, as he was of most of Carbo's antics. Joe Pittman was disgusted with the both of them:

"Bernie take a shit, Scipio gotta take a shit. Bernie throw up, Scipio gotta throw up. Bernie step on the card table, Scipio gotta step on the card table."

Pittman had been snarling all day. At the hotel this morning, waiting for the bus to the ballpark, just for fun he'd pulled out his pocketknife and waved it threateningly at Jim Bibby. While tourists looked on alarmedly, Bibby grabbed a signpost from the center of the lobby, raised it over his head, and dared Pittman to advance. The confrontation ended in a stalemate.

"You piss me off, Bibby," Pittman said now.

"Better to be pissed off than pissed on," Bibby replied, proving that, sometimes, men will be boys.

More roster moves. Spinks, parked on the taxi squad since November, was activated to fill the spot vacated by Bomback, who went on the disabled list. Also activated was Ed Clements, a thirteen-year veteran with the Sydney Sooners, a semipro team in Nova Scotia. Like Bill Lee, his teammate on the Sooners, Clements was a left-handed pitcher who could play the outfield when needed. In order to make room for Clements, someone had to go. So ended the five-decade professional career of Darrell Brandon.

Brandon's fate was made known to his teammates gradually, by the simple fact that he never bothered to get dressed for the game. There were those, once they knew, who made the mistake of trying to lighten the load: here a handshake and a "Whattaya say?," there a "Don't be afraid to stop by for a beer!" But Butch Hobson knew better, knew not to react. No gushy good-byes, no false condolences. Say good-bye if you must, but spare the theatrics. *Act like nothing was changed.* It was the honorable thing to do.

When I asked Brandon what his plans were, he said he didn't have any other than to remain in Florida at least long enough to work the upcoming Red Sox fantasy camp in Winter Haven. Later during the game, I noticed him sitting alone behind the dugout, drinking a beer. The next day he was gone.

THIS WAS ONE THE SUPER SOX ACTUALLY HAD A CHANCE TO WIN. Down 6–2 in the seventh, they chased starter Rick Waits with a flurry of hard-hit balls. Gene Richards's single scored Ron Dunn, and another single by Joe Pittman scored Tommy McMillan, which brought up Al Bumbry with the tying runs on base. Bumbry connected solidly on a one-one pitch from reliever Steve Luebber and might have tied the game but for Fort Myers's outstanding third baseman Ron Jackson, who knocked the ball down and made a strong throw to first to end the inning.

In the ninth, McMillan was robbed at first on a terrible call by Don Trentalange, an injustice more deeply felt after Richards followed with a double and Pittman singled. Again Bumbry came up with a chance to be a hero. This time he grounded straight back to the pitcher for a double play.

Game over. Sun Sox, 6, Super Sox, 4. Losing streak now at six games. Afterward, an undertone of desperation could be detected in the voices of the sad Sox.

"He ought to make the right call," McMillan said of Trentalange. "He ought to bear down because we're trying. He's not giving it all he's got."

"Umpiring, all you got to do is see," said Spinks. "I hope that motherfucker can't sleep tonight."

"I'll find out where he lives and put a pit bull on his dick" was Lee's opening remark. "Can't fucking believe it! Shit, we win that game if that fucking guy calls that play safe. That was the curse of that fucking woodpecker."

Lee had sighted a woodpecker. It flew over the practice field yesterday and again today, landing both times on a pole by the batting cage. Lee talked to the woodpecker. He decided that the woodpecker was, in fact, the ghost of Tom Yawkey, come to Fort Myers to pass on the dreaded curse of the Red Sox.

"Tom Yawkey is a bird because Tom Yawkey killed most of the woodpeckers on the Carolina Coast with pesticides, all that stuff that he sold to St. Regis. I talked to him about it before he died. He cried. Then he died. Saw him first as a pigeon and now he's an endangered species. I talked to him for a while"—Lee meant the bird—"and he looked at me, kinda nodded in acknowledgment, then he was on his way."

Lee looked pale. He was acting skittish. Twice during the game I watched him change his shoes, once to go running on the practice field, then late in the game because he was still hoping he might get a chance to pinch-hit.

"I still think if we hadn't a made any moves the first week of the season we'd still be playing with them," Lee said, still unable to accept having been fired as manager. "That's my personal opinion. I know everything about every one of these guys. I know what they can do, what they can't do, when they have to have a day off. I knew Bumbry's leg was hurt before he batted the last time up. I examine every player, everything about them. I see things that other people don't see.

"I had a pretty good idea about how to manipulate this ball club for the long run, and I haven't had that opportunity. That's my own personal opinion. I have said my input, but it's never accepted so I have ceased to put input. I just go out and dick off, kick footballs around, run my butt off on back fields, and every pitch I see in batting practice I try and jack the shit out of it. And I yell at fucking umpires until I'm blue in the face."

Finally, Lee was spent. "I'm gonna have so many fucking milligrams of Motrin in me tomorrow they won't fucking touch me," he said. And with that he was off, home to Winter Haven to sleep with his wife and rest up for tomorrow's doubleheader in Orlando.

The rest of us trouped onto the bus.

"THAT YOU, BRUMMER?" SAID FERGUSON JENKINS. "THAT'S A HOLstein fart." Jenkins, a cattle rancher in Oklahoma, would know.

"Somebody light a cigarette."

"Bernie"—this shouted over a shoulder at the back of the bus—"light a cigarette!"

While Brummer snickered, the rest of us suffered. His was the latest release into an atmosphere already polluted beyond a level thought to be safe for children, the elderly, and those with respiratory ailments. The soup was made of cigarette smoke, perspiration, beer vapors, and the countless farts of others. Everybody had the same headache.

We left Fort Myers at 10:30 P.M.—one hundred twenty miles north on I-75 to Tampa, then east on I-4 eighty-four miles to Orlando, a journey through the night of three and one-half hours. The main topic of conversation this evening around the cooler that served for a boo-ray table was the Hall of Fame. It so happened that included in the present company were two names on this year's ballot: Jim Bibby and Jenkins. The results would be announced in New York at 11:00 tonight, half an hour from now.

Bibby, who twice during his twelve-year career with the Cardinals, Rangers, Indians, and Pirates won nineteen games but never made it to twenty, was not regarded as a serious candidate (later I found out he received only one vote). But Jenkins was an interesting case.

Over a nineteen-year career, Jenkins won two hundred eighty-four games, sixteen shy of the magic three hundred but still more wins than thirty-one of the forty-eight pitchers already in the Hall of Fame. Seven times he won twenty games, including six seasons in a row in the late sixties and early seventies, and that while pitching for the Cubs in Wrigley Field. He was an all-star three times and won the Cy Young Award in 1971 with a record of twenty-four and thirteen, a 2.77 ERA, and thirty complete games. And, as Jenkins himself pointed out, he was the only pitcher in the history of the game ever to combine more than three thousand strikeouts (three thousand one hundred ninety-two, ninth on the all-time list) with fewer than one thousand walks, a testimony to the fine control that was his hallmark.

But admittedly there were a couple of problems with Jenkins's candidacy. In nineteen years with the Phillies, the Cubs, the Rangers, and the Red Sox, Jenkins never played on a team that won anything, not even a division championship. You might argue that Jenkins's record—unlike that, say, of Whitey Ford—was that much more remarkable considering what little help he received, but that's an abstraction. It's hard to shine if you're never in the spotlight.

Then there was the sticky matter of Jenkins's arrest on drug charges. On August 24, 1980, Jenkins flew with his Ranger team-

mates on a chartered airplane from Milwaukee to Toronto for a
series with the Blue Jays. Somewhere along the way, luggage
belonging to four passengers, including Jenkins, was lost. The
next day, after the bags turned up at Metropolitan Airport in
Toronto, they were opened and inspected by Canadian authorities, a routine procedure for which Jenkins gave his permission
in advance. But when Jenkins arrived at Exhibition Stadium for
the 12:00 game, he was arrested by the Royal Canadian Mounted
Police and charged with possession of four grams of cocaine, two
ounces of marijuana, and two grams of hashish.

Despite the fact that in Canada the maximum penalty for simple
possession was six months in jail and a one-thousand-dollar fine,
before the trial baseball commissioner Bowie Kuhn chose to sus-
pend Jenkins for the remainder of the season, a decision overturned
by arbitrator Raymond Goetz. Jenkins was later convicted on the
single charge of possession of cocaine. Unlike Vida Blue, Jenkins
never served any time. Later, his record was wiped clean.

Who knew what the upstanding members of the Baseball
Writers Association of America were thinking? The recent rev-
elation that Pete Rose was a compulsive gambler who consorted
with thugs and cheated on his income taxes had, unfortunately,
made "character" an issue in balloting for the Hall of Fame. If
it mattered that much, the voters would do well to consider that
only two months before his arrest, Jenkins, a native of Chatham,
Ontario, was awarded the Order of Canada, among the highest
civic citations bestowed by his native country.

Fergie, for his part, refused to let himself get too excited. "You
can't bank on what's gonna happen," he said. "You can't rule
your own destiny. It'd be nice. It'd really be nice. I told my dad,
before he passes on, I'd like to have him there with me if it
happens. My dad's eighty-four. He was a good athlete, but he
never got a chance to play."

"Fergie, I love you," said Joe Pittman after he had a chance
to look at the draw dealt him by Jenkins. "I hope you make the
Hall of Fame."

At 11:00, Rick Wise and Tommy McMillan put on earphones
and scanned the radio waves for election results. If either of
them learned anything, they kept it to themselves.

"We're gonna go to the hotel," Pittman predicted. "There'll
be Hall of Fame banners all over the hotel waiting on Fergie
Jenkins."

The bus rumbled on through an eerie tropical landscape, illuminated by a lantern moon two days shy of full. With only reading lamps to light the interior, it was darker inside than out. One by one the miles accumulated. One by one the readers and the radio listeners drifted off to sleep. The card players pressed on. Except for occasional outbursts, what noise they made was muffled by the roar of the road. Tuesday became Wednesday.

"Where the fuck are we?" came a groggy voice from the back of the bus. "Take me home. I wanna go home."

At a few minutes before 1:00 A.M., I borrowed a radio from Wise and picked up a newscast out of Memphis, Tennessee. They didn't say anything about the Hall of Fame until the very end, and then I almost wished I hadn't heard: Jim Palmer and Joe Morgan, both in their first year of eligibility, were in; Gaylord Perry, not yet, though he missed by only thirteen votes; and not a word about Jenkins. (Later I found out Jenkins received two hundred ninety-six votes, thirty-seven short of the required 75 percent of all votes cast.)

"ALL-NUDE REVUE!" THE VOICE BELONGED TO SCIPIO SPINKS. IT shattered the stillness of the early morning and woke everybody up. "Pull over! Pull over!"

Evidently, we had arrived in Orlando. Evidently, in a neighborhood far removed from the Magic Kingdom. Where was Bussie taking us?

"All topless!" Spinks again. "Pull over! Pull over!"

Bussie would not be swayed, and a short while later we pulled up not at the hotel but outside Tinker Field.

"What are we doing?"

"We got a workout, we got a fucking workout."

No, thank God, just a pit stop at 2:00 in the morning to unload the gear. Seems that Bussie wasn't comfortable with leaving the equipment in the bus all night, not at the hotel where he was planning on taking us.

We continued on, down dark streets lined with strip joints, liquor stores, and used-car lots, and arrived shortly at our hotel, which was not a hotel after all but a motel. "Welcome Florida Valve and Pipe Fitting Company and Orange Bank," the sign said.

The keys to our rooms were waiting at the front desk, arranged in sets of two. I was paired with a former Red Sox player, now a coach in the minor leagues. What impressed me most about my roomie was the speed with which he was able to locate from a wide array of choices the best that television had to offer at that hour. Within minutes, we were settled in our beds, enjoying the dramatic conclusion of *Pretty Smart,* a pretty dumb titty movie all about what went on behind the scenes at a beauty pageant.

Just before sleep came, a cackle, obviously female, erupted on the walkway outside our room. My roomie sprang from his bed, clad only in his briefs, and peered through the slit in the curtains.

"One of our guys has got a whore," he announced matter-of-factly, then corrected himself. "Nah, somebody else."

He climbed back under the covers. At the first sound of snoring, I got up and switched off the TV.

ORLANDO • *January 10*

Morning in Orlando. The motel coffee shop was wall-to-wall ballplayers, ours and Bradenton's. The Explorers, come to find out, had finished up a series with the Juice last night. Tonight they had a game in St. Lucie. The reason they were still in Orlando was simple: The Raddison in St. Lucie charged thirty-five dollars a night, double occupancy, while the Ramada here was a bargain at twenty-three fifty. So what if everyone had to get up a little earlier today? Was it so awful to have to spend two hours on the bus before a game? Evidently not. After all, it wasn't every day management saw a chance to save maybe two hundred fifty bucks. (You could say it was no coincidence that the Explorers lost to the Legends later that night for the first time this season, but you'll never be able to prove it.)

Bill Lee drove up from Winter Haven and beat the bus to the ballpark. He was waiting in the dugout when we got there, dressed in black jeans, a long-sleeved T-shirt, and a red baseball cap—college cool, circa 1975. He still looked pale. Lee lounged at one end of the third-base dugout with a group of teammates and talked bass fishing.

A short while later, today's other scheduled starter, Mike Marshall, arrived. Marshall stood at the opposite end of the dugout with Rick Maxwell and talked umpires.

"The problem with the umpires in the league," Maxwell was saying, "as far as I'm concerned, is they feel threatened all the time so they feel the only way to handle it—"

"Yeah," said Marshall, interrupting, "they're too intimidated by the hitters to call them out with two strikes. You see Billy Williams the other night? I loved it. It was major leagues again. He's standing back there, the pitch is this far out"—he held his hands six inches apart—"and he says, 'Strike three!' That's it. You see anybody arguing with him? Fuck no. Because if you watch every major-league game, what does an umpire want to do? You get two strikes, 'Strike three!' If you're ahead in the strike zone, the plate widens. If the hitter's ahead, it's a different story.' "

Maxwell, himself a man who liked to be heard, tried to get a word in; he just wanted to make it a conversation. Marshall merely raised his voice a decibel or two.

"Over half my major-league strikeouts were *called* strikeouts. They wouldn't swing because they couldn't hit the thing; that's too fucking close, 'You're outta there!' See, we don't have the fastball to live in the center of the plate anymore. If I still had a ninety-five-mile-per-hour fastball, I wouldn't be standing here talking to you."

"How old were you when you quit?" Maxwell managed to interject.

"Thirty-eight. And I didn't quit. I had a 2.61 earned run average that year. Could have done it for another four or five years."

It was then that Leon Roberts appeared at the end of the tunnel that led from the locker room to the dugout. Purposefully, the manager approached his starting pitcher. He came right to the point: "Does it make a big difference which game you pitch?"

Marshall stiffened. "Pretty big, yeah," he answered, while managing to avoid making direct contact with Roberts's eyes.

"I mean a *big* difference. Does it make a big difference to you whether you go in the first game or the second game?"

This time, Marshall said nothing. Roberts looked defeated.

"Sort of mentally programmed to go the first one?" Roberts asked weakly.

"Yeah, that and other commitments."

"If I have to make a switch will you go with it? Pitch at four? I mean, I'm leaning toward not doing it."

Marshall was silent. Then, "I'd have to make some calls."

"Well," said Roberts, "as of right now let's leave it this way."

"I'd appreciate it," Marshall said, polite now in victory.

Later I found out what happened. Lee, apparently, was acting up. First he tried to convince Roberts to let him pitch both ends of the doubleheader. When that didn't work he asked to pitch the first game so that he could play the outfield in the second game. Roberts balked. Lee pressed. Voices were raised. That was when Roberts tried to talk to Marshall.

"You can't give in to Lee," Rick Maxwell once said, "or he'll end up running the show."

At 12:25, thirty-five minutes before the start of the double-header, Lee left the ballpark saying he was going to get something to eat. Marshall would start the first game, after all.

"Managing in this league is damn near impossible," Marshall said before he went down to the bull pen to warm up, " 'cause you got twenty managers on the bench second-guessing everything you do."

Yeah, him and Lee and nineteen others.

THE SOX WERE LETTING ME WATCH FROM THE BENCH TODAY. AND I thought press boxes were filthy places. In the dugout you saw peanut shells, sunflower seeds, used-gum balls (orange, green, pink), used tobacco (brown, black), tobacco juice, spit, snot, gurgled water, gurgled Gatorade, some of it ground or smeared into the cement floor, some of it clinging to the walls. You smelled sweat, farts, and fetid breath. You contended with ants, spiders, flying insects, and sundry communicable diseases.

First inning: Marshall huddles with catcher Doug Simunic to go over the signs. "One fastball, two curve, three slider."

The demand for autographs never lets up. Even as the game begins, hunters hang their heads over the roof of the dugout, scanning the bench for likely trophies. One of them passes Ferguson Jenkins an eight-by-ten glossy of a smooth-faced kid in a Cubs uniform, portrait of the pitcher as a young man. "I thought I was Bob Gibson in pinstripes," Jenkins says, smiling and showing it around before he signs it and passes it back. Another hands Rick Wise his rookie card; incredibly, now over a quarter century old. "Good-looking kid, huh?" says Wise, and he, too, shares it with his teammates. With so many youthful images in general circulation, is it any wonder ballplayers have a hard time letting go?

"Slider?" someone wonders out loud after Bumbry homers off Juice starter Bob Shirley, scoring Joe Pittman, who reached on a bunt single.

"Slid right on outta here," comes the answer. Sox lead, 2–0.

In the bottom of the inning, the Sox give one back. The jury on the bench decides who's to blame. Agreed, Tony Scott made a weak throw from right; still, first baseman Pete LaCock should have been there to cut it off, which would have saved the run. This one's for you, Pete.

"Anybody know [Randy] Bass?" Marshall asks when he comes back to the dugout.

"Yeah, dead-pull hitter."

"I threw him a slider down and in. It was like I put it on a tee for him." Then to his shortstop, Ron Dunn: "Looks like [Ken] Reitz was trying to shove the ball the other way. Might make sense to shade him a little next time."

Second inning: Fergie is muttering to himself and shaking his head disgustedly. A minute ago he warned Marshall that Jerry Martin likes to wait on breaking balls; therefore, it might make sense to begin by pushing him back off the plate with a fastball. Marshall nodded, then walked out to the mound, threw Martin a screwball on the very first pitch, and nearly got his head ripped off with a line drive. Now Martin's standing on first base.

Larvell Blanks, trying to advance the runner, squares to bunt and misses. Should be a strike but the umpire calls, "Ball." Gloom settles on the Super Sox bench. When you've lost six straight, calls like that begin to seem like fate.

"Same old shit," comes a plaintive voice, somewhere down the line. "Why does this shit have to happen to us?" Orlando ties the game, 2–2.

Marshall may be stubborn, but he knows when an explanation is required. "I figured he's never seen a screwball," he tells Jenkins between innings, "so I'll throw him a screwball, *then* bust him inside." Fergie nods and pats him on the back.

Third inning: Carbo, singing along with the PA system: "And I sawww herrrr stannnnd-ing there." Then, "I hated the Beatles. I was an Elvis Presley man."

Fergie: "Can you whistle?"

Carbo tries, but he's been eating peanuts. The best he can do is spray shell fragments on his shirt.

Fergie: "Better than you can sing."

Fifth inning: Juice winning, 4–2. Pittman singles to right, makes too wide a turn, and is thrown out going back to first by José Cruz. "I can see why Pittman didn't play much in the big leagues," says Carbo, as harsh a judge as any tabloid columnist. "He makes a lot of fucking mistakes." Lucky for Pittman, it's the third out; he's better off not facing his teammates just yet.

Sixth inning: Marshall, under orders now to throw more fastballs, does, and walks Martin. Roberts asks Fergie to get Jim Willoughby up in the bull pen. No phone, of course, so Fergie waits until after the next pitch is thrown, then takes off running down the left-field line.

Grounder to Pittman at second base. He bobbles the ball, then recovers and flips to Dunn covering second for out number one. Dunn has it in his head to complete the double play but drops the ball while he's taking it out of his glove. On the bench, heads are shaking again. "Jesus Christ, what a circus," says Carbo. "Put a tent over it."

Left fielder Gene Richards throws out Bruce Bochy at the plate and the Sox are spared any further damage. It's just a two-run ball game. They're still in this one.

Seventh inning: Dugout sounds are metal cleats on cement, the PA announcer (muffled, hard to understand), birds singing. Birds? Today's attendance is in the low three figures: one hundred forty-five. The songbirds are making a bigger racket than the fans.

Bass homers off Willoughby and the Juice go on to score four more. Much moaning and groaning. Roberts sends Fergie out to make another pitching change. Now pitching for the Super Sox, making his first appearance in the senior league, Ed Clements. Carbo started calling Clements "Electro" when he saw how he wrapped electrician's tape around his legs to hold up his baseball socks. That was before anyone knew his first name was Edison. "He's a little dry, but his eyes are bright," Fergie reports to Roberts when he gets back to the dugout. "He's tense."

Clements walks the first batter on four pitches. "The ball was not high!" yells Lee, back now from lunch. "He's a grown man with a family! He's almost as tall as you! Bullshit!"

The ump turns to face the bench. "The ball was not *high*," he says, motioning with his hands that, in fact, it was *outside*.

"Oh," says Lee, grinning back. "Okay."

A ground ball and the side is retired. Juice's lead is now 8–2.

Eighth inning: Double by Ron Dunn scores two, Sox cut the lead to 8–4. Dare we hope?

Ninth inning: One out, then three straight singles to load the bases. Pittman batting now with a chance to redeem himself. "Don't hit a ground ball, Shoes," Fergie prays softly. Shoes does not, hits a soft liner to second instead. The Sox are down to their last out.

Bumbry batting. "A grand slam'll do," someone says. No, but Bumbry walks. Eight-five now and the bases still loaded.

"Soup," says Roberts, who has seen enough to at least begin making plans for the bottom of the inning. Bill Campbell was signing autographs; now he sprints down to the bull pen, just in case.

Scott walks on four pitches. Eight-six, bases still loaded. So long, Shirley. Hello, Doug Corbett. Dunn singles up the middle! Tie game!

Tenth inning: LaCock is called out on strikes, gets ejected for arguing. "Yeah, I'm gonna go!" LaCock bellows at the home-plate ump. "I'm gonna get my last word in, though."

Up and down the bench, his teammates prick up their ears.

"You stink! You stink, and everybody here knows it!" Lucky for the ump, there aren't too many here.

Twelfth inning: Carbo on third, one out. McMillan hits a fly ball to center. Carbo tags up and heads for home, chugging like a truck in low gear. Slides headfirst, but the ball is there waiting for him. "Aw, shit," he says, back in the dugout. "Throw beat me, didn't it?" Then he drops his pants to empty out all the dirt he scooped up.

"Bernie!" says Fergie, reprovingly, sounding like a mom. "People in the stands!"

Bernie, indicating his underwear: "It's like the beach."

Fergie: "This is *not* the beach."

With two outs in the bottom of the inning, Reitz singles, Bass doubles, and suddenly the game is over. Back in the locker room, LaCock still can't understand why he got thrown out of the game. "I didn't tell him 'Your mother sucks dick' or anything like that. I told him he was umpiring scared."

One down, one to go.

I was looking forward to the second game. Vida Blue would be making his first start since coming over to the Juice from the Legends for Bill Madlock—your basic I'll-give-you-my-headache-if-you'll-give-me-yours trade. But Blue didn't show up until right before the game so the Juice went with Gerry Pirtle instead, a right-hander whose major-league experience consisted of twenty-six innings for the Expos in 1978. Oh, well, at least Lee was pitching for the Sox.

To the extent that a crowd of one hundred forty-five could thin out, this one did. With so little noise from the stands, I had no problem hearing Lee, who chastised himself after almost every pitch. Sometimes the curses made sense, but when Lee lit into himself after retiring the batter on a pop-up to second base, I turned to Jenkins for guidance. "Sometimes he doesn't think the hitter should even *touch* that pitch," Fergie explained. "He's in his own world."

More injuries. Dunn made a running catch on the foul line behind third base, threw hard to the plate to try to get the runner tagging up, then fell to the ground, clutching his elbow in agony. Later Tommy Cruz strained his knee running down a fly ball in left and had to come out of the game. "We need four hot tubs and no doubleheaders in this league," Brummer said.

Down 5–0, the Sox reached Pirtle for a run in the seventh, then added one more after Blue came on in relief. "Tie it up, I'm still fucking loose!" Lee exhorted his teammates after setting down the Juice one-two-three in the eighth. Quickly there were two outs, then Butch Hobson walked, sending McMillan, who singled, down to second. Shoes's single scored McMillan. Up came Bumbry with two on and the score 5–3.

"I'll get another knock," he promised from the on-deck circle.

"If you do, it will be a big one."

"I know."

Bumbry fouled out.

So much for the Sox. The time now was 7:05. They'd driven here in the middle of the night, played twenty-one innings of baseball, labored for six hours, and now all they had to show for it was two more in the loss column.

Back in the locker room, the Sox gnawed on fried chicken, quietly browsed through the league's best collection of skin mags (maintained, for tips, by the local clubhouse staff), and pondered their fall: from five games under .500 to thirteen, from five and one-half games out of first place to eleven and one-half, from hope to surrender.

Only three weeks remained in the season. Nothing left for the Super Sox now but to play out the schedule.

PORT ST. LUCIE · *January 14*

WOKE UP TODAY WITH A COMPELLING URGE TO HIT THE ROAD. Checked the schedule—Orlando at St. Lucie, 6:00. Perfect. But then I looked in my St. Pete *Times* and the paper said, "Orlando at St. Lucie, 1:35." Better call. The woman who answered the phone at the Legends' main office said, "I really don't know. Let me give you the number for the ticket office." I called the ticket office: "The Legends' ticket office is open Monday through Friday from ten A.M. until . . ." I checked my watch while the recording droned on; it was 10:15. Then, ". . . Sunday, St. Lucie Legends versus St. Pete Pelicans, six o'clock." *Pelicans?* What the hell, the day was fine. I was going no matter what.

THE ST. LUCIE COUNTY SPORTS COMPLEX DIDN'T LOOK SO DEPRESS-ingly like a complex this afternoon, not when it was lit by the sun instead of floodlights and the sky overhead was a deep, hard blue like the waxed finish on a car. I entered through the gate by the bull pen out in left field and walked down to the dugout. There was Jerry Grote, standing around without a shirt on, his gut hanging over his jeans. Good, must be a game tonight. I was afraid maybe I'd driven all this way for the scenery.

The blue plastic seats that matched the sky were all empty, of course; it was still three hours before the game. It didn't look as if they'd be filling up anytime soon. At this moment, the AFC championship game was winding down in Denver (and in living rooms everywhere) while in San Francisco the NFC version waited in the wings, ready to carry viewers the rest of the way to bedtime. It hardly mattered that the Legends had a pretty good show planned for tonight; the Juice (not the Pelicans) were in town and Vida Blue would be making his first start against his old teammates. But Vida Blue in his prime would not have sold out this park, not tonight. This particular Sunday was reserved for football; in St. Lucie, Florida, and everywhere else in America.

Roy Thomas came out of the Legends locker room and sat down beside me on the bench. We had talked before. Thomas was thoughtful, quiet, introspective. He was keeping a diary, and he'd let me look at it a couple of times. It was a spiral-bound notebook filled with chicken-scratch script, double-spaced, and it chronicled the ups and downs—mostly downs—of laboring for the worst franchise in the league. He wrote about the weather: "Cold + windy! Cold + windy!!!"; about the working conditions: "None of the uniforms fit. The shirts were small, the pants were short but the waistbands were abnormally large. Some guys pinned them up, I finally turned my jock waistband out over the back of my pants, that seemed to work very well"; and about the pain of losing: "I was so upset that I felt like—just for a moment—like giving up. I work so hard—and it just seems to all be pissed away . . . I've given up trying to get my ERA down. Hits to innings ratio—forget it. I'm going for the strikeout lead. What else is left?" He talked about maybe getting it published one day.

Thomas was six-five and skinny. He sat with his shoulders hunched over, his hair hanging out of his hat, his shirt hanging out of his pants. His eyes were green and sad, like a dog's eyes. He wore his hat so low it almost touched his eyebrows. The hat helped him concentrate, he said, kept him focused on the sixty-foot tunnel between the mound and home plate. It was one of the tricks he'd taught himself over the course of a long, obscure career—seventeen years, fourteen different professional teams. Another trick he'd picked up was never, ever, referring to hitters by name.

Whenever he talked to his catcher, Thomas said, "I just say, 'First baseman, right fielder.' Even in the big leagues, I didn't like recognizing them, knowing that was Jim Rice or that was Johnny Bench. Got to keep those little thoughts out of there that you don't need."

Thomas was the first-round pick of the Philadelphia Phillies in the 1971 amateur draft, the sixth player chosen overall. The Phillies gave him seventy-five thousand dollars to sign and packed him off to Walla Walla in the Pioneer League. "Pitched my first game on my eighteenth birthday," Thomas said, remembering. He grew up in Lompoc, California, north of Santa Barbara, and spoke like a Californian—without an accent. "Walla Walla, Washington. 'A place so nice they named it twice.' Seven years before I made it to the big leagues and then I was up and down. Long haul. It's been worth it, but I would have changed a few things. That's how life goes, I guess. I'm a better person for it."

He chuckled at the last part, not really meaning it, knowing it was a cliché.

"I got traded to Houston and they sent me down in '78, through waivers, and the guy said to me, 'I hope you don't quit,' you know? And I looked at him, I said, 'I never even thought about it.' It never even crossed my mind to be out of baseball. That was some other dimension somewhere, wasn't even registering as a possibility. It was just a job, what I always did. If they released me that would have been a complete shock. So I just kept on going.

"I remember a lot of small things. Lou Brock coming up to me one time when I got a big save against the Dodgers, '79 I think. I got two outs, runner on second, and [Manny] Mota's pinch-hitting; he was having a great year. And [Ted] Simmons is catching. He calls fastball in, fouls it off. Fastball in, foul, foul. Kept calling fastballs. I'm thinking, 'What's he doing?' But [Mota] wanted us to go away so he could just lay the bat out and get a hit to right. So we stayed hard-in and I popped him up in left. Brock made the last out. Came in and he said, 'Don't ever leave the field when I'm coming in trying to give you the ball,' you know, the game ball. Kinda mad but kinda having fun with me. That was neat."

In two and a half weeks, the season would be over. Thomas would be going back home to his wife in Seattle ("No kids, dog just died"). He'd be looking for something to do. What he really wanted was to start a baseball school, that being what he knew best. But if that didn't work out, he'd have to find a job outside the game. "When I was fifteen, I had one," he said. "For about a week, got fired. Cleaning up in a travel agency and stamping addresses on flyers." One thing he knew for sure, though: if there was a senior league next year, he'd be back.

"It's so great, man. You're *alive*. I get out there and I come in and it takes me half an hour to wind down after the game. I'm just fired up, man, I mean, my body's alive. I'm out there full speed. To be able to go to your job and get a great mental and physical workout. That's what I miss, just groaning and getting it all out. When the game's over, I'm tired. I'm *tired. Exhausted,* sometimes, depending on how the week's been going. But it's great. I love it."

Thomas had to go get ready. But first he wanted me to have something. I waited while he went inside, and when he came back out he handed me a piece of paper, folded in half. "Just something I wrote," he said:

> *Echoes come from out*
> *of the past, reminders*
> *of tools that some*
> *knew would not last.*
>
> *But hope is sometimes*
> *eternally misled. By*
> *the echoes we want to*
> *hear inside our head.*

WATCHING FROM THE PRESS BOX, RAY NEGRON, THE BABY-FACED general manager of the Legends, had little that was positive to say about his former ace, Vida Blue. "Vida just totally lost interest in pitching over here," said Negron. "The last game he started in and played in for us, he was getting hit and [catcher Floyd] Rayford felt that he really wasn't throwing like Vida Blue. So he went up to the mound and he said to him, 'Listen, Vida, if you don't want to pitch, get the fuck outta here!' and then right after that we took him out of the game."

And right after that they traded him. Since then, Blue must have found a new attitude to go with his new uniform. Over the last week, the Legends had won five of their last seven, very impressive considering that their overall record was sixteen and forty-one. But tonight Blue went the distance against them for the first time all year and was the beneficiary of an offense that rapped out nineteen hits as the Juice won in a romp, 16–6.

"I just know that we had a situation in which the team wasn't going anywhere," Blue said after the game, "and it was eating me up on the inside to be on a losing team like that and I was lucky that

they worked a deal for me to come to the Juice. I wish that everything could be hunky-dory for them as well as for everybody else in
the league, but unfortunately the world is not like that. There's
always going to be good and bad. Right now I'm with the good."

Good for Blue.

Two tantalizing news bits to report. First, Negron happened
to mention before the game that the proposed sale of the Legends to Lenny Woolf was off. Woolf invested more than four
hundred thousand dollars in the team—some of which Negron
had already spent on new players—before deciding suddenly last
week to pull out. If Negron knew anything more about the deal
than that, he wasn't sharing it with me.

Then there was the mysterious meeting that took place in the
Juice clubhouse immediately after the game. Wynne Dillard and
Ben Kaufman, of the Juices' front office, closed the door to all
outsiders and addressed the players in private for about ten minutes. Tomorrow was payday, which naturally led to speculation
among the uninformed out in the hallway that the Juice were
unable to meet payroll. Dillard and Kaufman were no help at all;
both looked grim, neither said a word. So I asked a player.

"We're getting paid," Larvell Blanks said, "just in a different
style."

"What does that mean?"

"Keep your eyes and ears open," he said right before he left
to board the bus. "You might learn something."

WEST PALM BEACH, PORT ST. LUCIE · *January 15*

THE GROUNDSKEEPER IN WEST PALM BEACH LIKED TO DRESS UP THE
on-deck circle. One day he made it look like a baseball, gave it
seams and stitches, not all two hundred and two stitches but
enough to get the idea across. Today he gave it a happy face,
matching the prevailing mood at 11:00 on a winter morning
when the sun shone naked in the sky and the temperature
climbed toward eighty degrees. Tom Spencer, here with his
teammates from Fort Myers for a split doubleheader with the
Tropics, chatted with a nonuniformed, hair-slicked-back, walkie-
talkie-toting acquaintance. Joe Mincberg, the lawyer who would

be first baseman, did sit-ups in the damp grass while the trainer held his feet. The song on the spectacular sound system was "The Wanderer."

A win by the Tropics today would clinch the first of four available berths in the senior-league championship series, scheduled for the first weekend in February. Faced with the twin challenge of involving as many teams as possible (to keep the fans interested) and compressing the entire postseason affair into one weekend (to satisfy Prime Network and maximize national exposure), the owners had come up with a bizarre solution. On Friday night the second-place teams in either division would play each other for the right to go against the division winner with the lesser record on Saturday afternoon. The winner of Saturday's game would then go on to meet the team with the best overall record on Sunday. It was ridiculous to crown a champion in baseball on the basis of a single-elimination tournament—the players knew it and so did the fans—but it was already decided.

The Tropics, six games ahead of St. Petersburg in the race for the best record in the league, clearly were confident of earning the double bye and going straight to the championship game. So confident, in fact, that they were offering their fans an excursion package to the tournament site in Fort Myers with tickets for Sunday's game only.

I wandered over to the Sun Sox clubhouse and went inside. Here there was no hint of the glorious day unfolding in the world outside. The room had no windows. It smelled of excrement and sweat. A portable TV on a high shelf was tuned to a morning soap opera. Wayne Garland was not watching the TV. He was tugging at his right shoulder with his left hand and staring off into neutral space with that same haunting, vacant expression. Garland was pitching today, and already he hurt.

"There's no doubt in my mind, something's wrong inside," Garland said, "maybe tore it again or something like that. But the only way you can find out is to scope it and if you scope it you're gonna be out for a while."

Lately, to preserve himself, Garland had stopped throwing between starts, stopped using his right arm altogether if he could help it. Yesterday in Winter Haven he forgot and reached for the coffeepot, but then he felt the jolt and was reminded. He used to warm up for fifteen minutes before every game; now he rarely went more than ten. He faced today's starting assignment knowing there was no chance he'd be able to finish. There would be pain first, a shooting pain that ran down his arm on every pitch, and sometimes down his whole body. Pain he could cope with. But after pain came the end of feeling altogether, and then it was time to stop.

"You never know when that'll be. It just depends on how many pitches. Could be as early as the fourth inning, or the sixth inning, or something. What it is, it gets heavy. It just doesn't get any nerves down to it or any blood or anything. It just gets to the point where it's too heavy."

Garland wore no shirt. The scar on his shoulder was from the last time he was operated on in 1978. He was in no hurry to go through that again, but he knew sooner or later he would probably have to.

"It's getting to the time right now that if I have any aspiration of doing this next year, I'm gonna have to make a decision to find out what's wrong with it. I can't go on pitching like this. It just depends on what happens today, maybe one more start, two more starts. I'll have to see how it feels."

Garland fell behind the first four batters he faced today: Mickey Rivers walked, Jerry White grounded out to first, Mike Easler and Ron Washington hit hard singles straight back up the middle. That left two men on base, one run in, and Dave Kingman the batter. Kingman flied out to center. When Lee Lacy grounded into a fielder's choice, Garland survived the first inning with little damage.

More trouble to start the second: Toby Harrah and Randy Johnson walked. At that point, Ron Jackson and Dan Driessen converged from opposite corners of the infield and met at the mound, where they spoke briefly with Garland. Rodney Scott followed with the Tropics' third base hit, yet another hard single up the middle. Bases loaded now, nobody out, Rivers again at the top of the order. Rivers hit Garland's first pitch right at shortstop Jerry Terrell; one out. White followed with a fly ball to left that scored Harrah. Then, with the count two balls and one strike, Easler drove Garland's next pitch deep to right, where Larry Harlow made a running, reaching, World Series catch for the third out of the inning. Garland had thrown forty-one pitches through two innings. He had faced twelve hitters, fallen behind on eight, allowed six to reach base, and yet he was only down 2–0. Guts or luck, I wasn't sure which.

Whatever it was, it wasn't long before it ran out. The Tropics pushed across another run on a double by Washington and a single by Harrah in the third. In the fourth, White hit a two-run homer to right: 5–0. And in the fifth, after Kingman led off with a homer into the teeth of the wind in left and Lacy followed with a single, manager Pat Dobson emerged from the dugout. He had not taken two steps toward the mound before he gestured to the bull pen. Garland was finished, for the game (which the Tropics went on to win, 7–0) and possibly forever.

The next day, the Sun Sox would place Garland on the disabled list, where he would remain for the rest of the season.

Eᴅ Rɪᴄᴋꜱ ᴡᴀꜱ ᴛʜᴇ ᴡᴏʀꜱᴛ ᴘɪᴛᴄʜᴇʀ ɪɴ ᴛʜᴇ ꜱᴇɴɪᴏʀ ʟᴇᴀɢᴜᴇ. Tʜᴀᴛ wasn't opinion, that was fact. He knew it. He told you it was so. In fact, he went beyond that.

"I seen guys have a bad year," he said with more awe than self-pity, "but this is the *worst* I ever seen a guy have a year and I'm the one to have it. I never seen a guy have it as bad as this."

I drove back to St. Lucie from West Palm Beach this afternoon and found Ricks sitting in front of his locker. He was happy to talk. He just didn't know why anybody would want to talk to *him*.

Ricks had the kind of low-four-figures ERA that pitchers sometimes had after one bad outing at the beginning of the year. But this was the end of the year, and Ricks's ERA was 13.79. You couldn't say it was because he got lit up early and they stopped using him, either. Ricks was currently fourth among Legends pitchers with seventeen appearances. In thirty-one and one-third innings pitched, Ricks had served up four home runs and unleashed five wild pitches, which together equaled three-quarters of his strikeout total. He'd given up forty-eight earned runs on fifty-one hits. When you figured in the thirty-seven walks, you came up with an average of 2.64 base runners per inning. A small number, yes, but one that speaks eloquently of disaster; all you have to do is ask anyone who's ever played Rotisserie baseball.

"Just terrible," Ricks said.

Of course, it wasn't *all* his fault. He was pitching for the Legends, after all. Ricks was willing to concede that he had not had a whole lot of support, but he absolutely refused to make excuses.

"I had some bad breaks, but everybody can have bad breaks. As a pitcher you should be able to get *somebody* out. I'm just not getting *nobody* out."

Ricks came from Bastrop, Louisiana, a piny-woods town of about fifteen thousand residents up on the Arkansas border. He went to college at Grambling. They don't just play football at Grambling; ask Tommie Agee or Ralph Garr. Ricks was drafted out of college by the Yankees in 1972. At twenty-two he was old for a prospect, but he was already well developed. He quickly advanced to the Yankees' AAA farm team at Syracuse. Then it was as if he hit a wall, and no matter how hard he tried, he couldn't get over the top.

"Every year I went to spring training, I thought I was gonna stay. I was always either the last guy or one of the last guys to be sent out. I wanted out in '77, but they wouldn't let me go. Seattle came into the league that year, expansion team, and I was one of the fifteen guys the Yankees protected. I went to spring training that year and did well again, and they sent me back to Syracuse again. They said, 'You made the team, but we're taking eight outfielders and eight pitchers.' They never take eight outfielders, and they always take ten pitchers. They said I was gonna be the first to get called up, but that didn't happen either, they called another guy up, [Gil] Patterson. They said, 'We want you to get some work in AAA.' I went up in April, but I never pitched. I was there for eighteen days. I was gonna start the second game of a doubleheader in Cleveland, but it was so cold they canceled the game and they sent me back to Syracuse. One day they called me back to Baltimore. [Ken] Holtzman was pitching, and they had me warming up in the bull pen for six, seven innings. He struggled through to about the eighth inning and then they put Sparky [Lyle] in. My mom got a chance to see me on national TV in the bull pen, you know, my name was flashed on the screen."

Ricks laughed. It really was funny now. "Same thing happened in New York, against Baltimore. My mom saw me on national TV and they went to Sparky. I think the game was about eleven-two, Baltimore. For some reason, Billy [Martin] just decided not to pitch me. The Mets and the Yankees, they have like a Mayor's Trophy game every year in New York. I was gonna start that. That particular year they canceled it 'cause it was raining. I don't know, it's been a weird career for me. There was no doubt the ability was there. Guys used to rave about my ability to throw. I always had a great arm, I always could pitch. A lot of people were interested in me during my minor-league career, but I guess I was just such a highly regarded prospect that the Yankees decided to hold on to me, hold on, hold on, until finally it was too late."

Ricks finally quit in 1979. He had some arm problems, but that wasn't really it. He was tired more than anything else. Tired of being so close for so long and not making it. "I decided to give it up because it seemed like I wasn't going anywhere," he said.

These days, Ricks was living in Orlando, working as a private investigator. He did a lot of workmen's comp cases, some divorces. He liked divorces best because sometimes with those you ended up in a nice hotel with nothing to do except lie around by the pool and keep your eyes open. He dealt with a lot of crazies in his line of work, but he didn't mind. It was usually exciting.

Then he'd heard about the senior league. In some ways he was like all the others who came back. But for him it was a little different. Ricks wasn't here to relive the glory of the old days. What glory? Ricks was here to give it one more try.

This time he scaled the wall. He made the team. He just had no idea what he'd find waiting for him on the other side.

"I can't say it's been fun. You do some soul-searching and you work. I'm a hard worker. Luis Tiant has helped me a lot. In his major-league career his arm went dead and he came back and won twenty-two games. That's an inspiration to, like, keep on trying. Anything's possible."

He smiled. It amused him that he'd caught himself talking as if he still had a future in the game. "Where am I going at thirty-nine? But as long as there's life you gotta keep pegging, keep trying. It hurts, though, when you go out there and embarrass yourself. I done did it too much. I think a lot of my teammates. They're still behind me, you know, keep patting my back. It's good to see guys sticking with you. Overall, fans seem to like me 'cause I been so terrible, you know? You want to do good for yourself, but you want to do good for them, too.

"Before, they said I was a mean, nasty guy. They used to say, 'Get mad and pitch.' I don't want that attitude anymore. Maybe I should. But that was too much pressure back then, all those ulcers and stuff. I haven't shown that at all this year. I don't want that. Even if it takes that to win I still don't want it. When you're young, something like this happens, it really does a number on you. But now, there's life without basball. I experienced it. I went out and got a job, I'm doing okay, something that I like.

"There must be something good gonna come out of this. I don't know when or where. But I'm not quitting. I quit before, but I won't quit this time."

ON NIGHTS LIKE TONIGHT, WHEN THE DENSITY OF FANS IN THE stands was less than that of players on the field, the press box was the happening place to be. Traditionally, cheering is heavily frowned on in such quarters because the noise would disturb other members of the working press and because reporters were supposed to be objective. But on those occasions when there were no bona fide members of the working press actually in attendance, or maybe just one or two, protocol was ignored and the press box became more like a luxury box, where team officials gathered with friends, family members, visiting dignitaries, stadium employees, and anyone else who could get past the guard—assuming there *was* a guard—to root, root, root for the home team.

Rick Horrow was here tonight, making his presidential rounds. He was just back from a foray into Arizona with the league's expansion committee (Jim Morley and Rick Maxwell were the other members) and was brimming with enthusiasm. "All the owners are committed to year two," he assured me. He was of the opinion that the value of an existing franchise was "at least two, two and a half million" and an expansion franchise would bring "a million, a million-seven." (I thought, if that was the case and I owned a team, I'd sell right now and take the sure million-dollar profit, but then I didn't own a team.) The only time Horrow clammed up was when I asked him about Curt Flood. It was rumored around the league that Flood was not doing his job. Protests, requests for rulings, and other administrative tasks were said to be piling up on his desk. And he wasn't showing up at the ballpark to sign autographs as often as some of the owners would have liked. The latest I'd heard was that he was on the way out. Was it true?

"We'll deal with that in February," Horrow said. "No matter

what you think of Curt today, when he's there, his office is next to mine so I gotta be real careful." And that's all he had to say about that, at least for now.

Having dispensed with serious topics, Horrow loosened up fast. He had arrived at the ballpark in full business regalia, but now the jacket came off, the tie was put away, and the top button was unbuttoned. He discovered he was thirsty and so persuaded Chuck Malkus, PR director for the visiting Gold Coast Suns, to fetch him a beer.

Now that he was grown, Horrow was no longer content simply to cut box scores out of the newspaper, as he had when he was a child. He liked to score games himself—not necessarily the ones he attended but the ones he watched on TV. "Only football," he explained. "I used to score baseball games, but everybody does that and I have a novel scoring system in football. I'll use different colors, different codes for different offensive and defensive formations. I'll score a hundred games a year. It's my relaxation."

"So when you watch a football game you actually sit there—"

"Sit there and score it. Chart it, staple it, color-code it, cut out the box scores, put the numbers on it, quarters, time of game, officials—"

"You're not married, are you?"

"Separated. I've been separated for about two years. I'll be divorced in a period of time when my wife realizes that it's much more important to give the name away and start finding somebody. I'm trying to help her find somebody."

Horrow was ready for another beer. Since Malkus was not handy, he went himself. After he was gone about a minute, he came back for his portable telephone. "Long line for beer," he explained. "I can check my messages."

When Horrow returned, he showed me his appointment book. Actually, it was more than simply an appointment book. Horrow used it as a kind of diary as well, a place to record significant events that had already taken place. For example, "Every game I score I put in my book to indicate that I scored it."

He opened the book to the beginning. The box for January 1, 1990, was completely filled. It took me a moment to recognize what that meant. "You sat and watched and scored *all* these games on New Year's Day?"

"That's right. Shit, who won the Hall of Fame Game? I forgot to fill that in." Horrow paused, concentrating. "Auburn won, yeah, they beat Ohio State. But I forgot the score. Do you remember it? I think it was, like, thirty-one to thirteen, but I'm not gonna put that down until I call."

I examined Horrow's book more closely. The markings were fine-lined, precise, and multicolored. Horrow explained that he assigned one of four different colors to each event he set down, depending on the extent to which it made him happy. "So a green event is something you're *very* happy about?" I asked.

"Right."

"That's the highest form of happiness? Nirvana?"

"Right, and then orange is next."

"You're pleased with orange."

"Uh-huh, and then kind-of-brown is a shade of it. Blue is next."

"What does this mean," I asked, pointing to an orange entry. " 'Herald Senior League?' "

"Miami *Herald* did a story on the senior league."

"And if it had been a really terrific story—"

"It might have been in green. And then every racquetball or tennis game that I play, I have the results here. Let's see"—thumbing through—"what else?"

"I don't see any mistakes. Do you ever make a mistake when you're writing things down? Oh, here's one. You crossed out 'St. Pete' and had to write in 'Winter Haven.' "

"Oh, well, yeah. That's because the scheduler, [Peter] Lasser, made a mistake. Here's the Caribbean series [another one of Horrow's projects], here's my first Harvard class [Horrow would be helping lead a seminar on sports and the law at Harvard Law School in the spring]. I still speak at colleges. That day I'll be in Niagara."

"You haven't color-coded it yet?"

"I don't know what it's gonna be like yet. I'll circle it when I see . . . Hmmmm, slow week . . . We're going to Palm Springs to talk about expansion that week . . . That's a meeting of the Sports Lawyers Association, I'll be elected president. You should see my '89 book. My '89 book had *five* color codes in it."

Meanwhile, on the field, a pretty good ball game was unfolding. The Legends' bats were hot. Floyd Rayford collected three hits and two runs batted in. George Foster had two hits. Jerry Manuel and Willie Aikens each hit two-run homers. When Al Holland came on in relief of Bill Travers in the seventh, St.

Lucie was protecting an 8–4 lead. Then the roof fell in. Holland faced only five batters but gave up five runs on four hits. A ninth-inning rally by the Legends came up short and Gold Coast won this first of a three-game series, 10–9.

The loss dropped St. Lucie's season record to sixteen wins and forty-two losses; the mirror opposite, it so happened, of West Palm Beach's record. By winning two today against Fort Myers, West Palm nailed down the first available spot in the play-offs. And by losing tonight to the Suns, the Legends became the first team to be mathematically eliminated.

PORT ST. LUCIE • *January 16*

Tom Boswell, the baseball writer for the *Washington Post*, had a theory about why Earl Weaver got himself tossed out of so many ball games. "Nothing is more in character and calculated than the moments when Weaver pulls his own trigger," Boswell wrote in *How Life Imitates the World Series*. As long as the Orioles were winning, Weaver made himself invisible. But once the team had lost a few and the pressure began to build, Weaver intervened. "Weaver draws the electricity of defeat to himself like a lightning rod so his players can perform in calm," Boswell wrote.

"Well, let me say this, there's a little truth to that," Weaver allowed. He was relaxing in the visiting dugout at St. Lucie, sucking on a Raleigh while his players took batting practice. He spoke to the field rather than to his questioner. "Because you wanted to get thrown out before your, fuck, Brooks Robinson gets thrown out. Of course, Brooks never argued, but I wanted to get thrown out before Frank [Robinson] or [Paul] Blair, who did argue. I had to get out there in the middle. It's not motivating the players, but it's doing their arguing for them. That's the truth in that.

"But the real reason I got mad at umpires is because I'm sitting here and I think they missed it. And I gotta send my kids through college. And if those cocksuckers cost me a game and I get fired, then my kids can't go to college and my wife can't wear a mink. You know?"

Weaver was speaking right at me now—*listen to what I'm telling you.*

"I'm trying to keep a fucking job. We're supposed to win a
fucking ball game and if we lose because of an umpire's call—if
we lose because I'm dumb, that's okay; if we lose because I got
bad ballplayers on the field, then that's my fault, let me get fired
because of *that*—but don't let me get fired when the winning
run is crossing the plate in the ninth inning and my runner's
safe at first base, you understand?"

Weaver sat back and took a drag on his cigarette.

"So out of seventeen years that happened ninety-six times.
It's less than once a month that I got thrown out. Anyway, it
was only ninety-five 'cause one time a pitching coach, George
Bamberger, hollered, 'You rotten cocksucker!'—I've never cursed
an umpire—and the guy turned around and threw *me* out."

"You never cursed an umpire?"

"No. I never call 'em a name. Called 'em dumb, stupid, igno-
rant, low IQs, anything I can think of, but I never—well, let me
say this. I haven't since 1954 in Denver, as a player. I went out
and called an umpire some vulgar names, which today, naturally,
I'm ashamed of, that's one reason I haven't done it since. So
anyway, the manager got me after the game. His name was Andy
Cohen. He said, 'Hey, whattaya think that guy woulda done if
you called him them names in a bar?' I said, 'We'd a went to fist
city.' He said, 'That's right, but all that man can do there on a
baseball field is stand there and take it. You're taking advantage
of him.' I was twenty-one years old"—in fact, Weaver turned
twenty-four on August 14, 1954—"and it made sense to me. You
know what I mean? They don't like to be called stupid, either,
but at least I'm not using vulgarity."

"So not once since that day have you ever sworn at an umpire?"

That's not what he meant. "I say fuck," Weaver explained. "I
use vocabulary. But I don't call *them* a cocksucker, motherfucker, sonofabitch, or anything like that."

With Weaver, the conversation was liable to sudden shifts and
turns. He was almost always happy to talk about baseball, and
he generally answered your questions. But the minute he grew
bored he simply changed the subject, if need be, gradually raising his voice until he drowned out the competition. More than
anything, he loved to talk about his Orioles. He bragged about
them as if they were his own grandchildren, with pride but also

with wonder, knowing their accomplishments far surpassed the sum of whatever he may have contributed.

"Now Brooks mighta been the slowest guy in the big leagues," Weaver announced, apropos of nothing I was privy to. "It's just unbelievable that man was never thrown out, and took chances! Well, it wasn't chances 'cause he knew what he could do. He's on second base with one out. Now you see these bloopers, and guys holding up. Brooks would either go back to the bag knowing the guy was gonna catch it, or knew it was in there the minute it was hit. And many a time I'm sitting on the bench yelling, 'Hold up!' and the outfielder never got to the fucking ball. It was just unbelievable. So as a result, on that kinda hit, he'd be on third base where the fastest runner on my team might only be on second.

"Frank could do it all, he was the same way. I mean, he had good speed *and* he had the instincts. Donny Buford was a good base runner, but he's the kinda guy, if he's out on second and they hit the bloop, he'd only get to third. Brooks woulda scored."

"Hey, Speedy!" Speedy Hecht, Weaver's first-base coach, was walking toward the dugout. Batting practice was over. "Let's go finish looking at that schedule."

Weaver hopped off the bench with surprising agility. He waved at his coach to fall in behind him and disappeared down the tunnel to the clubhouse.

*B*ANG!

Maybe it was a car that backfired. Maybe a fan lit a firecracker somewhere in the stands. In any case, half a dozen people in the press box immediately shouted, "Somebody shot Joe!" Joe was Joe Sprung, the co-owner of the St. Lucie Legends. It was a joke. What made it funny was that so many people in the press box— not just reporters (there were two) but people who worked for Joe Sprung, especially his own general manager, Ray Negron— thought it was hilarious.

Since I had never met Joe Sprung, I asked Negron to point him out for me in the stands. Before I went down to talk to him, I asked Negron if Sprung was himself ever an athlete.

"When he's in bed with his wife," Negron said, and burst out laughing once again. "You shake his hand and tell me if he was ever an athlete."

Five minutes later I was shaking his hand. The evidence was

inconclusive. The palm was sweaty, but the grip was firm. Very firm. In fact, I had the sensation when we met that Sprung's springs were fully compressed. His eyes were hard, squinty, untrusting; his jaw, set. He watched the game with clenched fists. Whatever effect he was striving for with the horn-rimmed glasses and the polo shirt, he hadn't pulled it off. More than anything, he looked scared, like a gambler on a down slide.

I asked him if his first season had turned out the way he thought it would back when he and Burt Abrams, Sprung's partner in a New York accounting firm, bought the franchise.

"A little stormier," he said. Sprung was from Brooklyn; the word came out "stawmier." "I came down here Labor Day. We didn't have an office, we didn't have a staff, we didn't have anything. Just the fact that we're off the ground and walking—or crawling, if you want to say it—some people consider that a major achievement. Financially, we don't consider that a major achievement. We'd like to see more people in the stands. It's been a long season."

"I thought at one point you had sold the franchise to Lenny Woolf."

"He backed out of the deal. He didn't even call me to tell me he was backing out of the deal."

"But you were willing to sell?"

"Yeah, for the right price. See, three weeks ago I was in a different frame of mind. I was really tired. This back-and-forth traveling and all that, things weren't going great financially. But we've held on so far. I think if we make it through this season, there's a strong chance we can recapitalize for next year. 'Cause I think the franchises will have an inherent value at the end of the season. What do you think?"

I told him I really had no idea, although Rick Horrow's estimate yesterday of over two million dollars did seem high.

"I don't know if you're aware of all the building that's going on around here," Sprung said optimistically. "They're building a whole community here. In two or three years this place will be sold out."

While we watched from behind home plate, Clint Hurdle, the Legends' catcher, popped up to the third baseman. Hurdle already had one hit tonight and had driven in a run on a fielder's choice in the first inning. But the easy out reminded Sprung of how much he was paying Hurdle and how little Hurdle was doing to deserve it. After all, Hurdle was only thirty-two, he should have been a star in this league. Instead he was batting less than .200. It was a depressing thought, and, thinking it, Sprung looked scared again.

"Things are getting a little tight," he confessed. "Hopefully things are gonna turn around. It just might not turn around quick enough for us."

PORT ST. LUCIE · January 17

ED RICKS HAD TO DRIVE UP TO DAYTONA EARLY THIS MORNING ON a routine repo assignment. On the way back, he swung by the Port St. Lucie National Bank on U.S. Highway 1, arriving there a few minutes past 10:00. Ricks cashed his paycheck and afterward came to the ballpark.

Roy Thomas, who was scheduled to start today's game, must have just missed seeing Ricks at the bank; he got there at 10:15. But when Thomas presented his own mid-January paycheck for payment, the teller pushed it back.

"Sorry," she told him, "insufficient funds."

So it had finally happened. Joe Sprung did not have enough cash in his account to meet payroll. Thomas was surprised but not shocked. Some of the Legends had seen this coming for a long time, ever since they got their first paychecks back in November. Those checks were written out in longhand with no stub to account for the various deductions, and they were written on a New York bank, which meant that some of the players had to wait days before gaining access to their funds. "When you got an accountant, owns your team, that don't know how to write a payroll check, tell me something ain't wrong," said Bill Madlock, expressing what many others felt.

There had been plenty of signs for months that Sprung was in over his head. Players still talked about the day the team trainer asked for five thousand dollars to set up shop for the season and Sprung flew into a rage; evidently, training-room expenses were not included in his budget projections. Uniforms were a constant distraction. Either they didn't fit right, or there weren't enough to go around (some players wore different numbers at home and on the road), or they weren't ready in time for the game (during the December cold snap, when temperatures fell into the low forties, the Legends sometimes took the field in wet clothes). Once, Sprung had tried to motivate his troops by offering to pay meal money on an off day during a road trip, but only if they won. Later, he had to be told that he was obliged to pay it anyway.

When the players arrived at the ballpark today—angry and confused and looking for someone to blame—they found the toilet in the tunnel between the clubhouse and the dugout backed up. It was the perfect olfactory accompaniment to a shitty situation. George Foster, in his role as player rep, was making the rounds with a clipboard, asking, "Were you shorted? Were you shorted?" Tommy Moore got his money (he was at the bank at 9:15), but Willie Aikens was too late. Al Holland was paid ("I called his ass down, 'You want my ass in the ballpark, you gotta pay me' ") but not Tom Murphy.

Murphy, the Legends' other player rep, was fed up. He had a good job waiting for him back home in California, leasing commercial real estate. He worked on commission, and now was the time of the year when things were starting to get busy. If the Legends couldn't guarantee him a paycheck, well, he had to earn a living, Murphy was going home. He'd already packed up his gear and told manager Bobby Bonds he was leaving. As he stood in front of his empty locker, still wearing street clothes, his uniformed teammates stopped by one by one to shake his hand and say good-bye. "Autographs!" Murphy announced to the room at large. "Last chance to get my autograph!"

At 11:15 Bobby Bonds cleared the locker room of everyone but players for a team meeting. Even the taxi-squad members had to go sit in the dugout. The meeting lasted about ten minutes. When it was over, the players drifted out onto the field for pregame warm-ups. The warm-ups were merely a precaution. For at the meeting, the Legends had voted overwhelmingly (all except Dave Hilton, who was the lowest-paid member of the team) *not* to play until everyone got paid. Barring a credible, last-minute assurance on the part of club officials, there would be no game today. The Legends were on strike.

At 11:45, Bonds and Foster climbed to the top of the dugout steps and waved everybody back in for another meeting. Evidently, the players' vote to strike had achieved the desired result.

First, from Negron, came the assurance that funds adequate to cover all outstanding checks would be available after 11:00 A.M. tomorrow. And from Curt Flood—who spoke to Murphy by telephone from the league office—came the promise that if by January 23 the Legends did not have on deposit a balance sufficient to cover the final round of checks, due January 31, then the league itself would guarantee payment. The players were satisfied, the strike vote was reversed, Murphy unpacked his gear, and the game went ahead as scheduled.

Afterward, up in the press box, Negron was chuckling softly. "We're just buying time," he said, "and hope and pray. Maybe I can sell a car or something. Tell me where there's a bank around here, I'll go fucking rob it for eighty grand."

"You mean you *don't* have the money?"

Negron grinned sheepishly. He'd talked to Sprung, and Sprung had told him to say that the money would be available tomorrow. That was the sum of Negron's "assurance" to the players.

"Was I gonna tell 'em that?" Negron asked rhetorically. "We wouldn't be watching a ball game right now and I wouldn't be eating a hot dog."

I went looking for Sprung. He was right where I left him last night. In the light of day, his skin looked pale and pockmarked. He was smoking a cigarette. There were butts scattered on the cement under his feet. His shoes, I thought, looked old and worn; it was hard to believe the man inside them was capable of meeting a seventy-five-thousand-dollar payroll twice a month.

"I'm having money wired in this minute to cover the payroll," Sprung said right away.

"Will the players be able to cash their checks tomorrow?"

"I hope so."

According to Sprung, the reason for the shortfall had nothing to do with his being short of cash. "The whole thing happened because the account was frozen," he said. "When Lenny Woolf took over the club, he also took over sole signature authority. Then when he bailed out I had to freeze the account, get the signature authority back, get the corporate papers, the seals and all of that down here, right? Then I opened up a new Florida account. So now what I have to do is wire the money from New York into it. The money's in New York. It's being wired right now."

"But you must have known yesterday that there was going to be a problem."

Sprung looked disgusted. "When you get your paycheck, do you cash it or do you deposit it into your account? Normally, not every player cashes his paycheck. A lot of the guys mail it directly home to their spouses. We had a cushion, like thirty thousand dollars, so some of the players could cash their checks. I never realized that *all* these players would want to cash their paychecks at once. Thirty-three thousand dollars was cashed already between yesterday and this morning. I don't know why. Maybe it has something to do with this Orlando thing."

I knew if I was a player, *I'd* want to turn a piece of paper with Joe Sprung's signature on it into hard currency without waiting around for the ink to dry. But he was right. There was something else going on, and it did have to do with "this Orlando thing," for ever since the mysterious closed-door meeting that took place after the Juice game here last Sunday night, wild rumors had been flying all around the league. Sure, the players were anxious. After all, it wasn't every day that an owner vanished without a trace.

At 5:00 ON SUNDAY AFTERNOON, JANUARY 7, MITCH MAXWELL HAD finally gotten through to Phil Breen at his home in Beverly Hills, Michigan, a northwestern suburb of Detroit. Maxwell, the owner of the Super Sox, had been leaving messages for Breen for several days. The two owners were working on a deal to create a jointly owned company that would control the local broadcast rights for the Juice in Detroit and the Super Sox in Boston, with revenues to be shared fifty-fifty. Maxwell was anxious to make final arrangements, and Breen—now that Maxwell finally had him on the phone—sounded encouraging.

"Everything's all gonna happen," he told Maxwell. "I'd love to talk to you now, but I've gotta run."

Truer words were never spoken. Sometime between the end of the phone call and 3:00 the following afternoon, when he failed to appear at a scheduled meeting, Phil Breen disappeared off the face of the earth. "No sight, no sound, no peep, no nothing," as Jim Morley later said.

Not everyone was shocked. Breen's boss at Group One Mortgage Corporation, Douglas Hardy, must have smelled something funny. Otherwise, he would not have invited the FBI to that 3:00 meeting. And Kathleen Breen, Phil's wife of less than two years, surely had suspicions of her own. She filed for divorce within days of reporting him missing to the Beverly Hills police. But as far as everybody in the senior league was concerned, Breen's disappearance was a total surprise. Rick Horrow's first reaction when he heard about it from Maxwell early on the morning of January 9 was "You're full of shit, go back to sleep."

Breen, of all people. Together with Maxwell, Don Sider, and Mike Graham, Breen was part of the league's inner circle, one of the first to commit wholeheartedly to Jim Morley's farfetched notion of a new league for retired baseball players. The others looked to Breen for guidance in those early meetings, partly because he was in his early forties and therefore older than anybody else, and partly because he seemed to have strong ties to professional baseball. It was understood that Breen, like Morley, had played for a time in the minor leagues, in his case in the Tigers' organization. And judging from the way Breen talked about the business deals he'd been in on with Bill Freehan and Al Kaline, he was awfully well connected.

But what really gave Breen his standing was the fact that he was rich—cash rich. Breen was president of Group One Mortgage, but far from having all his money tied up in property he was the most liquid of anyone in the group. In late October, when Mike Graham looked as if he might not be able to come up with enough money to get the Fort Myers franchise off the ground, it was Breen who stepped in with an offer, which the league voted down, to offer Graham a $550,000 loan. "Breen, Berrie, and Sirota were the only guys in the league with enough money to buy a franchise," said Rick Maxwell, referring also to Suns owner Russ Berrie and Explorers owner Norm Sirota, who became involved later. "The rest of the guys were young, cocky assholes like my brother."

Some may have looked at the fact that Breen was only five-six and wondered how he ever could have played professional baseball. But then again, he had a muscular build and was definitely athletic. He was always off somewhere playing golf, and occasionally showed up at meetings wearing his tennis whites. Others may have thought that he smoked an awful lot for an athlete, even an ex-athlete, and that his drinking was perhaps excessive. "He was a drink-drink guy, not a beer guy" was the way one league official put it. And there were times they all remembered when he definitely went too far. But hey, a lot of guys drank.

In the end, everyone accepted Breen at face value, which was more than he was willing to do for them. Breen was the only one among them who took the trouble to run background checks. "He D-and-B'd everybody," said Jim Russek, one of Maxwell's partners, referring to the financial reports obtainable from Dun & Bradstreet. "He told us. Before he would even get into this league and write his checks, he made sure everybody sitting at the table was capable, either of raising the money by virtue of his past business history or had the money in the bank."

But no one looked at Breen's past. So no one knew that he was lying about having once played pro ball, a fact later confirmed by the records department of the National Association of Professional Baseball Leagues. No one knew that he was not a principal of Group One Mortgage, as he had led them all to believe, but only a salaried employee. And certainly no one knew that in 1978, while living in Lauderhill, Florida, Philip J. Breen was sentenced to nine months in jail for embezzlement, specifically, according to federal court records, for having "created a fictitious mortgage."

The first hint that something was awry at Group One Mortgage turned up during a routine internal audit in December 1989. Accountants going over the books noticed that payments due Group One from two other mortgage companies—First Oakland Mortgage Corporation and Franklin Mortgage Corporation—were in arrears. Group One had purchased a number of existing mortgages from First Oakland and Franklin. In what was a fairly common arrangement, those mortgages were in turn sold to the government's Federal Home Loan Mortgage Corporation, known as Freddie Mac. Ordinarily, Group One would advance the monthly payments to Freddie Mac, then collect from First Oakland and Franklin. But what the auditor discovered was that for the last three months, no payments had been made to Group One. The company was out approximately two hundred forty thousand dollars.

Douglas Hardy, chairman and sole stockholder of Group One, figured there had to be a simple explanation. Sometime toward the end of the first week in January, Hardy called Breen in Florida and told him of the auditor's findings. Breen did not sound concerned. He told Hardy not to worry, the payments would surely be made the next day. When the money failed to appear, Hardy again tried to contact Breen. This time Breen could not be reached. So Hardy called his brother, Thomas, the attorney for Group One. On Friday, Thomas called the FBI.

Finally, late Sunday night, after his hurried conversation with Maxwell, Breen called Douglas Hardy. He said he was back home now in Beverly Hills, that he knew what the problem was, that he would be happy to explain everything. "Why don't we meet at your brother's office tomorrow," Breen suggested before he hung up. And that was the last anyone ever heard from Phil Breen.

On January 9, the day after Breen's disappearance ("we really didn't think he would show," said Thomas Hardy), Douglas Hardy and Group One Mortgage filed suit against Breen in Oakland County Circuit Court. By now it was apparent that much more than two hundred forty thousand dollars was at stake. According to Thomas Hardy, Breen was the author of a multimillion-dollar scam that worked like this:

First Oakland and Franklin were both dummy corporations, controlled by Breen. The mortgages Group One bought from them were phony, nothing more than elaborate inventions on official-looking paper. As president of Group One, Breen okayed the purchases. And through his control of First Oakland and Franklin, he pocketed the proceeds. As long as Breen was able to keep up with the monthly mortgage payments, no one was the wiser. If he ever fell behind, all he had to do was create a new mortgage and sell it to Group One.

Friends and business associates had often marveled at Breen's opulent life-style. The condo in Tavernier in the Florida Keys, the twenty-six-foot Bayliner, the forty-two-foot Jefferson. Breen's explanation was always simply that he'd been lucky in the market. He was even able to produce account statements that appeared to document fabulous profits from trading stocks. He probably did make a lot of money in the market; after he disappeared, Group One identified a brokerage account in his name containing approximately one million dollars in cash and securities. But that was nothing compared to the value of all those phony mortgages. By the time they were tallied up, they were found to be worth more than ten million dollars. Group One, under pressure from Freddie Mac to buy back the bad loans, sued Breen to recover its losses.

Eight months after the disappearance, Group One had made claims on various of Breen's assets—the boats, the brokerage account, the condo in the Keys, a house in Ann Arbor—which together came to "a million five, maybe a million six," according to Thomas Hardy. All such assets remained frozen, however, pending the outcome of a counterclaim filed by Breen's wife, Kathleen. A spokesman for Group One expressed little hope for a speedy resolution.

Breen himself remained a fugitive. "We'll keep looking for him until we find him," said Larry Kuhl, head of the FBI office in Oakland County, Michigan, "whether it's six months or six years."

Breen's disappearance had immediate consequences for the senior league, which quickly took steps to protect the franchise and its assets. Unfortunately, there was not a lot to protect. The Juice had some money in an operating account, though not nearly enough to meet payroll, which was less than a week away. "I wish Phil had sent me two hundred thousand dollars before he left," said a stunned Wynne Dillard, the Juice's general manager.

What the Juice did have, in accordance with league bylaws, was a one-hundred-thousand-dollar letter of credit. With approval from the other league owners, Dillard cashed in the certificate of deposit—held as collateral against the letter of credit—and issued bank checks to all his employees. The Juice met payroll, "just in a different style," which explained Larvell Blanks's cryptic response. As for the final payroll on January 15, the league definitely had a problem. But for now, at least, that could wait.

OF ALL THE PEOPLE WHO CROSSED PATHS WITH BREEN, PERHAPS none was more affected by the fact that he suddenly disappeared than Lenny Woolf. Within days, Woolf reneged on the deal to buy the St. Lucie Legends. That act led directly to Joe Sprung's failure to meet his mid-January payroll. What was the connection between Woolf and Breen?

They were friends, that much everyone knew. "Lenny Woolf told us he met Phil about a year, a year and a half ago," said Jim Morley, "that they'd become friends and their wives became friends, and Lenny said he felt a little betrayed [when Breen disappeared]. He put a lot of money in the St. Lucie deal basically on Phil's recommendation, then Phil absconds."

Morley's explanation made sense. And like most stories intended to put the best possible face on a bad situation, it was partly true. Yes, Woolf and Breen were friends. Yes, Woolf got involved in senior baseball on Breen's recommendation. But no, Woolf did not invest a lot of money in St. Lucie. Someone did—over four hundred thousand dollars—but it wasn't Woolf. "If I was to invest my money," Woolf admitted much later, "very honestly, I wouldn't put it in a [senior league] team."

So whose money was it? Woolf kept his peace for many months after Breen disappeared. He felt besieged by the FBI, who wanted to know about certain large deposits made into Woolf's bank account from an account controlled by Breen. But the FBI eventually concluded that Woolf, like so many others, was no more than an unknowing participant, a pawn in one of Breen's grand schemes. These days, Woolf has nothing to hide.

The St. Lucie franchise, Woolf explained, was in trouble from day one. Sprung and his partner, Burt Abrams, had had "maybe three hundred thousand dollars" at their disposal when they bought the team. It was barely enough to get started. "They were hoping that the thing would take off immediately," Woolf said. "When the league suffered through losses and it looked like each team was gonna go down for a million in losses the first year, neither Burton or Joe was prepared to deal with that."

Neither was the league. If St. Lucie were to have folded in the middle of the first season, it might well have brought the rest of the senior league down with it. It was at that point that Breen went to Woolf with an amazing offer.

"Phil brought me into this whole thing," Woolf said. "You have to understand my relationship with Phil. Phil was my mentor and Phil was my friend. We sat down in late November.

"He said, 'We got a franchise that's in trouble.'

"I said, 'Okay, what do you want me to do?'

"He said, 'Well, I want you to run it.'

"So now you can put two and two together and come up with all the answers."

Then the four hundred thousand dollars Woolf put into St. Lucie was really Breen's?

"That's correct."

Whether Breen intended the money as a gift or a loan was not clear. Either way, from late November until he turned up missing the second week in January, Breen effectively controlled two franchises: the Orlando Juice, which was his all along, and the St. Lucie Legends, through Woolf. Of course it was a violation of league bylaws, but at the time no one outside of Woolf and Breen knew the real story.

"When we first got involved, I was just gonna be a stockholder and Joe [Sprung] was gonna run the team, that was the extent of it," said Woolf. "As I got deeper into the thing, I found out that the whole thing was a façade. [Sprung and Abrams] were about to hand me the whole franchise. They had no other choice. It was absolutely unbelievable."

Then Breen disappeared. "At that point it made no more sense," said Woolf. So he pulled out of the deal, as quickly and easily as he got involved in the first place. And since the money was never his anyway, Woolf didn't bother to ask for it back. Sprung and Abrams were puzzled, but they kept quiet. In the end, they were left with a four-hundred-thousand-dollar windfall, enough to stay in business through the end of the season.

"In essence," said Woolf, "for whatever it's worth, the league was able to maintain itself through the graciousness of our friendly thief. He was a very good benefactor for the senior league."

Almost a year after he last talked to Breen, Woolf admitted he held out little hope of ever seeing Breen again. Not that he believed Breen was dead, which was one persistent rumor. Just permanently missing. "I think he's resourceful enough" to stay hidden for the rest of his life, was the way Woolf put it.

After baseball, Woolf went back into the construction business outside of Detroit. Whenever he thought about Breen, his memories were happy ones. "I found Phil to be a very personable friend," Woolf said. "Everybody liked him. Nobody knew what he was. How many friends do you know that go out of their way to make you the owner of a baseball team?"

Woolf's laughter came loudly over the phone line.

"I'm coming in, I was gonna be the owner of a baseball team! You know, that's not a bad line of work, lemme tell you."

A DRIZZLY SUNDAY EVENING AT AL LANG STADIUM, AN HOUR OR two before the start of the final game of a series between the Pelicans and the Explos. Bradenton, continuing its late-season surge toward a play-off spot, had won two games here already on Friday and Saturday. They were now within four games of first-place St. Petersburg and only half a game behind Orlando, which so far this weekend had lost two in Winter Haven.

It was the time of year when players watch the scoreboard. There was something in the air. Not pennant fever, exactly. More like pennant queasiness. Bobby Tolan, who happened to be wandering in the vicinity of the visiting dugout, saw Hal McRae, his friend and former teammate on the Reds, sitting alone on the bench. "Did you hear the Orlando score?" he asked him.

"I heard they were winning, three-nothing," said McRae. He sat hunched over with a bat in his hands, looking up at the top of the steps at Tolan.

"I heard they were losing nine-four," said Tolan. "Dock [Ellis] just called, said they were winning fifteen-thirteen."

McRae's report was accurate. So was Tolan's, almost. Winter Haven had indeed rallied to take the lead, 9–5 in the third. But Orlando came back to score five in the fifth and five more in the sixth and eventually won, 13–11. That, coupled with a Bradenton loss later tonight, would temporarily stall the Explos' drive.

Then Tolan told McRae a story about the time Jim Morley put on a uniform and got three hits off Bill Lee and Lee was so angry that he threw the ball all the way into Lake Lulu. "That's the hardest ball he's thrown in his fucking life. Cleared the whole fucking stands. The next time he comes up, we're thinking he's gonna drill Morley, right?"

"Right," said McRae, a smile creeping across his face.

"Somebody said, 'He's gonna hit Morley.' I said, 'What's Morley done?' All we did is try to get the ball for the man. Next pitch, he had Morley like o-two and Morley hits a ball out by third base that hits the third baseman in the jaw. Shoulda had four hits."

"Is he playing? I saw him in the stands the other night."

"We took him off the roster."

"He's a good guy, Morley."

"Yeah. You know, he played, not a whole lot, but he played in the minor leagues a little. He has an idea about things."

McRae nodded in agreement. "He was a minor-league player so it's not like this is a joke."

"He's not like some of them other owners that go out and take BP and don't know which end of the bat to hold."

McRae raised his eyebrows and nodded once again.

Then Tolan said, "I understand they're trying to find the Orlando owner."

"Yeah, he left the company and embezzled ten million dollars. They ain't gonna find him."

"Now the league gotta come up with the money."

"League done already paid once," said McRae, " 'cause UL [Washington] says they got a cashier's check the other day, when he got paid. It came from the league."

"Yeah."

"Good thing the season ending."

"You ain't lying."

"If he'd a booked a month ago—"

"They talking about having that same problem with St. Lucie—"

"St. Lucie, yeah."

"They said they were monitoring that situation *every* day."

"Yeah."

"There was rumors that when Christmas break come, them motherfuckers wouldn't come back! Hah!"

"*Heh-heh-heh!*"

There was silence for a moment after the laughter died out. Then McRae looked out over the damp infield and up at the dark sky and asked Tolan, "So, we ever hitting tonight?"

"Far as I know, yeah."

"Oh, I see, you want to hit and then hope it rains."

Tolan smiled. "We're gonna hit and then I think we're gonna probably shut it down."

"We don't need to hit!"

"I know, you motherfuckers do yours in the game anyway."

"*Heh-heh-heh*. We just need a Pelican out there, we don't need to hit!" Then, "West Palm won again?"

"Yeah, four-three."

"They got a machine down there."

"We kick their ass almost as bad as you guys kick ours."

"Yeah?"

"We go six and three against them."

"Yeah, I noticed that."

"And a couple of those games we coulda won. Shit, we play them good. There's two teams that we just can't beat and that's you guys and motherfucking St. Lucie. It's bad enough having one, when you got two!"

"Well, we got two! Winter Haven and West Palm we don't beat."

"Well, good thing you guys don't play them anymore."

"We play Winter Haven again. Winter Haven scraps us at our place. We haven't beat 'em in our place. And Orlando, that was the first time we beat them. We swept them."

"Where do you get this 'we' shit from?" Tolan said now. It was a cheap shot. McRae had been out since the beginning of the season with a torn rotator cuff. His only job these days was to coach first base. "You ain't played in two and a half fucking months."

"But it's the team," said McRae, suddenly serious. "WE as a team. It's still WE."

EVER SINCE HE JOINED THE EXPLOS' ROTATION IN MID-DECEMBER, Dan Boone had pitched brilliantly. His record now stood at four and one and his ERA, 3.20, was falling with every start. In fact, it was Boone's success—together with the healing of Omar Moreno's stress fracture and the recent signing of Jerry Royster—that was responsible for keeping the Explos in the race. People were beginning to pay attention. According to rumors that were going around, several big-league clubs had an eye on Boone. The fact that he was the only knuckleball pitcher in the league made his age, thirty-six, seem less of an obstacle. In any case, his expressed hope of returning to baseball after an eight-year absence, while still farfetched, was at least less so now than a month ago. He certainly hadn't done anything to hurt his cause.

Now, as always, Boone's biggest problem was convincing the

rest of the world that he was big enough to face major-league hitters. It so happened that Boone's rookie year in San Diego, 1981, was the year Frank Howard was manager. At six-seven, Howard was nearly a foot taller than Boone, a fact that was never more apparent than on those occasions when Thomas visited the mound.

"It used to crack everybody up," Boone said as he sat in front of his locker underneath the first-base stands at Al Lang. "He'd come out to talk to me, and he'd stand right in the highest place on the mound, right by the rubber, and he'd put his hands on my shoulders. People, they'd just bust up. They loved seeing that."

Boone laughed when he told the story, but it took some effort. In the short time since they'd known him, his teammates had learned that Boone was more tightly wound than most. Once he'd entered a game as a pinch runner, only to trip and fall on the base path. It was a clumsy move, and his teammates got a big kick out of it. But the laughter died fast when Boone refused to join in.

Throughout his career, Boone had tried all sorts of ways to compensate for his size, everything from wearing lifters in his heels to working out with weights. "But I don't think gaining weight, being bulkier and stuff, helps you throw the ball any better," he said. "You only have so much in your arm, and you're not gonna throw any harder."

Boone still had not gotten around to writing back to his boss, who had fired him last month. He thought of sending some newspaper clippings, just to let him know how well things were going, but in the end he decided that probably wasn't such a good idea. If and when he went back to California, he'd just have to find another job.

"So has it been worth it?" I asked him.

"So far, yeah. I tell you what, my heart's still in baseball. I would love to go somewhere to play for somebody. I don't feel like I'm done. Some of the older guys in the league, with five or six ERAs, they probably know they can't compete. But I think with my knuckleball I can compete in the big leagues. That's a tough pitch to hit when that sucker's working."

Then he lowered his voice, as if he were speaking confidentially.

"*You never know.* As bad as pitching is in the big leagues the last few years, there's no doubt in my mind I could win a spot. It's always gonna be a challenge for me. I gotta be at my best every time out, and obviously you can't. But I think that's really helped me along the way, having to prove myself. Every time, everywhere. It's always a battle. It keeps me on edge all the time."

WINTER HAVEN • *January 25*

WHATEVER HAPPENED TO THE SENIOR LEAGUE NEXT YEAR, THERE would be no Super Sox in Winter Haven, that much was certain. So this was it: the last day of the season, the last day ever. And it was sad.

The game itself meant nothing, just a make-up between two teams buried at the bottom of their respective divisions. The visitors' bus arrived only half an hour before the scheduled start, which then had to be pushed back to give the old men time to stretch out. The Legends, as they disembarked, wore the grim looks of men who wished they were someplace else. According to Bill Madlock, there was talk before the team left St. Lucie of taking up a collection. If everybody kicked in twenty bucks, the players surmised, and offered the money to Joe Sprung, there was a chance he'd let them forfeit the game and blow off the two-hour bus ride. Who knows, Sprungbrenner might have gone for it; chances were good he'd have grossed more than whatever turned out to be the visitors' share of today's gate.

Across the diamond on the home side, the feeling you got was more poignant, even sentimental. When the players arrived at the ballpark this morning, each received a little going-home present from the club: a manila envelope filled with newspaper clippings (personalized for each player), plus a boxed set of senior-league baseball cards. Posted on the clubhouse bulletin board were instructions on how to collect up to two hundred fifty dollars in travel expenses for the trip home ("see Rick if you need more"), plus an open invitation to the team party tonight at the Grove Lounge.

The talk was of plans for the future. Catcher Doug Simunic, who applied for a manager's job in the Pioneer League but didn't get it, wasn't sure what his next move would be. "Baseball when it ends is always empty for me," he said. "I like coming to the park every day." Mark Bomback was hoping to get his old job back at a bakery in Rhode Island. "I called my boss up the day I made the club," said Bomback, who was dripping sweat from his forehead after having run his sprints. "He said, 'When you come back, I'll see what I can do for you.' I gave them a good two and a half years. If they want to give me a hard time, I told my wife we'll just move down here. There's plenty of bakeries in Florida."

I found Scipio Spinks alone on a bench in the bull pen, his back to the batting cage. It was a clear, bright winter day, the temperature just cool enough so that it felt good to be sitting in the sun. Spinks was picking up little handfuls of gravel and tossing the pebbles, one at a time. His knee hurt, he said, "and my elbow's killing me. I feel great other than that. Lost some well-needed weight. Trimmed up, burned out, broken down." He laughed, a deep belly laugh that sounded like a truck horn.

Spinks had managed to keep his spirits up through most of the season, despite a pitching record that was frankly abysmal. He'd appeared in only five games (all in relief), retired just seventeen of the forty-one batters he faced, walked eight, struck out one, and compiled an ERA that was so high it made you dizzy: 20.65. Yet I never saw him crack until a week ago in St. Petersburg. Spinks thought he deserved a chance to start that day. When he learned that he'd been passed over in favor of Ed Clements, the amateur from Canada, he lost his composure.

"If he's a major-league ballplayer or a professional ballplayer, I can deal with that," Spinks said to me, only because at the time I happened to be the one sitting next to him. "I can't deal with nobody who never fucking played in the league. This league is not called 'Y'all Come over Thirty-five.' It's called 'Senior *Professional* Baseball League.' It's for me to come back and regain some of *my* stardom, not somebody who never fucking played, who only dreamt about it. Bullshit. They want to know why I'm mad!"

Now, one week later, Spinks tossed another pebble in a soft arc and grimaced. "Oh, man," he said, rolling his right arm, "same elbow." Then he leaned over and rubbed his right knee. Same knee.

"What happened that day?" I asked him.

Spinks didn't have to ask, 'What day?' He smiled, but he didn't laugh. He looked at the field, squinting, still quiet. Then he told me his story.

"It was a day I wasn't supposed to pitch, Fourth of July in Cincinnati. One of the other pitchers was scheduled, and he had a cold, couldn't pitch—it was raining. Now I was always told by Ernie Banks when I was a kid, 'Never refuse the baseball.' So they came to me and said, 'Scipio, can you go?' and I told 'em, 'Sure.' I just got out of New York and I was fighting Jon Matlack for the Rookie of the Year in '72. Beat New York, seven-one, struck out thirteen Mets. I was on a pretty good high then, I was feeling real good, so I said, 'Yeah, I'll get 'em.'

"I went out there that day, and I was really wild, about as wild as I been in the big leagues for a long time. I was like, walking two guys, base hit, two runs scored, walk a guy, bases loaded, strike out two guys. It was probably my worst game. In the third inning with the bases loaded and two outs, Johnny Bench came up and I struck him out. He said something to me, and I said something back to him. In the fifth inning I was wild again. Cincinnati had the bases loaded again and Bench came up again with two outs, and this time he popped up, and when he popped up he ran down the line hollering at me. I said, 'Hey, man, go sit down, you ain't the only person in the world who can play baseball, God didn't give you all the talent!'

"We're losing five-nothing, top of the sixth inning, and I figure I'm going to the clubhouse. Red Schoendienst said, 'Scip, get your bat.' I said, 'All right,' got my bat, got up there, and got a base hit. Ross Grimsley was the pitcher, pitches in this league now. Threw me a curveball, I hit it up the middle, and with my enthusiasm, trying to get everything going, I was jumping up and down having a good time.

"Lou Brock, next hitter up—I'm on first base with no outs—hits a long fly ball to right field. It didn't go out. If that ball a went out I'd probably still be in the major leagues, or else a longer time than I was. Next guy up was Luis Melendez. They put on a hit-and-run. I take off, he hits a line drive to left-center field, Pete Rose playing left field at the time. I saw the ball in front of me. I hit second base, I said to myself, 'I'm gonna score, I'm gonna try to get us on the scoreboard and get us moving.' I got to third base, and as I was getting to third base, the third-base coach was raising his hands for me to stop. I ignored him, and I kept right on going through third. I just seen Rose going to left-center field, and I'm figuring he can't get there before I can get to home plate.

"They always tell you in baseball, 'When in doubt, slide.' So I'm coming around third base, and Johnny Bench is what they would call deking me. I mean, he was standing up like he didn't have a play at home with his hands on his hips. Probably what I should have done is run into him—hit home plate and just run into him. But I didn't, I slid. And when I slid, I was coming up from the slide and Bench comes down with the shin guard, hits me in the knee. And I see the ball bounce in front of home plate, hits off his shoulder. I look up and the umpire says I'm safe. I didn't know I was hurt—I get up, I holler something at Bench, and I run in the dugout. I coulda scored standing up, but I didn't know where the play was after I rounded third base. The adrenaline was pumping so hard, after I hit third base I couldn'ta stopped. Plus it was raining that day, too. If I'd a stopped I mighta slipped and fell.

"I got ready to go out and pitch the next inning, bottom of the sixth. I got ready to stand up, and I fell right on my face. So I called Gene Gieselmann, who was the trainer, and I said, 'Geno, wrap it up for me, put an ace bandage on it, I'm going back out there.' So he wrapped it up, I try to put my weight on my right foot, fell down again. They told me to go to the club-house. Diagnosed it that day as a bruised knee. Next day we diagnosed it as torn posterior cruciate ligaments. I was operated on the next day. That was it."

"This was before arthroscopic surgery?"

"Oh, yeah. They were using saws and hammers and nails and drills and everything else they could. What I was told by the doctor who performed the surgery was that they'd only done ten previous operations like that before, none on an athlete, so this was something experimental. But it worked. I came back the next year. They wanted me to be out a year, I was out six months. But in the back of my mind, instead of pushing off with my right leg, I would jump and I would throw the ball, and what I was doing, I was putting all that pressure on my triceps, and about four weeks later I tore my triceps muscle in half, in Atlanta. It was enthusiasm, me hurrying back, me wanting to be the great big Cardinal baseball player that they wanted, the pitcher that they were hoping that I would be. It just didn't turn out the right way.

"What I found out after I did all that, they just pat you on the back and send you down the road. There's no compensation, there's no, 'We're sorry,' or, you know . . ." Spinks threw another pebble. Again he grimaced, and he rubbed his elbow. "Hell!"

By now, Spinks's teammates were drifting by on their way to the same patch of outfield grass where, before every home game for the last three months, they'd done their stretching together. Spinks watched them pass. He was obviously in no hurry to join them.

"What's up next?" I asked him.

"Huh? Nothing. Going back to Houston. I'm not gonna do anything for about a week, two weeks, just to see what's gonna happen. I'm gonna still work out, just to get my arm back in shape."

Spinks threw another pebble.

"When I get out of this baseball world and go back into the other world, in car dealerships where there's no team, every guy's for himself, it kinda blows my mind, you know?"

Another pebble.

"It's hard, it's hard to get along with sometimes."

Another pebble.

"So I don't know where I'm gonna go, what I'm gonna do. I'm just glad this league came about."

Another pebble.

EPILOGUE

THE SENIOR-LEAGUE CHAMPIONSHIP SERIES WAS held the first weekend in February at Terry Park in Fort Myers. Among the forty-plus names on the league's press-credential list were exactly two members of the national media: Tracy Ringolsby, the veteran baseball writer for the Dallas *Morning News*; and Bruce Dobler, a freelance writer on assignment for *Memories* magazine. Headquarters for the event was the Sheraton Harbor Place in downtown Fort Myers, which happened to be hosting two other groups that same weekend, Greenpeace and Jews for Jesus. The whales were covered, so were the wayward souls, but who would save the senior league?

Friday afternoon started out looking beautiful, but by game time the skies were leaden. The last thing the league wanted was a rainout. By now, everybody—players, managers, me—wanted to go home. Many had already made plane reservations. There was concern that if rain forced a postponement of the conclusion of the series until after Sunday, there might not be enough players left in town to get up two teams.

Fortunately, rain was not a factor; a downpour delayed Friday night's game for almost ninety minutes but in the end the game was played, and thereafter through Sunday the weather was dry and warm. Unfortunately, the other nightmare shared by league officials came true. Bradenton eliminated Fort Myers in the first game, leaving the home fans with no one to root for the rest of the way. The league, anticipating such a possibility, originally tried to make fans buy tickets for all three games at once. How many thirty-dollar packages the league sold was not known but very soon tickets were made available on a per-game basis. As a result, nearly four thousand fans saw the game Friday night, but only twelve hundred came back Saturday to watch St. Petersburg defeat Bradenton and advance to Sunday's final.

Sunday was not as bad, but still the stands were only half full. West Palm Beach, with a record of fifty-two and twenty, was ten games better than St. Petersburg and had already proved itself the best team in the league. But the championship was determined by one game only, on a day when neither starting pitcher had his best stuff. Juan Eichelberger of the Tropics, voted the league's top pitcher, left with two outs in the fifth after giving up seven runs, six of them earned. Milt Wilcox lasted only five and a third himself, but by then the Pelicans were comfortably ahead and on their way to a 12–4 victory.

"We are not old men," insisted Pelicans manager Bobby Tolan, chugging champagne in the champions' locker room. "We are major leaguers in my heart."

After the season, most players went home to their families and back to their old jobs. Some, like Tolan, who hoped his experience in the senior league would lead to a full-time job in baseball and eventually an opportunity to manage, waited for calls that never came. Wayne Garland, who was diagnosed with a torn rotator cuff, was operated on in the spring.

For a handful of players, the senior league was a springboard for a return to baseball, however brief. Paul Mirabella, a middle reliever and occasional starter for the Tropics, was invited to training camp with the Brewers and made the team. Mirabella appeared in forty-four games in 1990, mainly in relief, and finished the season with a record of four and two and a 3.97 ERA. Ozzie Virgil, who joined St. Petersburg late in the season, went north with the Blue Jays, was hitless in five at-bats, and eventually was sent down to AAA Syracuse. There he batted .143 in twenty-eight games and was released in August. Ron Washington, signed over the winter by the Rangers, failed to make the team and was assigned to Oklahoma City, where he batted .238 in one hundred eight games. Roy Thomas, who did achieve his goal of leading the senior league in strikeouts, was signed by the Denver Zephyrs of the Brewers farm system. Thomas was two and one with a 5.23 ERA for the Zephyrs in seven games before being released. The Suns' Joaquin Andujar, who was cut by the Expos in spring training, thanked the Expos for the opportunity, and went home to the Dominican Republic. Dwight Lowry, the Pelicans' backup catcher, spent 1990 with the Expos AAA affiliate in Indianapolis, where he caught thirty games and batted .310. Willie Aikens of the Legends returned to play another year in Mexico. Jim Morrison of the Explorers went to Italy.

Three senior-league veterans were invited by the Orioles to spring training. Pelicans' starting pitcher Randy Lerch was soon released. The Juice's Randy Bass impressed scouts with his bat but reinjured his knee and finally went home to Oklahoma, convinced at last that he could no longer play. And then there was Dan Boone.

Boone was signed by Orioles' scout Birdie Tebbetts. After a strong spring, he was assigned to Rochester, the O's AAA affiliate, where he finished the season with a record of eleven wins and five losses, eight saves, and a 2.60 ERA. On September 1, 1990, eight years after he last pitched in the major leagues, Boone was recalled by the Orioles. He appeared in four games down the stretch, including his first career major-league start, a no-decision against Cleveland. After the season, Boone was invited to play winter ball with the Orioles' top prospects in the Dominican Republic. Boone was flattered, but in the end he said no, choosing instead to return for one more season in the senior league.

He was joined by Ferguson Jenkins, one among scores of senior-league veterans who came back to play another year. On January 8, 1991, by the narrowest margin in history—a single vote—Jenkins was elected to the Hall of Fame. His father, still living, shared in the celebration. Four days after the election, Jenkins's wife, Maryanne, died from injuries sustained in an automobile accident.

Meanwhile, the senior league struggled to stay in business. None of the league's three top officials survived past the end of year one. Vice president Peter Lasser was unceremoniously let go, a victim of cost-cutting. President Rick Horrow was given the nebulous title of special consultant to go along with a drastic reduction in pay. And Curt Flood was fired. "He was a very well-intended, good-souled, good-hearted man," one owner said of Flood, "but he didn't have a clue of what to do. I think he became unhappy in his job and was unable to do it properly."

When Flood refused to go quietly, league officials charged him with having double-billed almost eight thousand dollars' worth of travel expenses, and withheld payments due him under his contract. Flood, who went home to Los Angeles with his family immediately after the season ended, chose not to return my phone calls.

As expected, all eight original owners reported heavy year-end losses, ranging from seven hundred thousand dollars in Fort Myers to one million four hundred thousand dollars in Bradenton. Over the summer, four franchises folded, including St. Lucie, Gold Coast, Winter Haven, and Orlando, whose final January payroll had to be met jointly by the other owners. That left only four teams in Florida—St. Petersburg, Fort Myers, Daytona Beach (formerly Bradenton), and the Tropics (formerly West Palm Beach, reorganized as a "traveling team" playing only road games). To round out the league, two western expansion franchises were added, the Sun City (Arizona) Rays and the San Bernardino (California) Pride.

The senior league opened its second season on Thanksgiving weekend. The schedule was shortened to two months, rosters were trimmed, and player salaries were lowered from a maximum fifteen thousand dollars per month to twelve thousand five hundred. Still, the losses mounted. Attendance was little improved, if not worse in some cities. A hoped-for infusion of corporate sponsorship money never materialized.

In mid-December, the owners asked the players to accept an immediate 16-percent cut in pay. "We're trying to help," Milt Wilcox said on behalf of the players. "If we need to take a pay cut, we will. If we have to rake the field and stuff like that, we're willing."

It was a nice thought, but it would not be enough to save the senior league. One the day after Christmas, Fort Myers owner Mike Graham, embroiled in a bitter dispute with two of his limited partners, threw in the towel. Now only five teams remained, one less than the minimum required by the league's television contract. That did it. Within hours, Jim Morley announced that the senior league was "suspending" play for the remainder of the 1990–91 season. The ball game was over.